THIRTY YEARS OF SAUSAGE, FIFTY YEARS OF HAM

THIRTY YEARS OF SAUSAGE,
FIFTY YEARS OF HAM

Jimmy Dean's Own Story

JIMMY DEAN AND **DONNA MEADE DEAN**

BERKLEY BOOKS, NEW YORK

A Berkley Book
Published by The Berkley Publishing Group
A division of Penguin Group (USA) Inc.
375 Hudson Street
New York, New York 10014

First Edition: October 2004

Library of Congress Cataloging-in-Publication Data
    Dean, Jimmy.
        Thirty years of sausage, fifty years of ham :
Jimmy Dean's own story / Jimmy Dean and
Donna Meade Dean.—1st ed.
            p. cm.
    ISBN 0-425-20106-6
        1. Dean, Jimmy. 2. Country musicians—United States—
Biography. I. Dean, Donna Meade. II. Title.

ML420.D436A3 2004
782.421642'092—dc22
[B]
                                        2004046316

Printed in the United States of America

10 9 8 7 6 5 4 3 2 1

This book is dedicated to my mother, Ruth Taylor Dean . . .
the toughest lady I've ever known.

❦ Contents ❦

PART THREE—FAMILY MATTERS

ᜓ Preface ᜓ

I **CERTAINLY HOPE** this will not be your ordinary autobiography. In the first place, I promise not to bore you with the usual "I was born and this is what happened to me in this order" kind of stuff, mainly because I can't always recall exactly *what* happened *when*. Remembering dates has never been my long suit, but I *can* tell you stories from the past like they happened yesterday.

I've been accused on many occasions of having a steel-trap mind for trivia. If it's not important, I'll retain it forever. But if it is important, I'll forget it in ten minutes. And though I've never thought my life was interesting enough to write a book about, I'm going to try to relate things that I hope will be of interest.

The fact is, people have been trying to talk me into writing a book for ages, and for years they've said, "Jimmy, why don't you write a book about how you got into the sausage business?" or "You should write a book about your experiences in the entertainment business," or "I wish you'd write a book about all the interesting people you've known" and so on. Some have also suggested that I write one that included the many country sayings I've used, like "He's as dumb as a box of rocks," or "It was so cold outside I saw a goose running around with people bumps." In this book I've tried to honor some of these requests, and I guess you'd say it's a catchall for the folks who are interested in any of those things.

And so, with the help of my wife, Donna (who was left with the daunting task of researching dates, people and places and putting it all on paper), this is a stab at what I've been putting off for a long time—a book that is not necessarily a rags to riches story, but a collection of stories with a few memories, some good and some not so good, that I'd like to share with you. I hope you'll find it entertaining, enjoyable and in some cases informative. But more than anything I hope these pages will furnish you with a few smiles.

~ PART ONE ~

A BORN ENTERTAINER

1

FROM WHENCE I CAME

IT'S HARD TO believe how stories can get twisted around sometimes, and just how screwed up they can get. For instance, take a newspaper story that was written about me many years ago. Somehow a reporter got confused about my name and the place where I grew up. I was born in the Texas Panhandle town of Olton, but when I was a small boy my family moved about three miles away to a neighborhood on the outskirts of Plainview, Texas, called Seth Ward. The reporter got the story mixed up and said that my real name was Seth Ward, and that I had it changed to Jimmy Dean. Now I ask you, if I had a name like Seth Ward, would I change it to Jimmy Ray Dean? The name Seth Ward conjures up visions of a virile, movie-star-leading-man kind of hunk, and Jimmy Ray—well, definitely West Texas farmer.

Not that there's anything wrong with that. I'm extremely proud of my heritage and the fact that I come from a long line of West Texas farmers. In fact, the greatest man I've ever known, my grandfather William Jasper Taylor was the best farmer in Swisher County, Texas . . . or at least he was in *my* eyes. He and my grandma Ludie raised nine good kids, my mother being the oldest. I guess you could say that Papa Taylor was my father figure while I was growing up. My daddy left us when I was eleven and my brother Don was nine years old.

Ruth Taylor Dean was probably the single most influential person in my life. Mom was the strongest, wisest and most proud woman I've ever known, and I'm sure I'll be referring to her a lot in this book. Along with poverty—my greatest motivating factor—I can honestly say that she has been the main inspiration for what I have become in this life.

After helping to raise her younger brothers and sisters and then marrying my dad, she gave birth to me at home on the tenth of August in 1928. I was a healthy baby other than the fact that Mom's milk didn't agree with my system, so I was raised on the milk from our cow, an old Holstein we called Ol' Spot. Two years later she gave birth to my brother Don, and for a while we also had my half brother Chester living with us (from my father's previous marriage). We never had any money when Dad was around, but when he left my mother, we were down about as far as we could go, and at the ripe old age of eleven I became the man of the house.

I don't remember much about my father, but I do recall that he was gone a lot and that I didn't like the way he treated my mom. Dad liked the ladies, I'm told. He was quite a rounder and apparently a rather horny ole boy, and not much of a husband to my mother. He wasn't much of a provider either. I remember that once my mother let Don and me save enough money from working after school so we could buy some boxing gloves for Christmas, but when we left the money lying on the piano, Dad put it in his pocket and we never saw it again. And then there was the time we were over at old man Holcomb's place. I guess I was about five or six years old at the time. He said he'd sell us one of his baby goats for a dollar, and I remember begging and pleading with my dad. I thought they were the cutest things I'd ever seen and I really wanted one, but Dad said no. Even when we were offered one for fifty cents, my father still wouldn't budge. Finally, Mr. Holcomb could see how much I wanted this cute little black-and-white one and he gave him to me. I loved that little goat. He was my pal and my buddy and he followed me everywhere. He'd even let me lay my head on his belly and go to sleep when we'd lay down on the porch for a nap, and he wouldn't move until I got up.

I'd had my goat for a couple of years when the unthinkable happened. We hadn't had any meat in a long time and my dad decided he was gonna kill my goat for food. I remember watching my father chase him as I stood there in tears. It made me sick to my stomach to think that he would do such a thing, and naturally I couldn't eat a bite. It broke my heart.

Dad had his good points, I guess. It was said that he was a man of many talents and it was true. G. O. Dean tried his hand at being a songwriter, inventor, singer, preacher and author—anything to get him out of doing an honest day's work. For a while he traveled and performed with Harley Sadler's Tent Show, and he did, in fact, write a book, called *The Only Sure Steps to Success and Happiness.* In it he quoted a lot of Bible scriptures and proclaimed that "success and happiness can only be attained by a closer walk with God and a high plane of Christian living." Guess he "talked the talk" all right, but he sure didn't "walk the walk."

The only other thing I can remember about my father is that he beat the hell out of me a lot . . . and as Forrest Gump would say, "that's all I have to say about that."

———•———

I have a lot of memories from when I was a kid, some rather painful, mainly because of the fact that we were so poor. We were probably one of the poorest families around back then. In fact, if steamboats had been selling for a dime a piece, all I could have done was run up and down the riverbank and say, "Ain't that cheap!"

The house we rented for eight dollars and fifty cents a month was wired for electricity, but we couldn't afford to have it turned on until I was thirteen. And we never did have indoor plumbing when I was a kid. A real adventure was taking a bath in a luxurious number three washtub. Surviving a storm in our house was a challenge too. We learned quickly where to put the buckets when it rained, and where to stuff old newspapers in the cracks in the walls and under the windows during a sandstorm or when it snowed.

In spite of all the hardships, Mom did her best to make a home for us, keeping a garden with vegetables she'd put up in Mason jars for the winter, and making our clothes on her old treadle sewing machine. Mom had noticed that our local merchant would order sugar in one-hundred-pound sacks and then discard the sacks after

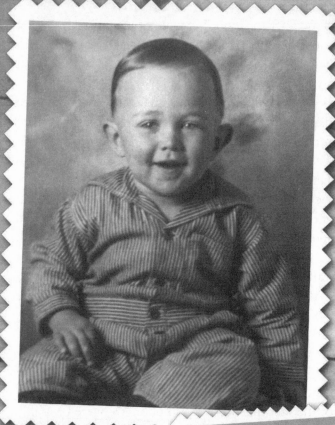

My first "publicity shot"

That's me at age 12 in my sugar sack shirt and bib overalls

they were emptied. She would buy them for little or nothing, bleach and wash them with lye soap until the lettering disappeared, and then dye the material with Ritz Dye. We'd wear the shirts that she'd make from that material with our bib overalls and brogan shoes— not exactly the most desirable fashion statement to make, and because of this, I didn't win many popularity contests. Many times I would come home from school in tears from being ridiculed and humiliated about my clothes. Nobody wore shirts made out of sugar sacks but me. I was an outcast and the butt of other kids' jokes. My mother's only retort was, "They're clean and you've got nothing to be ashamed of; you go to school every morning with clean clothes on your back, and you can stand tall and be proud of that."

Mom was a proud woman, indeed. I remember one time when the WPA—Works Progress Administration—came to Plainview with a program set up by Franklin D. Roosevelt to distribute free clothing to the needy. Being a child and not realizing how much it would hurt her, I said, "Mom, why don't we go down there and get some of those free clothes? They gotta look better than what *we're* wearing." And boy howdy, did I get a piece of her mind! She stomped her foot, turned and glared at me and said, "No sir! If we take that, boy, that says we're charity, and if we're charity, that says we give up. And *we don't give up, boy.* Do you understand what I'm telling you? *We don't give up!"*

Those words are indelibly etched in my mind, and to this day I don't know what the word *defeat* means. I can tell you an awful lot about temporary setback, but the word *defeat* is *not* in my vocabulary. As I've said many times, "You can't change the direction of the wind, but you *can* adjust your sails and reach your destination."

———•———

How well I remember growing up in Plainview. In the summertime it was hot and miserable with no air-conditioning, and in the wintertime it was cold and miserable with little heat. And it seemed like the wind blew all the time. There's an old saying there that goes, "The wind blew so hard that an old hen got her back to the wind and laid the same egg three times." And then there's another saying, "Plainview is the only place in the world where you can stand in mud up to your ass and dust'll blow in your eyes." (Don't ask me to explain that *last* one.)

Hailstorms were pretty much a regular thing for us too. Many times I'd see Mom standing at the back door crying as she watched a hailstorm destroy our garden, knowing it was taking our canned goods for the winter. I remember seeing some really strange weather there too. We had what people called Blue Northers that came through in the wintertime, where it would snow like hell and the wind would be blowing so hard that the back of our house would be covered with snowdrifts, but the front door would be free and clear. We'd have to go out the front door and dig ourselves out at the back of the house—that's how bad the snow had drifted. Sometimes the drifts would be twenty feet high, which always reminds me of that story about the guy who was walking along on top of one and looked down and saw a hat. When he picked it up, there was a head under it. He said, "Just a minute, and I'll go get a shovel and dig you out." And the guy in the snow says, "You'd better get a big 'un . . . I'm riding a horse!"

Plainview is also smack dab in the middle of Tornado Alley. One time a tornado came through, and afterward I noticed that a piece of straw was stuck in the side of a telephone pole. The only thing I could figure was that the rotation of the wind must have opened the grain of the wood, permitting the straw to lodge in it. And then there were those notorious West Texas dust storms, where it's been told that the dust was so thick that a groundhog was seen diggin' a hole, and he was forty feet in the air!

Besides its bizarre weather, Plainview, Texas, in the thirties was not exactly the gateway of opportunity. There wasn't much for us to do there back then but farm work. I remember one of the first jobs I had. I must have been about six years old when I started working in the cotton fields. In West Texas you don't pick cotton, you pull bolls. The climate is so dry there that the whole boll breaks off of the plant and you grab it all, cotton and burr.

After school and on Saturdays, Don and I would put on our work clothes and grab the heavy canvas sacks that Mom had made us, throw 'em over our shoulders and head out to anybody's field that needed boll pullers. On the best day I ever had, I pulled five hundred pounds of cotton, and at fifty cents for each hundred pounds, I had made two dollars and fifty cents.

When there wasn't any farm work around, I would do a variety of jobs, including cleaning out chicken houses. Now *there's* a job. Just thinking about it always reminds me of the story of the little old country boy who was late to school, and when the teacher asked him why, he stood there for a minute, diggin' his toe in the floor, and replied, "I've been pickin' chickens." She said, "Pickin' chickens! At this hour of the morning? How come?" And he said, "Well, last night Pa thought he heard something in the chicken house, so he got up and put on his boots. All he had on was his boots and long-handle underwear with the flap down in the back, and he took his shotgun and lantern and went out to the chicken house. He was bent over looking inside when our old dog Blue eased up behind him and cold nosed him, so I've been pickin' chickens since midnight last night!"

During planting time I'd work in the fields, planting, plowing, loading or whatever there was to do that would pay a few dollars a day. Every dime I made would go to help Mom with household expenses. She made money with her work as a barber too, cutting people's hair for fifteen cents in a spare room at our house. I remember one Saturday counting forty-eight customers. She'd stood so long that her feet and legs were swollen and killing her. She did a good business, though. Still today when I go back home, someone will invariably say they remember when Mom used to cut their hair.

Life as a kid in West Texas during the Depression wasn't *all* work and no play. I'll always remember the first dollar that Mom let me keep. My favorite lunch meat was bologna—still is—and I made a beeline to McCartie's Store and bought six pounds at fifteen cents a pound. It was in a brown paper bag and I ate the whole thing walking home . . . no bread, no nothing. For the first time in my life I had my fill of bologna.

Once a month Mom would give me a quarter on Saturday and I'd walk three miles to town to the Quick Lunch Cafe, where I could get a soda pop for a nickel and the best hamburger in the world for a dime. Then it was off to the Fair Theater to watch Western movies. You could stay there all day for a dime, and I made sure I got every penny's worth. Like a lot of other folks in those days, my favorite movie star was Gene Autry. I always did like to hear him sing.

The old Fair Theater is still standing today, and during an August 2000 visit to Plainview for Jimmy Dean Day, I was proud to be honored by the mayor and townspeople with a ceremony that unveiled my likeness on a plaque embedded in the sidewalk of the theater entrance. Not exactly Grauman's Chinese, but not too bad for an old boy from the poor side of town.

———•———

One of the most vivid memories I have from my childhood is riding a horse to school with my older half brother, Chester. He would drive the horse, and I'd sit behind him while holding the bail that held our lunch in a gallon bucket at the end. Sometimes the bucket would slip off the bail and there would go our lunch all over the road, which didn't mean much. We'd just get off and put it back in the bucket, 'cause you had to have lunch.

Horses were the usual mode of transportation back then, and I still consider them just a beast of burden. I've always maintained that if you own a horse you don't have to make an ass of yourself, he'll do it for you. You name it and I've had it happen.

One of the funniest things was the time I was riding with our neighbor Edwin Howell, sitting behind his saddle. The horse stepped in a hole and stopped short, and the two of us took off like birds. I landed on Ed's back and we were both a little shook up, and as Ed came to he looked over at me and said, "You can get off now; this is as far as I'm going."

As kids, my brother Don and I couldn't help but get into our share of mischief. There was the usual stealing watermelons and turning over the occasional outhouse, but most of the whippings I got from Mom were not for doing what I shouldn't have, but for *not* doing what I was told to do. I deserved most of them, except when I was punished for something my brother Don had done. He would do something wrong and look Mom square in the face and say, "Jimmy did it and I think he needs a whipping." For some unknown reason she would believe him. At the risk of sounding like one of the Smothers Brothers, I'll say Mom always *did* like him best.

In those days they used to give whippings if you misbehaved in school, and Mom would always say, "If you get a whuppin' there, boy, then you'll get a *good* one when you get home, 'cause *I* know how to do it." And that she did. Our neighbor Betty Jo Ward never cut me any slack either, and if I got in trouble at school she would always beat me home to tell my mother.

My best friend when I was growing up was a neighborhood boy by the name of Calvin Garrett. Cal and I were the same age, the same height, and wore the same size shoe, hat and shirt. Two peas in a pod I guess you might say. We sure did have fun, and for some reason, our brand of fun always came with a healthy dose of trouble. Actually, it was more like mischief—we didn't have enough money to get into any serious trouble. Now living with his, wife, Jan, in Hereford, Texas, he and I are as close as ever and still talk on the phone nearly every day.

Like most young teenage boys during those times, I was about thirteen years old when I began smoking cigarettes—nonfiltered Lucky Strikes. Don and I were working the harvest for my aunt Merle and uncle Frank at the time and they taught us all about cigarettes. Smoking was the cool thing to do back then, and I was hooked for the better part of thirty-five years.

And then there was my first cigar. Mom's brother, my uncle M.T., used to smoke them, and at that point I liked the aroma. M.T. handled a cigar in such a way that he made it look so good, and one day after visiting Mom he left over a half of one lying in an ashtray. I immediately filched that sucker and went out to the back of the well house to light it up, but it didn't taste nearly as good as it smelled. Shortly after having put the red end on it, I was as sick as a dog and began to throw up. Nobody ever knew about it and I never did get caught, but years later I read a poem that I still love because it always takes me back to that time. It was called "When I Smoked My First Cigar," and it was about a boy who was caught smoking a cigar by his father. I don't remember the whole poem or who wrote it, but my favorite line in it was "I knew he knew, *I knew* he knew, I'd smoked my first cigar . . . "

With not much else to do in Plainview, I used to ride around with my buddies Doug Cox and Melvin Bramlet. They had cars and that was the big thing, to ride up and down Broadway. Hanging out with the guys was really all the socializing I ever did, because the way I looked in my bib overalls I could forget about having a date or a girlfriend. There was this one girl by the name of Ann Stanton who I liked a lot and had set a date with one time, but she stood me up. After that I didn't have the nerve to ask anybody else out.

———•———

Seth Ward Baptist Church was a big part of our lives back then. Just about everybody we knew was Baptist. I've always maintained that being a Baptist won't keep you from sinnin', but it'll sure as hell keep you from enjoying it.

We'd walk to church every Sunday morning and Sunday night, and again to Wednesday night prayer meeting. Our Sunday best was old suits that were handed down from my uncle M.T. that Mom would cut down to fit Don and me. She made sure we were clean and presentable, as she'd scrub and dig with that old washcloth until it felt like she was gonna take out half of your ear.

Don and me in our Sunday best

Church was where I became acquainted with music—hymns—and I still love to sing those songs to this day. They bring back such fond memories of when friends and family would gather around to sing in our living room on Sunday afternoons. Mom would play the piano and we'd all sit around munching on popcorn and parched peanuts that came from our garden. That same old Broadman Hymnal that we used back then sits on the piano in the living room of our home today.

Music became more of a hobby once I was in my teens. I enjoyed singing with my buddies Glen Rainer and Orville and Clint McCarty, and I guess I was about fourteen or fifteen years old when we began singing in a quartet together. On Saturdays we'd go to town and watch a movie, then we'd walk over to the old First National Bank building and stand inside its alcove out front. We'd discovered there was an echo and great acoustics inside that alcove, and we loved to go in there and sing hymns.

It was with our little quartet that I remember singing harmony for the first time. I don't know just how it happened, but I knew it was different because it gave me goose bumps all over. It's hard to explain, but if you've ever sang harmony, then you understand just how much fun it can be.

———•———

Growing up poor and fatherless during the Great Depression weren't my only challenges as a kid. A great student, I was not. In school I was just too restless to concentrate on much of what the teacher had to say. There was a great big world outside of that classroom, full of opportunities that I was quite aware of, and most days it was difficult for me to think about anything else. I remember going to the pencil sharpener and looking out the window, dreaming of what it was like down that road to Amarillo. I thought if I could get to Amarillo I could get anywhere. All I could think about was having a better life, and getting out of the boll patches and wheat fields of West Texas.

2

THE MILITARY YEARS

I **SPENT MY** seventeenth birthday in Lima, Peru. Mom had signed for me to join the Merchant Marine because I was still too young for the military, and since I'd never been away from home or my family, joining the Maritime was the boldest thing I could have ever done. Being from the plains of Texas, I found ship life totally foreign, but it was a way to escape pulling cotton bolls, milking cows, cleaning chicken houses and all the other despicable jobs I'd had. My adventure had taken me from Plainview, to Dallas, to Catalina Island in California for boot camp, and then on to just south of Tacoma, Washington, where I was assigned to a ship called the S.S. *Heigara*.

I landed the glamorous job of wiper in what was known as the "black gang," and I had to get used to being covered with black oil from cleaning up the ship's engine room—hence the name. I discovered that being in the Maritime was no day at the beach, although an eight-hour day did seem pretty easy. I was used to working a lot harder and longer than that back home, so I would regularly volunteer for overtime. I especially enjoyed the extra pay.

The best part about my Maritime duty was mess time. I'd never had such good food as we had on that ship. The cook on board was a Swede who loved to bake. Pies were his specialty, and after a day or two of eating just one piece and trying to wrangle him out of another, I learned a little trick. I'd eat most of my pie and then leave a little piece of the crust. Then I'd pull a hair from my head, stick it in the piecrust and yell, "There's a damned hair in my pie!" Sure enough, I'd get a replacement.

The trip to Peru found our ship in stormy seas that tossed us around pretty good, and when we returned to Tacoma, I was glad my year was up. Being at sea was my first real adventure and an experience I'll never forget, and to this day I still love being around the water. I remember saying to one of the old salts on that ship, "Man, that's a lot of water," and he said, "Yeah, and you're just looking at the top of it!"

Back in Plainview, I signed on with the Peerless Pump Company installing irrigation wells six days a week. It was a tough job, but it was gratifying knowing that helping to bring water to a farmer's crops could mean his livelihood. It wasn't long until I was laid off, though, and that meant having to find more work. With not much opportunity around for a kid with no high school education, I decided to join the Army Air Corps, which today is the United States Air Force. In 1946, at the age of eighteen, I hopped the bus for Amarillo.

My physical was conducted at English Field, and for a sheltered and shy kid, the experience of parading around in the buff was unsettling. And you know, I've noticed that when you're put in a situation like that, where everyone is standing around in the nude, you don't know what to do with your hands—no pockets, no nothing, your arms and hands just dangling. And as I stood there I wondered, what does a nudist do with his car keys after he's locked his car?

Those were some cold marble benches in that building where we took our physical. I remember hearing some guy yell, "Sit down!" And when all fifty or sixty of our bare butts hit those benches it sounded like someone was applauding.

I'm sure the military has changed a lot by now, but they used to have showers that were just a wall with eight nozzles and no partitions in between. Taking a shower in the service was one of the toughest things for me. You stood there and showered right beside another guy, and that was the most embarrassing thing in the world to me. It was there I learned that all men are *not* created equal.

From Amarillo I went to Fort Bliss in El Paso, Shepherd Field in Wichita Falls, and then on to San Antonio for basic training at SAC Field, or today's Lackland Air Force Base. It was there that I became fascinated with airplanes, and to this day I still get a kick out of getting into a two-seater with a real jet jockey at the controls. I never took flying lessons, but I enjoyed learning about the different aircraft and becoming familiar with them.

One of the greatest thrills I would have came years later when I was traveling on American Airlines seated next to a guy by the name of John Hogan. He said he was a pilot for American but flew F-4s for the Air National Guard. I told him I'd give my eyeteeth to go up in one of those things, so a lot of pulled strings and six months later he made arrangements for me to come to Louisville, Kentucky, to fulfill my fantasy. I had to take a complete physical to do it, but it was the most exhilarating experience I'd ever had. He must have done every aerial maneuver you could do with that plane. And I remember that when we came down, John said, "Boy you're really something. You're the first person I ever took up that didn't get sick and throw up." I said, "Nobody told me I was supposed to get sick." Although they did tell me when I first got in that if I needed to throw up to use a barf bag, and if that wasn't enough, to throw up down the collar of my flight suit. It seemed it was a lot easier to clean me up than it was that airplane.

From basic training I went on to radio school at Scott Field in Illinois, where I became certified as an ROM, or radio operator and mechanic. I also learned Morse Code, about 95 percent of which I've retained to this day. The funny thing is I had seen Morse Code run people crazy because it was so tedious and frustrating. It was being phased out about the time I was learning it, though, and with all the new technology that was coming in at the time I can certainly understand why.

I didn't know it then, but my next destination would be one of the most important moves of my life. Uncle Sam shipped me off to Bolling Air Force Base in Washington, DC, where I would serve the remaining two-and-a-half years of my stint in the military. It was there that I launched my music career and met the woman who was to become the mother of my three children—but more on that later.

Private Dean

In Lima, Peru, on my seventeenth birthday

The military service provided me not only with invaluable experience and a steady paycheck, but unlike a lot of the other guys, I was having a good time. Though I wasn't the greatest linebacker around, I enjoyed playing Air Force football. For my job, I had become part of a team that did "test hops," and along with a pilot, copilot and engineer, I would go up in the aircraft to see that all the radio equipment was functional. Since the planes weren't ready until the afternoon, my job didn't call for me until later in the day, so I was able to sleep until noon. The food in the mess hall was good, too, and I was in the best physical condition ever. Not a bad life, I thought.

The accordion I had brought from home was beginning to come in handy. After seeing it in the window at Mary L. Spence's Music Store in Plainview, I had bought it for thirty-five dollars, thinking I could learn to play it like I had Mom's piano. When I was about ten years old, Mom had taught me a few chords on the piano, and since an accordion has the same kind of keyboard, I thought, why not? It would be easier to carry around. I actually think I fell in love with that accordion because it had this silver diamond in the bellows with lots of mother-of pearl, and I thought it was one of the prettiest things I'd ever seen. So now, for entertainment, a few of us guys would sit around on the bunks and I would play and sing for them in the barracks.

Brownie Callaway was one of my GI buddies who was also a musician, and he and a couple of his other buddies made up the house band at a nightspot in Washington called Harry's Tavern. Harry's was not one of your classier places. Okay, it was a real dive—but it had plenty of entertainment. The band played mostly old country favorites, and the place had its share of the usual fights and drunken brawls. The latter was practically guaranteed with the mixture of servicemen from different branches, along with the locals and the cheap beer.

One night, Brownie's band needed a replacement for their fiddle player, Scotty Stoneman (of the famed Stoneman Family), who was out sick. They thought I could play a fair accordion and asked me to take his place, and it didn't hurt that I knew the words to most of their songs either. I said yes and was offered a quarter of the band's tips, so for my first gig I made a grand total of four dollars.

I have to say it wasn't the money that I enjoyed most of all that first night with the band, but something more. I had a great time, and I think the folks in the audience did too. This show business felt good and *I was hooked.*

Since the owner liked how I was making the cash register ring, the Harry's Tavern gig turned out to be a regular thing when the band asked me to take Scotty's place permanently. Making music was great, but I especially enjoyed the fun we had bantering with the audience between the songs. I just loved making them laugh. The money had improved too; I was put on salary for twenty-five dollars a week plus tips.

The extra cash came in handy, as I was still sending some of my money home to Mom, and I learned quickly how to make the rest of it work for me. The master sergeants were making some serious cash by loaning money to the enlisted men in the middle of the month to be repaid on payday. Talk about loan sharks! They were getting twenty dollars for every ten dollars they loaned, earning 100 percent interest and taking advantage of the guys who were needing fast cash. But with the extra money I was making at Harry's Tavern, I was able to strike the guys a better deal. The word got out that I was lending twenty for twenty-five dollars on payday, and it wasn't long before I had quite a few clients. The master sergeants were pretty ticked off about it because I was stealing their business, but what could they do? We were *all* illegal.

I had to have a system, though. I had a policy that I would never loan money to anyone with a last name that came two names before or after mine on the pay list. That way, when I was collecting my loans, I could get into the pay line when my name was called and pick up my own pay, and then get back into position to collect from them. So with my regular pay, the money I made as a loan shark and the Harry's Tavern gig, I figured that by the time I was mustered out of the Air Force I was making more money than the commander of the base.

With Brownie Callaway's Band

At Scott Field in Illinois

Besides making money, having fun has always been one of my favorite pastimes, and I've never let anything get in the way of that, not even the military. I guess you could say I could be down-right mischievous. Like the day there was a doctor-ordered "short arm inspection" that was being held. This, of course, was an inspection of the most private part of your body. We would have to walk as a group from our own barracks to another for the inspection, wearing only GI shoes and an overcoat. They would then make us stand up on footlockers, take off our coats and throw them over the end of a bunk. So there we'd be, standing stark naked with everything hanging out.

Once, I thought it would be kind of humorous to get all the guys in our barracks to put on a necktie. Just try to visualize thirty guys standing on top of footlockers with nothing on but GI shoes and a necktie and tell me that's not funny. When we took off our overcoats the sight of our ties brought uproarious laughter from the other troops in the barracks, but the doctors giving the inspection didn't think it was very funny. That next week would find our entire group on KP duty.

I guess if I had to choose one memorable character from my time in the service, it would have to be my immediate superior officer, Lieutenant Stoneface. What a jerk this guy was. I didn't mind being told what to do by my superiors in the military, not as long as they were somewhat intelligent. But I resented being told what to do by a doorknob. He must have really liked me too, because he seemed to make it his life's mission to teach me a lesson or two.

A naturally miserable human being, Ol' Stoneface tried every way he could to get to me. Sometimes he succeeded and other times not. Once, as I was entertaining my buddies in the radio repair shop, I picked up a broom, hopped up on a workbench and began my comedy routine, which probably included a slam or two about our beloved leader. As I carried on to the guys, all of a sudden the laughter stopped, and I could tell by the faces in front of me that Stoneface was standing behind me. Yes, our lieutenant had come in and caught part of my act, and he didn't like it. In fact he didn't like it so much that he reported me to the commanding officer.

I would bet I'm the only guy in the United States Air Force that signed the 104th article of war with a charge of "habitual horseplay," all courtesy of Lieutenant Stoneface. It was pretty serious too, because the 104th article of war was just short of a summary court-martial. The punishment he gave me was to paint the orderly room after hours, but it ended up working out okay. The officer of the day whose direct supervision I was under ended up saying, "Dean, just bring your accordion and play and sing, and *I'll* paint the orderly room." And that's just what I did.

I can't say I was unhappy about leaving the Air Force, though I'll be forever grateful for the experience. That day when I went to pick up my discharge papers (honorable, I might add!), they asked me if I would like to reenlist. I said yes, that I would like to reenlist as a bird colonel with a guarantee of a promotion to brigadier general in three weeks. An absurd offer indeed, and I've often thought what an expensive mistake it would have been on my part had they accepted it. But thank God they didn't. They just laughed and I laughed, and then went on my way.

3

THE WASHINGTON, DC, YEARS

HARRY'S TAVERN WAS a long way from singing at the Seth Ward Baptist Church in Plainview, Texas . . . and I mean a *long* way. I continued to play with the house band at Harry's after I got out of the service in '49, having a pretty good old time "paying my dues."

One night, a guitar player by the name of Dub Howington came by the club and sat in with our band for a few sets, and I thought he was great. He must have liked what I did too, 'cause he told me we ought to form a new band along with his brother Roy, who played upright bass. I said yes, and our little band wasn't half-bad. Dub Howington and the Tennessee Haymakers included the three of us along with Herbie Jones, a really fine rhythm guitar player. We played Harry's Tavern as well as some of the other clubs around town, and I finally felt like I was in a real band with a real repertoire.

Now, the Howington brothers were good musicians and they sang a pretty good country duet, but nobody ever accused either one of them of being the sharpest knife in the drawer. I remember one time when the musicians' union, who referred to their members as "brothers," sent Dub a letter that began, "Dear Sir and Brother," summoning him to the union office because he hadn't paid his dues. He and Roy had asked me to go down there with them, and when we went in someone said, "Well, Dub, what'd ya bring Roy for?" And Dub said, "Because you *told* me to; your letter said 'Dear Sir and *Brother*'!"

The Howington brothers were always broke, fighting and usually drunk, and since Dub Howington would become a no-show with his own band after a while, we hired a lead guitar player named Jimmy Groves—a real super-picker. The band went on without Dub until we'd all had enough of his not showing up, and then something very important happened. As the front man for the Tennessee Haymakers, I was taking care of most of the business in Dub's absence, so we decided to change the name of the band, and with Herbie Jones on rhythm guitar, Jimmy Groves on lead guitar and Bob Elliot on bass, we became Jimmy Dean and the Texas Wildcats.

After a while our band really began to take off, and being the leader, I had the responsibility of finding work for my new "family." Besides singing, playing the accordion and fronting the band, I also had to learn how to negotiate, market, promote, collect, discipline, encourage and just plain organize this new business I was in. I liked the extra money I got from leading the band, and I became highly ambitious, intent on building a reputation for us.

We worked a lot, playing clubs all over Maryland and Virginia— the Dixie Pig, the Covered Wagon, the Famous Club—as well as dances at fire stations, lodge halls, church basements and junior high school gyms. We paid our dues at just about every joint around, from Rockwood Hall and the clubs at Belvedere Beach, Maryland, to the NCO clubs at Ft. Belvoir, Quantico Marine Base and Andrews Air Force Base.

Some of our band members would change now and then. Quincy Snodgrass would replace our bass player Bob Elliot after a while; and when Jimmy Groves went into the service in '52, we hired a fiddler named Buck Ryan. Buck was a Virginia State Champion, a two-time National Champion, one helluva musician and a good friend. Years later, the Virginia Folk Music Association would induct him into the Virginia Country Music Hall of Fame, and I was proud to be there to help make the induction in his honor.

Did I mention there were fights where our band played every night? Good ol' ball-bustin,' nose-bleedin' fights. And that was just with our girlfriends! I remember one time when a pretty good one

Jimmy Ray Dean, "Singing Cowboy"

broke out at the Harmony Club while we were on stage. Part of a light fixture from over the stage fell on me when some jerk threw a beer bottle and hit it. So I asked around in the audience and found out who the culprit was, walked up to the guy and asked him why he did it. Naturally, he denied it and we had a few words. Then, when he jumped up, I popped him, and when I did, his arm went around my neck as if he were trying to dig my eyeballs out with his fingers. Well, that's when one of his fingers went in my mouth and I bit down, heard a crunch and felt the bone break in my mouth—and he let go. They finally got him out of there, and the next night he came back and apologized to me.

I guess the worst brawl I ever got involved in was one night while we were playing a dance at a tobacco barn out in Maryland. These five young Amish men dressed in their black hats and traditional clothes had come in and were standing in front of the bandstand enjoying the music, and I had noticed that some old rednecks had started to pick on them. I told those guys to go away and leave these Amish fellows alone but they just kept on coming back and aggravating them. Then one old redneck grabbed one of the Amish kids' hats. That's when I walked to the end of the stage and placed the heel of my boot squarely in the middle of this guy's head. (Are you getting the idea that I was enjoying this?) Well, the old redneck went flying across the room, the band stopped playing and all hell broke loose. It was a *good* one!

There were many more nights that were memorable, and sometimes we'd end up in the middle of things, whether it was over some girl or just blowin' off steam. I guess I did enjoy a good scrap every now and then, and it's a funny thing . . . I found out that once you hit the first time, or you *get hit* the first time, it really doesn't hurt after that.

I figure it was about 1952 that I met a man named Connie B. Gay. Connie was a popular disc jockey, businessman, entrepreneur and reputed crook who hosted an afternoon country music show on WARL radio in Arlington, Virginia, called *Town and Country Time*. Besides having his radio show, Connie also booked nationally known country music artists to play show dates in the area.

Being the ambitious one, I got an idea to make a deal with him that would really help promote our band. One day I approached him at the radio station and said we'd play his afternoon radio show for free if he'd let us plug our nightly appearances. He liked the idea, especially since we agreed to personally go out and sell airtime for the show. The idea for the show worked out well, with Connie hosting and our band playing and singing, and I got to talk some too, as well as plug our up-and-coming dates in the area.

Live radio being what it was, naturally there were some glitches. I'll never forget the time there was some construction going on on the roof of the station and the workers were making noise while we were on the air. Not being used to having so many microphones around him and not realizing that the band's three mikes would pick him up, Connie pushed the mute button on his microphone and yelled, "Cut out that f——kin' hammerin'!" Boy did we get letters.

Getting to and from our gigs back then was nothing like today with bands and their fancy buses. It usually meant all of us having to pile in our cars loaded with musical equipment. So to make traveling to our gigs a little easier, Connie bought our band a vehicle—an old produce truck that we called the "kidney buster," for obvious reasons. He also bought a limousine for "the band," which he could write off his taxes, but he kept that for himself to ride around in.

The radio deal we'd made with Connie was beginning to pay off, as the crowds began to get bigger and bigger at our personal appearances. We started traveling abroad some too. It was in the fall of 1952 that Connie booked our group to entertain the U.S. Marines in the Caribbean and Panama Canal. Things were going great and I was having a pretty good time, until one day Connie said, "Jimmy, we need a comedy act in this troupe, so I want you to dress up and do some rube comedy." So complete with fright wig, blacked-out teeth and painted-on freckles, I gave it my best shot. And brother, was I *terrible*! I had to write my own material, and it was bad too. There's just some things a man should never ask another man to do.

It was also about this time that Jimmy Dean and the Texas Wildcats managed to get into a recording studio and record some songs. I had met a songwriter by the name of Fred Foster who worked as a carhop at the Hot Shoppe restaurant in Washington, and Fred hooked us up with a guy he knew named Ben Adelman.

Adelman had what he called a recording studio, but it was actually just a room over a garage with some cheap recording equipment. It was there that we recorded some demos that Fred sent to a record company in California called Four Star Records. They liked what they heard, but being a fledgling company, they couldn't afford to fly us to California to record for them. So we went to a place on Vermont Avenue in Washington, DC, called Sound Studios, and recorded some songs for them there. Our first record was a thing called "Bummin' Around," recorded with no stopping during the song and cut with a needle on acetate. We cut several other songs, including one called "Release Me." I learned many years later that I was the first singer to record what would eventually become a classic.

Another song we recorded then was called "Queen of Hearts." It was really a lousy record because of the fact that Bill McCall, the man who ran Four Star Records, had me sing it two keys too high. He wanted me to sound like Webb Pierce—a really hot singer at the time—but it sounded just awful (and people think that "cloning" country music acts in Nashville nowadays is something new). I wanted to promote the record on our radio show, but I couldn't hit the high notes, so every time I'd put the song on the set list I'd end up having Herbie Jones take it off at the last minute.

Other songs we recorded at Adelman's studio would later turn up on unauthorized albums and off-the-wall record labels, courtesy of Ben Adelman himself. Those were the albums that had a bunch of songs you'd never heard of (and that I never saw a penny from). But the worst thing about those bogus albums was that they usually used the worst picture of me they could find for the album cover.

———————

We recorded "Bummin' Around" in the summer of 1952, and by August we had heard that it was being played on radio stations in Houston and Dallas. But little did we know that it was catching on around the country, and by January of 1953 it had hit the national charts. Before we knew it "Bummin' Around" was at number five on the charts and had sold over two hundred thousand copies!

It was also during this time that the band and I were tapped to entertain the troops overseas. In March of 1953, along with a square dance group called the Echo Inn Cloggers, we were sent for a month-long USO tour to perform for the GIs in Europe. Then, much to our surprise, we learned upon our return home from Europe, that "Bummin' Around" had sold close to a *million* copies!

After arriving back in the States, I had to take a train home to Washington, and I remember being in my berth sleeping when I was awakened by someone singing "Bummin' Around." I opened my curtain, and when I looked out there was the train's porter singing, "Got an old slouch hat . . . Got my roll on my shoulder . . . " He went on

An early publicity shot . . . they posed me with a guitar,
even though I didn't know how to play it

That's me with my old manager, Connie B. Gay

about his business, but I thought *how cool* it was that he was singing my song. It affirmed that "Bummin' Around" had become a hit record, and I wanted to stick my head out and holler, "Hey! That's my song!" but I didn't.

Since our little record had stayed on the charts for nineteen weeks and made it to number ten nationally, Connie B. Gay decided to call in a favor from a music publisher friend of his who had a lot of pull in Nashville, Cedarwood Music's Jim Denny. From what I under-stand, Denny was also involved with booking acts for the Grand Ole Opry. So with his aid, on Saturday night, May 16, 1953, I made my first appearance at the Grand Ole Opry!

Grand Ole Opry star Carl Smith made my introduction on stage at the Ryman Auditorium, and I was never more frightened before or since that performance. Besides being as nervous as I've ever been in my life, the one thing I remember about that night was Opry comedian Rod Brasfield walking by me before going on the air, say-ing, "I don't know what you're worried about. You've only got eight or ten million people listening to you." *Thanks, Rod.*

Having a hit record with "Bummin' Around" was a real break for us, but we still had to eat, so our band continued to play the radio shows in the afternoon and our club gigs at night. Still, having a hit gave us the encouragement to press on. We were fortunate to have gotten the record deal, and truly indebted to Fred Foster, who would go on to become one of the most successful people in the music industry, most notably the creator of Monument Records. I always liked old Fred, and we're still good friends today. In addition to being an astute businessman, he's always had a great sense of humor. I remember once during a visit to Nashville I went to see him at his office, and there in the lobby of Monument Records was a sign that read, "Will Rogers Never Met Larry Gatlin."

Our top ten record was indeed exciting, and it made Jimmy Dean and the Texas Wildcats instant celebrities. Finally, it felt like I was getting somewhere in this music business. However, because of the questionable business ethics of Four Star Records head Bill McCall, and a deal that gave me only a penny a record in royalties, I figured that for my first hit record I made approximately thirty-five dollars.

4

TOWN AND COUNTRY TIME

WITH THE POPULARITY that our band had gained in the Washington, DC, area, it wasn't long before Jimmy Dean and the Texas Wildcats were playing mostly all dances instead of the nightclubs and dives where we'd begun. And it sure didn't hurt *my* feelings any to get away from those seedy places and people. One of the worst was the Homestretch—a dive with a whorehouse upstairs and the occasional thugs in the parking lot threatening people with knives and guns. And then there was the guy who ran the Covered Wagon, Lou Miller, who used to hit people with a baseball bat.

I remember something Lou Miller told me one time that's always stuck with me. We had gone to work at his club on the contingency that if we filled the place up we'd get a raise. He agreed to the deal, but when we packed the place he reneged. When I asked him about it he said, "You think you can't be replaced, don't you?" And I said, "No, I didn't say that." "Well," he continued, "if you think you can't be replaced, I'll tell you what, you go home tonight, draw a tub of water and stick your hand in it. Then pull it out and see how big a hole you leave." Such a sweetheart, that Lou Miller.

Things were looking up for Jimmy Dean and the Texas Wildcats, with better places to play, a hit record under our belt and a successful radio show. So I thought since television was beginning to take off, why not try for a TV show? Now that would *really* be the Big Time. Once again I presented my idea to Connie B. Gay, and again he went for it. I suggested we do a television show with the same deal as before, with us playing for free as long as we could promote our dates. I found out pretty quick that you can get a lot of work if you do it *for free*.

Acting as our manager, Connie approached the ABC affiliate WMAL-TV in Washington, and they agreed to sign us up for a daily half-hour TV show in the afternoons. Now, *this* was exciting! Making its debut in January of 1955, *Town and Country Time* starring Jimmy Dean and the Texas Wildcats also featured a couple of other acts that Connie had signed as regulars: a singer who was just a young college kid from the University of North Carolina named George Hamilton IV and a ventriloquist named Alec Houston, a former member of the Echo Inn Cloggers. Buck Ryan and Herbie Jones were still in our band, and we had added a banjo player named Smitty Irvin. Smitty was a real talented guy who was able to fix or build anything with his hands, and he also played a little steel guitar with us until we hired a regular steel player named Marvin Carroll.

The show featured mostly all country music and some inspirational tunes, and aired locally in the Washington, DC, area. My costume was usually a tailored Western-cut suit with pointed-toe boots and a cowboy hat, and the band members would all wear matching uniforms of Western shirts and slacks with neckerchiefs and cowboy hats. We weren't a bad-looking group. I guess we all cleaned up pretty good, as they say.

It was about this time that we decided to add another guitar player to our band, and there was a certain fellow that we had in mind by the name of Roy Clark. Roy was really terrific. He'd grown up around Washington and had been playing in other bands in the area for a good while. In the past, he and I had worked on some of the same shows and we'd jammed together and traded a few jokes, and we got along real well. That "one of these days we're gonna work together" day had come, and Roy was an excellent addition to the Texas Wildcats.

Things were rolling along pretty well for us; in fact things had really taken off, but our schedule had gotten to be so hectic with the added TV show that we were beginning to meet ourselves on the highway coming and going. We had the daily radio show on WMAL and the local TV show five days a week in the afternoon on channel 7. Then in October of that same year Connie announced that we would also be starring in a three-hour live TV show at Turner's Arena (later called the Capitol Arena) on Saturday nights called *Town and Country Jamboree*. Along with all of this we were still playing our dances, show dates and regular weeklong gigs at the local clubs. In other words, we were busier than that proverbial one-legged man at a butt kickin'.

A typical day for our band began in the morning at the radio station, where we would rehearse and then do a live one-hour show at noon. From there it was off to the television station, where we would once again rehearse, and also do a run-through for the TV show, and then perform it live at five o'clock. Most nights, as soon as the

Buck Ryan, Marvin Carroll, Jimmy, Herb Jones, Roy Clark (seated) and Mary Klick

last note was hit on the closing theme song, we'd run downstairs from the TV studio, pack everything into the car and drive a hundred miles or more to do a live show for that night. Sometimes we wouldn't get back home until around three or four in the morning. Then it was up again early and back to the radio station for the next morning's rehearsal.

Our busy schedule went on practically seven days a week, and the guys in the band were real troupers. Although, I don't think Roy was as dedicated to the cause as the rest of us. In fact, his habit of being late was really starting to bug me. If you know me at all, then you know that that's my pet peeve in life. I am never late and I arrive as early as possible, because if I tell somebody I'm gonna do something *I do it*. I consider people's time their most valuable asset, and I am not privileged to waste their time, nor they mine. Roy Clark was not only wasting my time but a lot of other folks' as well, and it wouldn't be too long before the spit would hit the Spam.

So, as the story goes, Jimmy Dean and the Texas Wildcats were scheduled to headline a Saturday morning show for a big weeklong celebration at George's Warehouse Appliance Store (well, it was big to *us*), and we were to be there at 10 A.M. That morning, ol' Roy came rollin' in about his usual twenty minutes late, and I just walked over to him as he went to get his guitar out and said, "Don't bother to take it out of the case, Roy. You're through." He said, "Hey, Jim, you don't mean that." Then I told him that I'd had it with him and that this was it. Roy just gave me that mischievous grin of his and said, "Well, just let me pick one . . . you might like it!" I just grinned back at him, and then he packed up and went home. I found out later that he had gone to Connie B. Gay to try to save his job, but Connie was behind me all the way.

With Roy being young and a little on the wild side, we quickly found out that he wasn't going to go away without some sort of ado. One night shortly after he was fired he showed up at the Log Cabin, where our band was playing, and right in the middle of our set he drove his motorcycle through the club, across the dance floor and up to the stage. It was like Moses parting the Red Sea; people scrambled everywhere, some yelling and some laughing. It really was quite a stunt.

Roy and I remained friends after that, and today he readily admits that I was justified in firing him. He concedes that he pushed a little too far, and that if he had been in my place he would have fired him too. He'll also tell you that he learned some real lessons during his two years with us, especially about hard work, and that nothing "just happens" without a plan, that you have to *make* things happen. Roy never could get over how careful I was with money and the fact that I had put myself on an allowance. But back then he was just a kid, living it up, sleeping late in the day and playing music at night, and just generally playing around. But as we all know, the multitalented Roy Clark grew up and into one helluva showman and one of the biggest stars of our time, and I'm proud to be able to call him my friend.

To replace Roy in the band I hired another really fine guitar player by the name of Billy Grammer. Billy was also a good singer and a great guy, and he added a lot to our show. Years later he would have an impressive career of his own with hit records including the classic song "Gotta Travel On," as well as becoming a regular performer on *The Grand Ole Opry*.

───── • ─────

As *Town and Country Time* grew in popularity, we gained a new sponsor; a new product called Brigg's Ice Cream was to be introduced to the Washington area on our show. Our show was live, and in those days it was common for the performers to do the local commercials. So every week the ad agency for Brigg's Ice Cream would hand me a script and I would do my best to read it, but I knew it wasn't coming across very well. The script was poorly written, with a lot of advertising BS in it and a bunch of adjectives that added up to nothing, and I just couldn't read it with conviction. I knew I wasn't selling Mr. Brigg's product, even though I sincerely believed in it and knew it was the best ice cream around. The situation was really bugging me . . . and then I got an idea.

I decided to call Mr. Briggs himself and explain to him that I didn't think his commercials were good enough, that the scripts written by his ad agency weren't doing either one of us any good. I asked him to let me do them my way for a week, just the camera on Jimmy Dean holding a container of Brigg's Ice Cream, totally off the cuff. He gave me the chance I was asking for and said he would watch when I asked him to. I don't remember word for word exactly what I said on the next commercial, but it went something like this:

"I remember when my granddaddy would take down that old ice cream freezer, and Grandma would gather fresh country eggs and fresh, thick sweet cream to put in it. Papa Taylor would keep adding the ice, and he and I would turn that old crank until we could hardly turn it any more. And then finally he'd take the top off, and if you were real lucky he would hand you one of the paddles for you to clean. And boy, I'd take my spoon and run it down that paddle and pull off the best ice cream in the world.

"It still is the best ice cream in the world, but I've got to tell you, this Brigg's Ice Cream is the closest thing to it, 'cause it's got the same fresh ingredients, the same fresh country eggs and fresh, thick sweet cream . . . "

Well, by the end of the show the phone was ringing and it was Mr. Briggs wanting to talk to me. He loved the commercial so much that *he* wanted to go out and buy his ice cream! From that moment on he told his ad agency to "forget the scripts and just leave it to Jimmy." He didn't even want any of those people around me, and told them, "Just give him the flavor of the week and stay the hell out of the studio!"

The Brigg's Ice Cream commercial was the most important thing to happen to me as a result of that television show, because it taught me that if I believed in a product I could "sell" it. In my mind I always tried to sell a product to the one person that knew me best— my mother. I figured if I could sell it to Mom I could sell it to anyone, because Ruth Dean was hands down the toughest "sell" in the world. It's been said, and I believe it's true, that the TV camera is a mirror to the soul. I know it's true for me. People can usually tell when you're being dishonest anyway. That commercial was indeed a valuable experience, for which I'll be forever grateful, and a lesson learned that would serve me extremely well in the years to come.

In the early 1950s *Town and Country Time* was the most popular afternoon television show in the Washington, DC, area. I had even heard from several sources that President Harry Truman himself watched our show sometimes, that if he was in a meeting when the show came on at four-thirty, he'd say "Gentlemen, if you will excuse me for a little while," and then go back to the Oval Office and shut the door. Harry Truman was a good guy and I liked him a lot.

Along with our afternoon television show, our three-hour Saturday night TV show, *Town and Country Jamboree,* had become a success as well. With the televised portion from 10 P.M. until 1 A.M., it was a six-hour event that started at 7:00 every Saturday night, with fifteen thousand or so folks having a high old time drinking beer, dancing and enjoying the music. We were definitely the stars of the show and enjoying the notoriety.

One of my favorite memories from the *Jamboree* was its opening night. It was a pretty big do, with guest stars Bob Wills and the Texas Playboys, Marvin Rainwater and Autry Inman helping us debut the show. I was especially thrilled that my childhood idol Bob Wills was there, because where I come from in West Texas he was almost like a religion. But, I somehow never summoned the courage to walk up to him at that show and tell him how much I worshiped him as a kid. I was just too shy, I guess, and I've always regretted that.

To turn our band into more of a show for the *Jamboree,* Connie added a couple of girl singers to the Texas Wildcats for variety and to "purty up the stage." Dale Turner was a lovely and sweet girl who would sing a few numbers with us, and Mary Klick was a very talented musician and singer from Hagerstown, Maryland, who played guitar and upright bass.

We'd have occasional guest performers on our shows as well. Among them were Grandpa Jones (who lived in the area at the time), Eddy Arnold, Johnny Cash, Faron Young, Carl Smith, Ferlin Husky, Mac Wiseman, Hank Thompson, and the Wilburn Brothers, just to name a few. The broadcast, which in 1955 was actually America's first late-night musical variety TV program, became somewhat of a regional institution for Connie B. Gay.

By March of 1956 we would also add another regular performer to our cast, a girl singer by the name of Patsy Cline. Patsy was on our Saturday night show at the Capitol Arena for about a year, and then later on was added to our morning radio and afternoon TV shows.

I had met Patsy when she came into the Starlight Club in Washington one night while I was playing there. She walked in with a clothes bag over her shoulder and asked if she could sit in with the band, so we went over to the piano. Patsy sang a little bit for me, and I found out right then and there she was one hell of a singer. Later on, when we called her up to sing with the band, she had changed into a flashy cowgirl outfit complete with fringe and boots, and I thought, *Who the hell's gonna care that she went to all that trouble in* this *joint?* But that was Patsy. If she was gonna do something, it wasn't gonna be done halfway. And besides, Patsy Cline was *not* going to go unnoticed!

Patsy was a big fan of Kay Starr, and just listening to her sing you could tell she'd probably heard every record Kay Starr ever made. Besides working together on the television shows, Patsy and I, along with George Hamilton IV, would also work some package shows and road dates together that Connie would book.

George was a pleasant guy to work with, and Patsy—well, she was just a piece of work. I recall one time when we were on a trip to Canada, we were walking into the hotel lobby to check in, and Patsy saw a tall, good-looking Canadian Mountie standing across the room. She turned to me and said, "Dean, go over there and tell him I wanta f——k his boots off." I said, "Sorry, Patsy, but I'm not pimping for anyone this week." I guess flirting was just Patsy's second nature, 'cause she would come on to all the guys, including me.

There have been plenty of stories about Patsy Cline that have circulated over the years, especially about her foul mouth and how she could drink any one of us guys under the table. There were even times when she was so drunk she could hardly stand up and talk on the microphone, but when it came time for her to sing she had no problem. One night, during a performance in a club, she was slurring her words over the mike and said, "I want to thank you all for making me what I am today," and a guy from the audience yelled, "What's that, a goddamn drunk?" Then Patsy yelled back "Screw you!" and started after the guy.

I don't know if she ever got to that guy in the audience, but Patsy wasn't afraid to defend herself. She and her husband, Charlie Dick, would get into some hellacious fights and she'd come to the TV show in tears saying, "He beat me up again." But Patsy would fight back too; I don't think she was anybody's punching bag. She and Charlie would even fight during the show on Saturday nights, and he would

GUNTHER
Premium Dry Beer

PRESENTS Connie B. Gay's
TOWN and COUNTRY®

GUNTHER BREWING COMPANY • BALTIMORE, MD.

JIMBO ROPER

WMAL-TV CHANNEL 7
10:30 SATURDAY night

That's me and Patsy Cline backstage about 1957.

Me and Elvis
backstage

Elvis pays
a visit on *Town
and Country Time*

beat her up on the breaks. We'd all say, "Patsy, why don't you just have him thrown in jail?" But as far as we know she never did; she'd just pout and shrug her shoulders and go on.

It's often been said that Patsy was outspoken, brash and downright bawdy at times, and though she was too gruff for me, I don't think she meant a whole lot by it. She just wanted to be a "good old back-slappin' one of the boys" kind of girl. It's true she would cuss like a sailor, especially when she was mad, but she could also be warm and sweet, and I got along with her just fine. So much has been written and said about Patsy, and I could keep going on here, but I won't. I'll just say this: Patsy liked to sing and she was a good singer, and she *knew* she was a good singer. There have been many who have tried to copy her, but no one could ever improve on the original. As far as I'm concerned, there will always be only one Patsy Cline.

Throughout the years I've been fortunate to have had the opportunity to witness the beginnings of more than one musical legend. Occasionally entertainers that were performing in the Washington, DC, area would drop by WMAL-TV to do a guest spot on our show. One afternoon, we were paid a visit by a very young and inexperienced Elvis Presley, who was appearing on an excursion boat called the S.S. *Mt. Vernon.* The boat would make its run from DC, up the Potomac River to Mt. Vernon, where there was an amusement park, and of course the home of George Washington. Elvis was the featured entertainer on the boat that night and was booked on our show to promote the cruise, apparently because it wasn't quite full. I had the excruciating task of conducting the interview with Elvis, possibly the worst I've ever done. It went basically like this:

ME: So, you're gonna be on the S.S. *Mt. Vernon* tonight, are you, Elvis?

ELVIS: Yep.

ME: Have you ever worked on a boat before?

ELVIS: Nope.

ME: I imagine you're looking forward to this, aren't you?

ELVIS: Yep.

And that was it. "Yep, nope . . . " and that's all he would say. But I'm sure it didn't matter; all it would take would be for the gals who tuned in to that TV show to get a good look at him and he wouldn't have any trouble selling more tickets. Years later, when we were both playing in Las Vegas, Elvis would apologize profusely for leaving me hanging on that interview. He told me, "You know, Jimmy, I was so sorry about that but I was scared to death." It's hard to believe that Elvis could be shy or afraid of anything, but I guess even "The King" had those days in the beginning.

It had been a great ride with *Town and Country Time,* and the Texas Wildcats and I had experienced a lot of changes during the show's run. It was an incredible time in our lives in this business of television; and though our TV show would soon come to an end, we had no idea that our best years in the entertainment business were still to come.

🌿 5 🌿

NETWORK, SWEATWORK

I T WAS THE mid 1950s when the TV networks started having early-morning shows, with the first one being NBC's *Today* show featuring Dave Garroway. Naturally, the other networks would try to compete with them, and CBS had tried everything to top NBC in the ratings. They weren't too successful, though, even after trying morning shows that featured Walter Cronkite and Jack Paar.

CBS made another stab at it with *Good Morning* starring Will Rogers, Jr., and it had been on for about a year when there was an article in the newspaper saying they wanted to replace it with a country music show. The network was auditioning country music talent from all over the country and had received a half dozen pilot shows for review, including several from Nashville featuring stars from the Grand Ole Opry.

Our *Town and Country Time* show had been on WMAL-TV in Washington, DC, for about three years, and with such a great opportunity for national exposure, my manager, Connie B. Gay, and I decided to throw our hat in the ring. So using the cast of performers from our television show, we recorded a *Jimmy Dean Show* for CBS. I spent about three hundred and twenty-five dollars on a kinescope—the predecessor of videotape—and we recorded straight through with no stopping. We had no money for several takes or fancy editing. The people in Nashville had spent thousands and thousands of dollars for their audition tapes, with big stars, elaborate sets, production and writing, but thank God for the ignorance of the big brass at CBS in New York, because when we played our kinescope for them, they liked our show better than the others. They didn't know me from Adam or a big star like Eddy Arnold, and I remember there was a tremendous amount of animosity from the folks in Nashville over my winning that TV show.

What impressed the network, I was told, was my "folksiness and ease with error." It happened that I had flubbed a song on the audition tape, and during the chorus I forgot the lyrics and began to ad-lib. I knew we couldn't do it over again, so after the song ended I said, "I know those words are original, but I'd appreciate it if none of you folks would beat me down to the copyright office with them."

So there we were, playing in the Big Leagues, trying to knock television's "big boys" off their perches. I remember distinctly having read in a lot of publications the words that still stick in my mind: "Country Show Going Up Against the Firmly Entrenched Dave Garroway." Broadcasting from WTOP-CBS in Washington, *Country Style* starring Jimmy Dean became the first nationally televised network show to originate from Washington, DC, other than news programs.

I was certainly glad they decided to keep the show in Washington instead of moving it to New York, 'cause the Big Apple was just too fast for me. We basically used the same cast that was on the *Town and Country Time* shows, with one exception—no Patsy Cline. I'm not sure what happened there, but I know that she and Connie B. Gay got sideways with each other and he wouldn't use her on our new show. I think he got ticked off at her because she may have ended up on somebody else's audition tape instead of helping us with ours.

Country Style featuring Jimmy Dean made its debut on April 8, 1957, and aired every Monday through Friday from 7 until 7:45 A.M. It was followed by fifteen minutes of news and then *The Captain Kangaroo Show,* and because it was live television, we had to do two performances. The first one was at 7 A.M. for the East Coast, and then we repeated the entire show at 8 A.M. EST for the Midwest and central time zone, with a fifteen-minute break between shows.

The cast of our early morning TV show on CBS

It was a killer schedule, and since rehearsals began at 5 A.M., I'd have to get up every morning at 3:30. Breakfast was usually a Waring blender filled with cream, two eggs, vanilla and sugar—certainly no cholesterol *there* (and if I ate like that today, my arteries and veins would cough and choke and close up completely). After breakfast it was off to the studio in my purple '57 Oldsmobile, and the only people I'd meet on the highway were the drunks going home from the night before.

With the advent of the new show, Connie B. Gay would add some new performers to our cast of characters. Joining me and the Texas Wildcats—Billy Grammer, Herbie Jones, Mary Klick, Buck Ryan, and Marvin Carroll—were a former Miss Florida, Jan Crockett; ventriloquist Alec Houston and his company of dummies; a lovely and talented lady named Jo Davis, who incidentally was the only one on the show that could read music; and a duet called the Country Lads featuring Dick Flood and Billy Graves. It was a pretty well-rounded group and a whole lot of talent joined together.

Country Style featured mostly country songs and sacred numbers, with a pop song thrown in every now and then, and plenty of country banter peppered with y'alls and some other down-home sayings. I've always said that Lawrence Welk played champagne music and we played music to drink coffee by. I would handle the hosting duties and sing songs as well as some duets with Jo Davis and Mary Klick, and I also had the job of making sure the songs that the others would perform were appropriate, though I hardly ever made anybody change anything. All I asked was that they kept everything friendly and happy because we were playing to people who were just getting up, and I didn't think they would want to look at a bunch of sad, gloomy kissers.

The press tuned in to our show big time, and we made the papers everywhere the first few days we were on. And much to our surprise, we received great reviews from the New York critics. They didn't pan us like we'd thought they probably would.

We began to get calls for interviews, with them wanting to get to know us "country bumpkins" and what we were all about. They'd ask us about our favorite music, to which my answer was always "hymns," and when they asked if I had any favorite entertainers, I would tell them Ferlin Husky and Bing Crosby. Who did I pattern myself after? "Nobody." I'd tell them that maybe I tried not to copy anyone because of something my granddaddy always said: "Be yourself, son, because if people don't like you as you are, they sure won't like you as somebody you're tryin' to be."

One critic in *Time* magazine said, "Although Dean's corn is off an aged cob, he is photogenic, amiable and happy-go-lucky." Then there was the critic that gave us credit for "just being up, shaved, breakfasted, bright-eyed, cheerful and in full makeup at that hour, and ready to entertain the world." There were also some who would good-naturedly take a poke at us. I remember being described by one as a "handsome Texas Stringbean," and by another as being "real tall and slim [I'm six-foot-three] with a boyish face, not much of a voice but a real friendly personality." *Thanks*.

This new TV show was a real happening, it seemed, and it turned out to be more successful than any one of us had ever dreamed it would be. And when the Neilsen ratings were taken two weeks after the show had its debut, we were all ecstatic when they said we were ahead of NBC's *Today* show with Dave Garroway in every market. The press was having a field day with it, and the newspaper dailies were saying things like, "Within two weeks Jimmy Dean has become the first performer in three years to clout NBC in the morning ratings war," and "Until Dean, no matter how CBS brewed the morning coffee, the network couldn't take viewers away from percolating Dave Garroway on NBC's *Today*. "

It was also the first time in the history of the Neilsen ratings that the results were sent back to be checked. They just couldn't believe that we were ahead. Our popularity was obviously verified by the estimated two million people watching every week, and by the twenty-five thousand fan letters we were receiving weekly. We were all truly amazed at the immediate and overwhelming acceptance of the show by the big-city viewers.

After we had topped the *Today* show I remember a quote to the press that Connie B. Gay had made when asked about the reason for our success. He said, "That's easy. Garroway plays to the box office, and Jimmy plays to the grandstand."

I enjoyed this particular television show more than any other I'd ever done, mainly because we had total freedom.

We did what we wanted to do and we had fun. One time while we were singing "The Yellow Rose of Texas," Smitty Irvin was playing the banjo and led the entire group of us marching out of the studio. Of course, this left the director with nothing to shoot except picket fences, amplifiers, coffee urns and whatever else there was on the set. Then, when we marched back into the studio and the song ended, all we heard was a pause and a very irritated director coming over the studio's talk back speaker saying, "Very funny."

Our show was broadcast mainly from the studio in Washington, but would travel occasionally. For one week during the summer of '57, we took it to a ship's deck in Norfolk, Virginia, during the International Naval Review for a remote broadcast aboard the USS *Iowa*. The Review was highly touted because it was the first of its kind in over fifty years, featuring over a hundred ships from seventeen foreign countries and the United States. Television was playing a major role in its promotion and it seemed that all the networks were at the Norfolk event. In fact, I remember how the press made such a big deal about the NBC helicopter buzzing over the ship for a half hour, making noise and hovering over us during our show. When NBC was confronted by the CBS officials during an investigation, they pleaded pure innocence, saying they didn't know our show was going on there and that they were rehearsing for *The Home Show,* which was also originating from the event. Whether they were trying to mess us up or not, it worked out just fine, because it was our show and not theirs that ended up on the front page of the *New York Times Magazine* with a full-color spread.

An occasional gig without the band and entire show wasn't unusual. I remember one time being booked to do a show up in Pennsylvania and the only ones that went with me from the cast were rhythm guitarist Herbie Jones and our conductor, Joel Herron, who would lead the band we were to work with there. The job turned into somewhat of a nightmare, however, when an airplane pilot named Fred Johnson offered to fly us there in his plane and nearly got us killed.

I had known Fred from my early days in Washington when he had a Sheetrock business, and I'd worked for him hanging Sheetrock during the day to make some extra cash while playing the Dixie Pig at night. The four of us from the show and Fred's wife set out for the Pennsylvania gig in his plane, and everything was fine—that is until we were on our way home that day and we got fogged down between some mountains. There was so much fog we couldn't see over the mountains or how to get out, and we just kept circling around until Fred said, "Hey, there's a road down there. It looks clear of traffic, so we'll go down there and land on it."

Well, from the air the road looked flat, but when we got down there it was nothing but rolling hills. We bounced and bounced until Fred finally got the damned thing stopped, and we were thankfully able to walk away unscathed. Once we got out of the plane, we realized we were in some kind of military installation. We walked for the longest time, until the only person we saw was a guard at the guard shack, sitting in his truck eating his lunch.

I don't know whose idea it was at the time, but as we approached the guard, we decided to start singing so we wouldn't startle him and get our butts shot off. We must have looked pretty dumb and the guard must have thought he was hallucinating. When he saw us, I won't ever forget the double-take he gave us, as he whipped out his gun and jumped out of the truck, realizing we were on the *inside*. He ended up taking all of us down to the provost marshal office for a visit with the major there. That major gave me a strange look, obviously recognizing me from somewhere, and in a very stern and military voice he said, "I recognize you. Pentagon, wasn't it?" Guess I thought our TV show was a little more popular than that.

Little did we know how dangerous our retreat could have been. They told us we had landed in the middle of the Letterkenny Military Depot munitions dump, and had we gone a hundred feet to either side and hit one of the explosive-filled bunkers along that road, we could have started a series of explosions that would have lasted for weeks.

After having quite the military experience and going through every kind of scrutiny you can think of, we were finally released. It didn't take us long to get into that place, but it sure took us a long time to get out. Fred wasn't so lucky—it took them forever to let him get his plane out of there. Poor Fred. He was a good friend and a really nice guy, but either he didn't have the instrument rating to fly in those conditions or he wasn't a very good pilot, and he was unfortunately killed in that plane just two weeks later.

———•———

After a while our television show added the occasional guest performer that would appear every day for the entire week. Today one of my most prized possessions is an old upright piano that we used on that show, because on the guest star's last day he or she would sign it somewhere. I wouldn't take anything for that old beat-up piano with its collection of signatures. We had some really big names on the show, like Mel Torme, Les Paul and Mary Ford, Sam Cooke, Jaye P. Morgan, The Mills Brothers, Hoagy Carmichael, Billy Eckstine, Jimmie Davis, Porter Wagoner, Carl Smith, George Hamilton IV and Jim Reeves. And even though the Texas Wildcats didn't read a lick of music, they always did such a great job of backing them all.

I had to laugh when some of the guests would come in with their music charts for the musicians and our guys would just stare at them like a tree full of owls. But I think it was the singer Jerry Vale who got the biggest kick out of it and laughed the hardest, when he went to pull out his charts and somebody said to him, "Hoss, you might as well put those away . . . "

With the success of the morning show, the network was convinced that if there were that many country music fans up that early in the morning, there was no telling how many more there were later in the day. So to find out, they doubled my workload and added another show. In October of that same year *The Jimmy Dean Show* debuted live on CBS for an hour on Saturdays at noon EST. It also featured big name stars, like Steve Lawrence and Eydie Gorme and the Mills Brothers, and used basically the same format as the morning show.

Not only did the two TV shows keep me hopping, but I was making some occasional personal appearances as well. Before we had landed the network shows, I'd been signed to a recording contract with Mercury Records back in '55 by a man named Dee Kilpatrick. I'd released a few records and had some success with one called "Glad Rags," so every now and then I'd make appearances on other shows in the area to promote my records. I'd also have to hop up to New

York City to do *The Vic Damone Show,* as well as make the trip to Nashville every few weekends to record more songs for Mercury.

After my Mercury Records contract was up, CBS signed me to a record deal with Columbia Records, a division of the CBS network. I think it was Mitch Miller (of the famed TV show, *Sing Along with Mitch*) who did the signing, since he was A&R (artist and repertoire) director with them at the time. It was his job to find and match songs with the recording artists. Our first release was an album of hymns called *Jimmy Dean's Hour of Prayer* that I recorded with the cast of the morning show in the autumn of '57. Then in November of that year I had a single released called "Deep Blue Sea," and another one at Christmastime called "Little Sandy Sleighfoot."

Things were going along great for our shows on CBS, with wonderful ratings and lots of fan mail, but the networks couldn't sell time at that early an hour and our morning show would only attract one sponsor: Armstrong Quaker Rugs. It wasn't enough to pay the bills, however, and though it was the first time a network ever canceled their top-rated show, CBS gave our morning show the boot after nine months on the air. In spite of the more than seven thousand cards and letters begging the network to let it stay on, we were canceled and left with just the Saturday afternoon show. The folks over at NBC were having the same troubles, but I guess they were content to lose money just so they could get a jump on the morning ratings.

I think it was when we lost the morning show that the TV executives at CBS started looking very closely at moving things up to New York. They were just not happy with the production and sets at our DC television station. Indeed, the critics liked the entertainment, but there were times when they panned the small-time production and the minimal sets and lighting. And since the shows were done live, there was no way to fix it if something went wrong. Like the time I was sitting on a stool singing a ballad and an entire set fell down behind me. I just went right on singing like nothing happened, and then afterward I said, "Wait just a minute . . . Before we go ahead with this show, if anybody's got anything they want to drop, would you drop it now?!" The audience thought it was hilarious and roared with laughter.

In the past I had resisted the network's efforts to do the show from New York City and told them I thought the program would lose its flavor should it be moved there. Nevertheless, I could tell that changes were beginning to take place at CBS. To get me to go to New York, the network actually made me "an offer I couldn't refuse" as they say, and I was to move there to do a half-hour show on the weekdays. The format would change, the look would change, and Herbie Jones was the only one of the cast members that they wanted to take with us. Everyone else was history . . . There would be no more Texas Wildcats.

It was then that Connie B. Gay sold my management contract to CBS for what I understand was a "sizable amount." I never really knew the details, but there were several newspaper reports that said CBS was to pay him a thousand dollars a week for several years. Nevertheless, I'm indebted to Connie because he did indeed open a lot of doors for me. He would go on to become one of country music's most important people, as the founding father of the Country Music Association, and ultimately a member of the Country Music Hall of Fame.

I would miss those days in radio and television in Washington. It was a great place to go to "school" and the town was very good to me, but I think the thing I miss most about those times was the freedom I had in broadcasting, and just doing what came naturally on live TV. There's no doubt that living in Virginia and working in the Washington, DC, area was one of the most important chapters in my life, a chapter of learning and growing.

And when things didn't go so smoothly, I would have to take my own advice and reflect on a little saying that I used to end my television show: "Grin once in a while, it's good for ya."

6

NEW YORK CITY

IF ANYBODY'S EVER told you that New York City is a horrible place with too many people, buildings and weirdos, I guess it's really how you look at it. One of my first experiences there was on a cold, gray and rainy day as I was on my way to rehearsal for our new television show. I was commuting to the city on the train from Connecticut, and I would have to catch a taxi to the studio after arriving at Grand Central Station. This one morning in the cab, I said to the driver, "What a horrible day!" And this big, black taxi driver said, "Hey, man, it's a *beautiful* day! Any day the good Lord lets you get out of bed, put your feet on the floor and walk outside, it's a *gorgeous* day!" I've never forgotten that. It was then and there I learned that you can find good and decent people all over the world, including New York City.

It was late in the summer of '58 that I made the move north from Washington, DC, to New York City for my new job. CBS was determined to make our new television show bigger and better there, but I wasn't so sure it was going to work. I had sold our house on Roosevelt Street in Arlington, Virginia, but had held on to some farm property I owned in Loudon County just in case. The house I rented on the outskirts of New York City in Greenwich, Connecticut, was beautiful and spacious, and by this time I needed the room because

I had a wife and two children. (As I mentioned before, more about my family life later.)

Now, living and working in the New York area seemed a long way from the plains of West Texas, and after having visited there a few times, I'd always felt that the Big Apple just wasn't my cup of tea. Talk about a fish out of water! And I surely must have *looked* out of place.

Once, when I was on my way to the city on the train, a short blond-headed woman boarded at a stop in New Rochelle. Seeing that every seat was full, I stood up and gave her mine. Well, you'd have thought I'd committed a cardinal sin with the looks I got from the other men on the train, as they hunched down behind their papers. I was only doing what Ruth Dean would have me do, and that was to be courteous. But I found out later that it just wasn't done there. Several years later, the TV personality Joan Rivers would tell me that she never forgot my giving up my seat for her and that she loved me for it.

So here I was, this country bumpkin in New York, up against the big guns of television. I was especially filled with fear since a conversation I'd had with radio and TV personality Arthur Godfrey. Once, when the airport was closed due to a snowstorm, I took the train from DC to New York shortly before I moved there. I happened to be seated by Godfrey and knew him from when I had appeared on his show.

As we talked, Godfrey had a lot to say to me on the subject of New York television executives. He knew my situation and said, "Jimmy, I've watched ya, and I know who you are." And then he said, "When you get to New York, they're gonna tell you everything you've done in Washington was wrong, but you've got to remember that the only reason you're in New York is because of what you did in Washington. And you can stick to your guns, and have everybody call you a miserable son of a bitch like they do me, and you'll be tremendously successful, or you can listen to them, and let them change ya and break ya and bend ya, and you're gonna fall on your ass."

Godfrey did indeed have a bad reputation in the business, and everybody would tell me, "You know that Godfrey is such a mean, tough, lousy ass." And then I got to thinking about it: He had been nothing but nice and helpful to me. I made up my mind then and there that I wasn't going to care what people said about someone. I was going to judge people by the way they treated me, because if you're nice to me, I can't bad-mouth you. Nevertheless, Godfrey scared the hell out of me, and whether or not he was right about the big brass in New York, I would certainly never forget his advice.

It turned out that Godfrey was right, and sure enough the CBS executives had their own idea of how *The Jimmy Dean Show* was going to look and sound—slick and sophisticated, with a much bigger production than before. And I guess I did let them mold me and bend me, but I didn't think there was much I could do about it at the time. Besides, I thought I had it pretty good, with the banker's hours I was keeping, not having to come into town until 10 A.M. and returning home on the six o'clock train. My paycheck of about a thousand dollars a week didn't hurt either. And all and all, it turned out that *The Jimmy Dean Show* ended up being a pretty good little television show.

Our show went on the air September 22, 1958, and was seen live Monday through Friday across the country, in the afternoons from 2 until 2:30 EST. It featured a singing group called the Noteworthies and special guests that included a lot of actors and singers from Broadway, as well as popular singers of the day. I wasn't real pleased with the way the show was presented, however, since it was a lot more "uptown" than it had ever been. I felt we were betraying our country fans, even though the reviews we were getting were good. I remember one critic saying that I was so laid-back and comfortable on the show that I made Perry Como seem like a bundle of nerves.

We enjoyed some pretty big-name entertainers on the show—Sam Cooke, Patsy Cline, Della Reese—and I won't ever forget the time Sammy Davis, Jr. paid us a visit. I had gone down to the Copacabana Club to catch his show one night, and I told him, "Sammy, I sure would love it if you'd do our show." He said, "Well, when do you want me?" I said "Uh, tomorrow . . . " And Sammy said, "I'll be there," and he was.

Not only did Sammy Davis sing for us that day, but he also did a demonstration of his talents as a quick-draw artist; he always did enjoy doing his quick-draw act with his guns. He was good at it too, but of course Sammy Davis, Jr., could always do anything he set his mind to, and do it well. As far as I'm concerned, Sammy was the best all-around entertainer there ever was, bar none.

The Jimmy Dean Show had been on the air for almost a year and was going along really well, and since the ratings were so good, I felt like my "bending" for the network had been a positive thing. I made it a point to get to know the writers for the show and would invite them to my dressing room to chat and swap stories, hoping they would get familiar with my personality and somehow incorporate it into the scripts.

Joel Herron, Joe Bigelo and Larry Marks were three of the most talented people on the show, and they would join me for coffee or lunch, where we'd have a great time laughing and talking . . . that is until the producer made them stop. What a miserable and pushy SOB he was, a real know-it-all, this Barry *Somebody*. It happened that he wanted them to write what *he* wanted, and not what some hayseed from Texas wanted. I had been reduced to a pawn with no voice at all, and Godfrey's words would indeed ring true. They had bent me and changed me and tried to make a silk purse out of a sow's ear, and I was about to fall on my ass.

I'll never understand the inner workings of the networks or the reason behind some of their decisions, but I'm sure the bottom line has to be money. And even though our show was number one in its time slot and was attracting a sizable audience, I still got called into the CBS offices to be told that *The Jimmy Dean Show* had been canceled, making it the second time I had gotten the ax while being number one in the ratings.

The fact was, Art Linkletter (who'd had the successful *House Party* show on NBC) had somehow convinced CBS that he could do a cheaper show and get a better rating than ours. The show was called *Divorce Court* and had no musicians or guest stars to pay and a budget that was a fraction of ours, so the network decided to go with him. I was still under contract and would be paid, but our show was history. "Sorry," they said, "we'll call you sometime." Ultimately, CBS would also wind up being a loser, because *Divorce Court* ended up being a bomb.

Country-Music Singers Overtake City Crooners

There was a day when the smart boys in the entertainment field described a hillbilly singer as one who sang through his nose by ear for money. That's definitely not today.

There are so many country music compositions regularly in the top songs on radio, jukeboxes, and recordings that CBS set up a special new "Country-Music Show," and the other networks and individual stations have hillbilly time too. Some of the country-style singers who have made good include Elvis Presley, Pat Boone, Tommy Sands, Tennessee Ernie, Eddy Arnold, and now smiling Jimmy Dean.

Hottest New Throat

At the moment Dean is as hot as any of the new throats. As the relatively new host of the CBS-TV morning show, he is gaining more friends every day. And he also has a Saturday evening variety program.

Smiling Jimmy Dean

This ever-smiling young man won't be 29 until Aug. 10, but he has been entertaining for more than a decade—in fact, ever since he entered the air force in 1946. He began entertaining with piano, accordion, and guitar for the boys at his base. After his discharge he worked clubs and then got into country music. He toured Europe and worked many county fairs and carnivals.

After Jimmy's record of "Bummin' Around" hit the jackpot, he was tabbed for a television role and really picked up viewers fast.

Advocates a Grin

This young man, whose favorite expression is "grin once in a while; it's good for you," has a wife and two children. And the folks in Plainview, Tex., where he was born, figure that already he's a bigger star than was the late actor who also was known as James Dean.

Philosophy and patter seem to go with country-music singers, and Tennessee Ernie Ford now is almost better known for his pithy expressions than for his songs. Ole Ern, as he likes to call himself, really coined a national

Tennessee Ernie Ford

phrase when he said he was "scared as a long-tailed cat in a room full of rockin' chairs."

Ernie still does a warm job on his songs, especially his Bible numbers. He loves to sing.

I loved live television and still miss it, because when they tape the shows, an awful lot of spontaneity is lost. And sometimes I believe the TV audience would tune in not because I was so entertaining, but mostly to see how bad I could screw up— *and* if I could get out of it.

A perfect example was the time I opened the show with my first number and the zipper on my fly was down. While I was singing, I noticed that the cue card guy was flashing a card that said "YOUR FLY IS OPEN." Not paying attention to it, I kept right on singing, thinking it was a joke, one that he had pulled a jillion times before. Besides, there's an old adage that says, "Don't worry if the gate is left open; if the horse can't get up, he can't get out." I finished the number, but then while talking to the audience I noticed that I was getting laughs where I shouldn't have gotten laughs.

By this time the veins were popping out of the cue card guy's head as he frantically waved his sign, and then I realized he might not be joking. So I said to the audience, "If you'll excuse me for a moment I need to correct something," and I slipped behind the curtain to zip up. When I came back out, I said, "I want to thank the director for getting waist shots during that number . . . but now that I think about it, it may be the best 'opening' this show has ever had!"

Naturally, I wasn't too happy about losing that television show, but I had learned, though I don't know how, to never take setbacks personally. I had also learned that getting knocked down is a part of life, but then so is getting up. It's a little bit like being thrown from a horse: You've got to get right back on him and ride him again. But I guess the most important lesson I learned during this period in my life is that one year you can be as hot as a depot stove, and the next year you can be as cold as a deep-freeze turkey.

1

MAKING AND
BREAKING RECORDS

WITH NO REAL job and our television show down the tubes, my career in show business was now a bit uncertain, but as I've said a lot of times, *I've seen sicker dogs than this get well.* I knew one thing, however: Whatever happened, it would be better than choppin' cotton in West Texas. And even though I had left CBS and the television show behind, the recording contract I had with Columbia Records remained intact. I had released a couple of albums and some single records, but nothing that set the world on fire. In fact, I really hadn't had a hit record since 1953 with "Bummin' Around."

So now I would continue to record for Columbia, as well as make lots of personal appearances. My manager had been a sweet and elderly gentleman named Tom Martin, but soon after I left the network, Tom passed away and I signed with the Sheils and Bruno Agency. The two-man team consisted of Tom Sheils, who had managed Glenn Miller, and Al Bruno, Johnny Carson's manager. Since I didn't have an office at CBS anymore, they set up a place in their office for my secretary, Willie, and me, so it worked out real well. After a while we settled in with the new agency, with all of us getting to know one another.

I remember one time when Sheils and Bruno's old secretary was leaving, and the new one coming in was told, "Now, when Mr.

Carson comes in, if he speaks, you speak. But if he doesn't speak to you, don't say anything to him." Then the new girl asked, "Well, what about Mr. Dean?" And she said, "Oh, Mr. Dean? Well, you can say anything you want to *him*." At the time I was making more money than Johnny Carson, and I thought, *What am I, chopped liver?* But then I thought about it for a little bit and decided that it was quite a compliment, that I'd much rather be known as someone you could talk to.

Along with my new managers, I also had a new agent. In April of 1961 I signed with the William Morris Agency, where the president was a man named Abe Lasfogal. Abe was a little short guy who didn't have a neck, and if you worked in that office and you *had* a neck, you wore a shirt that made you *look* like you didn't have a neck. His wife was a darling little lady that was the biggest fan I ever had, and as agents go, I liked Abe just fine. Although to me, agents are merely a necessary evil who are only as hot as you are, and the truth is the majority of them are parasites.

I'm reminded of my favorite "agent story," which Bob Hope told me on the golf course a few years later. It was about the actor who called his agent's office saying, "I'd like to speak to Irving Schwartz," and the secretary said, "I'm sorry, but Mr. Schwartz has passed away." So he hangs up and the next day he calls back and says, "I'd like to speak to Irving Schwartz," and the secretary says, "I told you, sir, Mr. Schwartz is deceased!" And the next day the same guy calls back again and says, "I'd like to speak to Irving Schwartz," and the secretary says, "Sir, I've told you . . . Irving Schwartz is dead!" And the guy says, "Yes, I know, but I just love to hear you say it!"

As a recording artist, I finally got all my ducks in a row, and since I was a country singer, I told the powers that be at Columbia Records that I wanted to record in the country music capital of the world— Nashville, Tennessee. As a result, I would fly regularly to Nashville to record, though most of my business was conducted in New York City. I would also fly to performances around the country, usually on commercial airlines, and would occasionally run into other entertainers on my flights.

Once on a flight from New York to Dallas I was lucky enough to be seated in the first-class cabin across from the great Ray Charles.

One of the flight attendants came over to me and said he wanted to talk to me, so I went over and sat down beside him for a chat. I remember him telling me that he had just recorded an album of country music in Nashville, and I didn't quite understand it, because Ray Charles was just about the biggest rhythm-and-blues star around. So I asked him why he chose to do an album of country songs, and he said, "Hey, man, I'm from Georgia. I was raised on that stuff and I've *always* loved it." He said it was something he had wanted to do for a long time but his record company wouldn't let him, and then he told me, "I finally got big enough that I didn't ask them, I *told* them!" I don't think I have to tell you that the album he was talking about, Ray Charles' *Modern Sounds in Country and Western Music,* is legendary.

Another time I was on a flight with the "man in black," Johnny Cash, except this time I wasn't so thrilled to see a fellow entertainer. Johnny had a pretty bad reputation for doing drugs and destroying hotel rooms when he was touring back in those days, and I'd had a bad experience—courtesy of Mr. Cash.

It was late one night when I was on the road and I had just arrived in Calgary, Canada. With my suit bag over my shoulder and exhausted from traveling, I was glad to finally get to my hotel and check in. But when I got to the desk, the clerk acted rather strangely and said there was a problem with my reservation. Now, that was peculiar to me, because my secretary was highly efficient and had always organized my affairs perfectly. When I asked what the problem was, the manager came flying out and said, "Well, you see, Mr. Dean, last week Johnny Cash and his troupe were here and they destroyed their hotel room and literally wreaked havoc, so it is now our policy not to accept entertainers as hotel guests."

Well, as tired as I was, I could have ripped Cash's head off, and years later when I finally saw him on that airplane flight, I let him have a piece of my mind. I said, "John, what you do to yourself is *your* business, but what you do to our industry is *my* business, and I resent the fact that you have hurt our industry." Then I told him, "And I've heard that you've cleaned up your act and found religion, but I'm going to wait and just see how long your eyes stay clear." I understand that Johnny Cash told some people, "There are those who forgive and forget, and there are those who don't . . . Jimmy Dean don't." But that wasn't true—I always wished Johnny the best.

———•———

But back to Nashville. When it came to making records in those days, there wasn't the time spent on each song like there is today, with multiple overdubs and layer on top of layer of instrumentation. It was just go in there and do it. Usually we would go in, all of the musicians and singers together, and play the song a couple of times and then record it. Boom. That way we could usually record four songs, or two 45RPM records in one three-hour session, which is what most record producers would shoot for.

On one of those trips to Nashville, I only had three songs prepared for a recording session and needed one more song for a B side. So I was sitting there on the plane thinking about what I might do and I got this idea. A few months earlier I'd had my first acting experience working in a play, in a summer stock production of *Destry Rides Again*. It was there that I met and worked with an actor named John Mento. At six-feet-five-inches tall, John was the only guy who was taller than me and the only one I had to look up to, and each time I'd pass him on the set I'd say "Big Johhnn." It had a nice ring to it, so during that hour-and-a-half flight I decided to write a story around him, and I lyrically put him in a mine and killed him.

When I reached in the seatback in front of me for some paper to write on, all I could find was one of those certificates that American Airlines used to give a baby for its first flight. So on the back of it I wrote the song "Big Bad John." And being the brilliant son of a gun that I am, after I finished recording the song in the studio I promptly threw the manuscript in the trash can. I would venture to say that it might be worth something today—original manuscripts usually are. But then again, with my handwriting, I might have been the only one who could have deciphered it.

It was an interesting session that day when we cut "Big Bad John." We recorded it in the old Quonset hut down on Music Row that housed Columbia Records' studios, where incidentally in those days a young songwriter by the name of Kris Kristofferson worked as a janitor.

Grady Martin, a great country guitarist who later went on to play in Willie Nelson's band, helped me arrange the song. Grady not only played on the record, but also had a music publishing company in Nashville at the time, and in return for his help with the song I gave him the publishing rights to it.

My record producer was a man named Don Law, one of the most renowned in country music back then, and for musicians we had some of Nashville's finest super pickers on hand. Besides Grady on guitar, I remember there was bass player "Lightning" Chance, Grand Ole Opry drummer Buddy Harman, and The Jordanaires singing background vocals.

But the most memorable musician on the recording was by far my old friend, the wonderful piano player Floyd Cramer—who wound up not playing piano at all that day. During rehearsal of the song Floyd turned to Don Law and said, "Don, you don't need me to play piano on this song; I'd just be playing the same notes as the background vocals." Then when an obvious idea hit him, Floyd reached over and picked up a chunk of steel they used as ballast for a TV camera, tied a coat hanger around it and hung it on a coatrack. Somewhere in the studio he found a hammer and began to strike the chunk of steel, obviously looking for the sound of a miner's pick. He then pulled a microphone over to it and told the engineer to put some echo on it. Floyd Cramer worked magic that day, and that hammer sound became a very important part of our record. Brilliant!

Of course, there used to be a lot of that creative thinking and ability in Nashville, and Don Law got a lot of credit for being a genius. But the truth of it is, he was smart enough to let the musicians do what they knew how to do, that's all. He knew he had a bunch of creative people and he let them create. Floyd Cramer was indeed one of the best, and I would bet it was the first and last time that one of the greatest pianists in the world ever played hammer on a record.

By this time in my career I'd made about a dozen records and three albums, but nothing I'd done had come close to the success I would enjoy with "Big Bad John." I really didn't know how well it had been received until one day when I was driving into New York City in my purple '57 Oldsmobile convertible, and it came on the radio while I was crossing the George Washington Bridge. Never wanting to hear myself sing, I reached over to change the radio to another station and there it was again. And then before I could get across the bridge I turned the dial and heard it playing for the third time. I realized then and there that I had a pretty big hit record on my hands. It literally put me on the map.

It really kind of puzzled me, though. How could a song be so popular that had no tune and no sex? It was actually the flip side, "I Won't Go Hunting with You Jake (But I'll Go Chasin' Wimmin)" that I thought would be the hit. Just shows you how much *I* know.

In its first two weeks on the market, "Big Bad John" had sold over a half million copies, and in three weeks' time it was the number one song in America. And not only was it a smash on the country music charts, but it stayed on top of the pop charts for five weeks.

The funny thing was that unbeknownst to my producer, Don Law, my contract with Columbia Records had expired before we recorded "Big Bad John." I hadn't realized it either, and with Columbia being such a huge organization, their legal department had failed to let anyone know. Obviously the left hand did not know what the right hand was doing. But now we had the hottest record in the country and there would have to be a renegotiation and a new deal between us. I was in an advantageous position, and that's putting it mildly.

Of course when I shamelessly put the word out that I didn't have a contract, there were other record companies coming to me with some pretty sweet offers. Columbia was having to compete with them for their own artist, and to no one's surprise I ended up renewing with an exceptionally good contract.

Another bit of trivia about "Big Bad John" that some find interesting was that there were two different endings to the song. Now, you've got to remember that the year was 1961, and in those days you had to be careful about what you put on a phonograph record. Of course, nowadays they can say anything and *everything* on records—it's just amazing.

At any rate, the original ending that I had written for the song was, "At the bottom of this mine lies one hell of a man, Big John," and that's how we recorded it. The record was released that way and had sold about twenty-five thousand copies when Columbia Records decided that they wanted me to change it. They thought saying "hell" was a little too risqué, believe it or not, and had me go back into the studio to replace the ending with "At the bottom of this mine lies a big, big man." Except instead of flying me back to Nashville to just say one line, they sent me to a studio in New York City to record it. Subsequently the vocals on the record were recorded in two different cities.

Though what was *really* weird about them making me change "one hell of a man" was that I had already said the word "hell" early on in the song, as in "man-made hell." But that didn't bother them, only the ending. The original version was never released on an album, only on a forty-five, so if you happen to have one of those original twenty-five thousand records, it might be worth something today. I personally didn't have a copy of the original record until my friend Gary Ratcliff, a radio station owner in Staunton, Virginia, gave me a copy matted and framed for Christmas in 1999. *Thanks, "Rat."*

The song took me to stages everywhere, from the *Grand Ole Opry* to the London Palladium, the Hollywood Bowl, *The Ed Sullivan Show* and Jack Paar's *Tonight Show,* just to name a few. And besides all the wonderful doors it opened for me professionally, "Big Bad John" would also win many awards and accolades. In 1961, the Music Operators of America would name it Most Popular Juke Box Record of the Year, and it received numerous gold records, along with awards from Broadcast Music, Inc., my performance agency.

"Big Bad John" would also receive four Grammy Award nominations in 1961, for Record of the Year, Song of the Year, Best Country and Western Recording of the Year and Best Solo Vocal Performance for a male. And when it won the Grammy Award for the prestigious Best Country and Western Recording of the Year in 1961, well, I was on top of the world! That little gramophone still sits proudly in a crystal cabinet in our living room today, although a little beaten up from when my kids used to play with it when they were little.

Today it amazes me that people still remember that record after more than forty years. And I can't tell you how many men named John have come to me and said Big Bad John was their nickname, and then asked me to sign an autograph to them that way. But to me one of the greatest things is that John Tyler High School in Abilene, Texas, uses it as their school fight song. All those kids singing a song that was popular so long ago. I have to tell you, it's an awesome thing to hear a stadium full of kids singing your hit record.

I guess it was inevitable that in 1990 *Big Bad John*—the movie— would make its debut. It premiered in Nashville and starred a pro football player named Doug English as Big John, along with the two great character actors, Jack Elam and Ned Beatty. I also played in the movie as Cletus, Big John's nemesis.

Doug English had been All American at Texas University but had gotten his neck broken and couldn't play anymore, and even though he didn't have any acting experience at the time, I thought he did a pretty good job on the film.

In spite of its talented cast, the movie realized little or no success, simply because the guy who said he could produce it didn't know what the hell he was doing. And what was really weird to me was that he didn't use my record for the theme song on the soundtrack, but instead used a recording of my song by Charlie Daniels. That's one I've yet to understand. Regardless of all that, however, somebody must have thought the film was okay, because it still pops up on the cable networks from time to time.

After all the success of "Big Bad John," I wouldn't have felt right if I hadn't done something special for the man who was my inspiration for the song, John Mento. Shortly after the record became a hit, I had him go to my tailor so I could buy him a suit. Not a bad lick for just having a catchy name and being two inches taller than the farmer. And for a song that I didn't think was so special at first, at this writing "Big Bad John" has sold over eight million copies. Not too bad for what was supposed to be the B side of a record.

Trying to follow "Big Bad John" became my next challenge. We released records that were sequels, like "Cajun Queen" and "Little Bitty Big John," but nothing ever came close to its success. Recitations sort of became my trademark, and I had a string of hits with what they called "saga songs." In 1962 we would have five more top forty records; besides "Cajun Queen," there was its B side, "To a Sleeping Beauty" (written with Larry Marks for my daughter, Connie); "Dear Ivan," a Cold War–inspired recitation I wrote;

"Little Black Book," a peppy little song I wrote that was real popular with square dancers; and "P.T. 109," a song inspired by then-President John F. Kennedy's World War II Navy experience. Those were pretty good records for us, although I never did care much at all for "P.T. 109," even though it did garner a Grammy nomination. Since I had no faith in my own songwriting and had thrown away every song I'd ever written prior to "Big Bad John," I sometimes looked to other songwriters for material on my many trips to Nashville. One of my favorite writers was, and still is, Tom T. Hall, and I've let him know it on more than one occasion. He said to me one time, "Jimmy, you're a better songwriter than me; it's just that I'm willing to suffer and you're not." Maybe he was right. Tom would go out in his shed and stay there for days to write songs, and I never wanted to work that hard.

Among the young songwriters in Nashville whose songs I liked back then was Roger Miller. In fact, one distinction I'm proud to hold is that I cut the first song he ever had recorded, one called "The Good Lord's Happy Child." I think it must have sold about two copies in North Dakota and then tapered off.

Then one time a stutterin' Mel Tillis came to my hotel room in Nashville to pitch me some material. He played his guitar and sang several of his songs for me, but I didn't hear anything I really liked. Afterward he said, "Th-that's all right, ch-chief . . . I've got one m-more at home and I'll c-call you and p-play it for you over the ph-phone. So if your ph-phone rings and no-nobody answers, d-don't hang up, it's m-me." Indeed he did call me when he got home, and over the phone he played and sang a song for me called "Detroit City." "Well, honestly, Mel," I said, "to me it's just another country song, and to tell you the truth it's a little bit morbid." I probably don't have to tell you that "Detroit City" was a smash hit and sold a gazillion records for Bobby Bare. Brilliant, Dean.

Speaking of my good buddy Mel Tillis, I've always loved him and his sense of humor. One time he picked me up at my hotel in Nashville in his big old Lincoln to give me a ride to the airport, and there were some kids collecting donations at a traffic light. On the side of their gallon buckets were big letters that read "HELP THE HANDICAPPED." When we stopped, Mel rolled down the window, reached out and took the bucket from one of the kids and said, "Th-thanks!" I thought I would die laughing right there. (Well, *of course* he gave it back . . . along with a donation!)

There have been other songs that were huge successes that I turned down throughout the years: Charley Pride's big hit "The Snakes Crawl at Night"; the Mel Tillis penned "Ruby Don't Take Your Love to Town," a monster hit for Kenny Rogers; and "The Battle of New Orleans," a huge hit for Johnny Horton. Although, in my defense, when the latter's songwriter, Jimmy Driftwood, pitched that one to me I loved it, because I love American history, but when it came to me it had extra verses and was eleven minutes long. Besides being too long, I thought, *Nobody's gonna buy American history on a phonograph record*. Wrong again, Dean.

Actually, what a lot of people don't realize is that sometimes the songs aren't that appealing because of how poorly they sound on the demo tapes when they are pitched to you, or how badly the song-writers themselves sound when they sing them. For instance, many years before I recorded for Columbia Records, Connie B. Gay and I went to the legendary Hank Williams's home in Nashville for a visit, and he played us some of his songs. To begin with, I'll never forget seeing him there, sitting on his sofa in a pair of green boxer shorts, with those spindly little legs that he could have sued for nonsupport.

Hank was pretty full of himself that day and he'd been drinking, and as he was playing his guitar and slurring his words, he said, "Jimmy, I just wrote another f——king hit." Of course that wouldn't have surprised me any, because Hank Williams was so hot at the time he could have sung the Yellow Pages of the phone book and had a hit record. He then broke into this tune that sounded just awful, mainly because he could hardly remember the words or the chords to it.

As we were leaving Hank's house, I whispered under my breath, "Well, you Alabama dumb ass. This is one time you're not gonna get it done, 'cause nobody is gonna buy a song about a cigar store Indian falling in love with a mannequin in an antique store." Well, who'da thunk it? "Kawliga" has only been a hit forty-two times and has sold eighty jillion records since then. *Really wrong*, Dean.

Surely I'm not the only recording artist that's ever passed up a hit song; though I've never really let it bother me. In fact I used to sing a medley of all the hits I'd turned down through the years. When I would play the showrooms in Vegas years later, the audiences loved it. I figured they'd be saying to themselves, "Hell, he's as dumb as I am!"

——————•——————

Nashville has always been good to me, especially when they presented me with the key to the city in 1964. It was certainly the best town to find great songs too, and those were some fun days when I'd go there to record. Sometimes after a recording session a bunch of us guys would get together for a poker game that would last all night and well into the morning. Porter Wagoner was a regular at our card games, along with Mel Tillis, Grady Martin, Floyd Cramer and one of the Wilburn Brothers. Word would get out that there was a game and other players would drop in too.

There was this one guy that used to come in to play who owned a liquor store, and I remember he had a loose set of dentures where the upper plate was always falling down, and he'd push it back up with his bottom lip. One time during a game there was a big pot on the table and somebody bet a hundred dollars. Well, it got real quiet, but in a little bit you heard this guy's plate of dentures drop . . . *click* . . . and the next thing you know all hell broke loose. Grady Martin got so tickled that he reared back, hit the table with his knee, and money, cards and chips went everywhere. What a mess! We tried to straighten it all out, but nobody ever knew if they got the right amount of money back.

It was always a good time with those guys, and there are more stories I'd love to share with you but they can't be printed here. Let's just say there were some pretty good chunks of money that traded hands, and the competition would get hot and heavy, along with the language.

I enjoyed recording other writers' songs, but I found out that writing your own hit is a lot more rewarding, and certainly more lucrative. I have to say that the success of "Big Bad John" encouraged me to write more songs, and to keep them instead of throwing them in the round file. I ended up having some pretty good luck with one I wrote called "The First Thing Every Morning," my last record on Columbia Records and a number one hit.

After many albums and single records over a six-year period, my contract ended with Columbia, and in the summer of 1966 I signed with RCA Records. I was pretty happy about it too, because it gave me the opportunity to work with one of my favorite people, Chet Atkins.

As everybody knows, Chet was one of the greatest country guitarists of all time, but he was also one of the greatest record producers that Nashville ever had. In the 1960s he was credited, along with the legendary record producer Owen Bradley, with creating what was known as the Nashville Sound—a slick, more sophisticated production that was sometimes lush with strings in place of fiddles.

Chet produced most all of my records for RCA, and I enjoyed working with him a lot. Knowing whether or not he enjoyed working with *me* wasn't as evident; he was so quiet and never had much to say. When we were recording in the studio, there was hardly ever any feedback from him, and a rave review from Chet Atkins was "Not too bad."

Chet Atkins, Don Gibson, Jimmy & Floyd Cramer

We released several albums and singles for RCA, including one called "Stand Beside Me," followed by "Born to Be by Your Side" and "A Thing Called Love," a song written by the multitalented singer, songwriter and actor Jerry Reed. Another little tune that Jerry pitched to me was called "Aunt Maudie's Fun Garden." I recorded it because it was a fun, upbeat little song and I liked the melody, but only Jerry Reed would come up with a tune about a little old lady who raised pot in her garden and smoked it.

In 1971 I had several top forty records on RCA, including a duet with Dottie West called "Slowly," from an album of songs we had recorded together. I continued to record for RCA Records until 1972, and then after returning to Columbia Records for a brief period the next year, I dropped out of show business. It just wasn't fun anymore. Besides, by then I had my hands full with the business of making sausage.

———•———

I went headlong into the food business and devoted a lot of my time to the Jimmy Dean Meat Company (which I'll discuss later), but it wasn't too long before I was bitten by the show business bug again. It was while I was in Las Vegas, at a convention for the sausage company in 1976, that my old friend Robert Goulet was headlining at the Frontier. When I went by to catch his show, he coaxed me to the mike, and I had such a great time with the audience that I was hooked again. I had been considering a return to show business anyway and could genuinely say it wasn't for the money, because at that time our company was grossing sixty million dollars a year.

Consequently, that same year I signed with Casino Records, one of the small independent labels that are a dime a dozen in Nashville. One day, while preparing to go there to record, I was in my office in New York, and my secretary for the past eighteen years, Willie Bruffy, took out a song from the file cabinet. She said, "Mr. Dean, why don't you take this with you? You've always liked it and maybe somebody else will." It was a recitation I had written with Larry Marks back in '59 for a Mother's Day show on CBS, and for almost twenty years it had been tucked away in the file cabinet.

The song was called "I.O.U.," and I remember it had gotten such tremendous mail response after I did it on the television show that I wanted to put it on a record. It was not to be, however, because when I submitted it to Mitch Miller at Columbia Records, he turned it down, saying it was too corny, too schmaltzy and too long.

That wasn't the only time Mitch Miller did the farmer an injustice. Once when I recorded a song called "Sing Along," my record suddenly disappeared from the airwaves, and shortly thereafter the song turned up as Mitch Miller's theme on his new television show. Strange coincidence. I don't mind telling you that I disliked Mitch Miller intensely, and as far as I'm concerned he was one of the lousiest human beings I ever knew. If Mitch ever had any scruples, decency or ethics about him, *I* certainly never saw them.

Anyway, in 1976, I finally recorded "I.O.U." for an album on Casino Records, and after they released it as a single, it ended up becoming one of the fastest breaking records in the history of the music industry. It sold a million records in just three weeks, and in 1977 became my first gold record since "Big Bad John." It popped up on the charts again that year around Mother's Day, and again in 1983 as a reissue on Churchill Records. And since it was a tribute to Mom, I presented my mother with the very first copy and sent her a dozen roses when it was released. The song meant a lot to her *and* to me, and since her passing I get so emotional I just can't perform it anymore.

I don't think I'd realized just how popular "I.O.U." had become or the fact that it had gone global until I was doing an interview for someone in Australia. I remember the interviewer telling me, "Jimmy, until your record I thought my mom was the only one that ever said, 'Make sure you're wearing clean underwear in case you're in an accident.' " I guess we hit home with a lot of folks on that song. It makes me extra proud too, because every year since the record was released it has been the most popular song played on the radio on Mother's Day.

I.O.U.

You know, most people look through their wallets or their pocket-books and way down at the bottom, past the credit cards and baby pictures, green stamps . . . You usually find a little old dog-eared piece of poetry. I was cleaning out my wallet the other day and I ran across a whole bunch of I.O.U.s, some of them thirty years overdue. Funny thing is that all of these I.O.U.s are owed to one person, and I kinda feel like right now might be a pretty good time for an accounting.

Mom, are you listening?

Mom, I owe you for so many things . . . A lot of services. Like night watchman, for instance. For lying awake nights listening for coughs and cries and creaking floorboards and me coming in too late. You had the eye of an eagle, the roar of a lion . . . But you always had a heart as big as a house. I owe you for services as a short-order cook, chef, baker. For making sirloin out of hamburger, turkey out of tuna fish and two strapping boys out of leftovers.

I owe you for cleaning services, for the daily scrubbing of face and ears . . . All work done by hand. And for the frequent dusting of a small boy's pants to try to make sure that he led a spotless life. And for washing and ironing no laundry could ever do. And for drying up the tears of childhood and for ironing out the problems of growing up.

I owe you for service as a bodyguard, for protecting me from the terrors of thunderstorms and nightmares and too many green apples.

And Lord knows I owe you for medical attention. For nursing me through measles, mumps, bruises, bumps, splinters and spring fever. And let's not forget medical advice either. Oh no! Important things like "don't scratch it or it won't get well," "if you cross your eyes they're gonna stick like that." And probably, uh, most important of all was "be sure you got on clean underwear, boy, in case you're in an accident."

And I owe you for veterinarian services, for feeding every lost dog that I had dragged home at the end of a rope, and for healing the pains of puppy love.

And I owe you for entertainment. Entertainment that kept a household going during some pretty tough times. For wonderful productions at Christmas, fourth of July and birthdays. And for making make-believe come true on a very limited budget.

I owe you for construction work. For building kites, confidence, *hopes and dreams. And somehow you made 'em all touch the sky. And for cementing a family together so it would stand the worst kinds of shocks and blows, and for laying down a good, strong foundation to build a life on.*

I owe you for carrying charges. For carrying me on your books for the necessities of life that a growing boy's just gotta have . . . Things like a, oh, a pair of high-top boots with a little pocket on the side for a jackknife.

And one thing, Mom, I will never, ever forget. When there were only two pieces of apple pie left and three hungry people, I noticed that you were the one who suddenly decided that you didn't like apple pie in the first place.

These are just a few of the things for which payment is long over-due. The person I owe 'em to worked very cheap. She managed by simply doing without a whole lot of things that she needed herself. My I.O.U.s add up to much more than I could ever hope to repay. But you know, the nicest thing about it all is that she'll mark the entire bill paid in full for just one kiss and four little words . . . "Mom, I love you!"

After "I.O.U.," twenty years would pass before I would record again. And had it not been for a man named Buddy Killen, I might not have recorded at all. I knew of Buddy as a music publishing mogul, record producer, hit songwriter and bass player in Hank Williams's band, but he and I got to know each other and became best of friends through my current wife, Donna. Buddy owned the World Famous Stockyard, the restaurant and nightclub in Nashville where Donna sang for several years during the eighties, and our friendship began with a mutual respect for each other.

Donna and I have spent a lot of time with Buddy and his wife, Carolyn, at their home in Nashville, and they've been guests at our home and on our boat many times as well. We shared a lot of interests and enjoyed each other's company, and through the Killens we also became friends with another delightful couple, Dianne and Bobby Goldsboro. Bobby, of course, is the multitalented singer of hit records such as "Honey," and is one of the funniest human beings God ever put breath in. Most of the time when we were all together we'd play card games or dominoes, drink wine from the Killens' fabulous collection, and laugh at Bobby until our sides would hurt. On occasion during our visits with Buddy and Carolyn I'd be reminded of a piece of material and recite a portion of it, as I enjoy doing from time to time. Buddy always seemed to enjoy these bursts of inspiration, and a few years ago he encouraged me to record an album of recitations. So in 1996 we went into the recording studio with Buddy producing, and ended up with enough songs to fill two CDs.

We recorded the albums at the Sound Shop, Buddy's recording studio in Nashville, and negotiated a record deal for their release with Curb Records in 1998. Both CDs included some rerecorded versions of previously released material, including "Big Bad John," "To a Sleeping Beauty" and "I.O.U.," but they also contained some new songs as well, with the most popular being the one with the dumbest title, "Drinkin' from My Saucer." I found this wonderful poem at a diner in Phil Harris's hometown of Linton, Indiana, while I was there playing in his celebrity golf tournament some years ago. It was written on the back of a menu and was a little short, so I added an extra verse. It's about being grateful, and I've always loved it because it sort of sums up my philosophy of life.

Drinkin' from My Saucer

I've never made a fortune and it's probably too late now
But I don't worry about that much, I'm happy anyhow
And as I go along life's way I'm reaping better than I sowed
I'm drinkin' from my saucer 'cause my cup is overflowed.

Haven't got a lot of riches and sometimes the going's tough
But I've got three kids that love me, and that makes me rich enough
I thank God for His blessings and the mercies He's bestowed
I'm drinkin' from my saucer 'cause my cup is overflowed.

Oh, I remember times when things went wrong
and my faith wore kind of thin
But all at once the dark clouds broke and the sun
shone through again

So Lord help me not to gripe about the tough rows that I've hoed
I'm drinkin' from my saucer 'cause my cup is overflowed.

And if God gives me strength and courage when the way
grows steep and rough
I'll not ask for other blessings, I'm already blessed enough
And may I never be too busy to help another bear his load
Then I'll keep drinkin' from my saucer 'cause my cup is overflowed.

It's true I've had a lot of blessings, and my association with Buddy Killen is certainly one of them. I thank him for believing in me and for his encouragement to record again.

I'm also grateful for all the opportunities I've had during my recording career, and for all the doors it opened for me. But as much as I love to sing, the truth is I never really enjoyed making records. I hated recording in the studio and was always intimidated by it, mainly because I didn't think I was very good at it. I also hated to hear myself sing—and I still do. I thought if I was a singer, then the woods were full of them. I thank God a lot of *other* folks didn't think so too.

ABC-TV'S
THE JIMMY DEAN SHOW

IT HAD BEEN two years since I'd hosted my own television show on CBS, but fortunately the success of some pretty good records had kept me busy. During that time I did a lot of traveling around the country, performing and promoting my records, as well as making guest appearances on other television shows.

Those were some fun times, and guesting on other TV shows definitely helped my visibility. Hosting *The Tonight Show* played a particularly large part in landing my next television show, and because of my exceptionally high ratings (and high ratings mean big bucks), the networks were looking at ol' JD with dollar signs in their eyes. It wasn't long before I got the call that ABC was offering me my own TV show.

I think it was Bob Banner, the executive producer of the show, who broke the news to me, that at age thirty-five I would be one of the first country music entertainers to have my own nighttime, prime time variety show. I had met Bob about five years earlier and had always wanted to work with him. He had produced the *Today* show with Dave Garroway (the one our old CBS morning show was up against back in the late fifties), and he'd also had a string of successes that included *Candid Camera* and variety shows with Garry Moore, Carol Burnett and Dinah Shore. Needless to say, I was happy and excited about having *The Jimmy Dean Show* on ABC, and the fact that it would be the forerunner to every country music television show since. This was *definitely* the Big Time.

The show was taped at the network's Studio Fifty-One and used more than seventy people in the production, including four cameramen, a full orchestra with musical director, talent coordinators, technicians, writers, a floor manager, hairdressers, makeup artists and thirty-one crew members. The stage teemed with people, and the sets and scenery were much more elaborate than our previous show in Washington.

Our producer was Tom Egan, a very creative guy and good friend, who produced Tim Conway's "Dorf" videos. Also on the show was a really fine director named Hal Gurnee (who would later direct *The David Letterman Show*), the tremendous award-winning set designer Jan Scott, costume designer Al Lehman, choreographer Tony Mordente, and Will Glickman, Buddy Arnold and Buddy Atkinson as writers. Our original music director and conductor was Peter Matz, and then after about a year Don Sebesky took over.

The orchestra included about thirty musicians, with Larry Grossman as our musical consultant and pianist. Larry was and still is an extremely talented guy, and he and I hit it off pretty well, becoming good friends and buddying around together some. Also in our orchestra was the legendary harmonica player Toots Theilemans, who in the past had played on many of my recording sessions.

There would be plenty of singing, comedy skits and banter on the show, and like any other variety show of that time, we'd have productions with singers and dancers. And of course each show would feature celebrity guests.

We planned the show for months before it premiered, with informality being the theme and the key. And though it would be aimed at a mainstream audience, the show would focus squarely on country entertainers. We had a five-day workweek, Sunday through Thursday, with rehearsals every day until late each evening. On Thursdays we would tape the show early that evening before it would air nationwide that night at 9:00 EST. Preceded by *The Flintstones, The Donna Reed Show* and *My Three Sons*—all prime time shows back then—and with competition like *Perry Mason, Dr. Kildare* and *Hazel, The Jimmy Dean Show* premiered on September 19, 1963.

This new show was a little too slick to be believable at first, and I realized that it would take time to find ourselves during those first few weeks—especially for *me* to find *myself*. Gone were my flashy Western suits and cowboy hat, replaced with gray flannel suits that were tailored to perfection. They even took away my cowboy boots and gave me regular shoes to wear. I just wasn't me for the first six or seven shows; everything was too sophisticated and overproduced, and the entire show lacked warmth.

The producers also felt our show got off to a poor start, and word had it that they would cancel me after the first season. But in a *TV Guide* interview, the president of ABC-TV would later admit, "We made a mistake. We'd put Madison Avenue suits on him and the writers gave him sophisticated lines. The notice for closing went up and we didn't think he was going to make it. We were looking for a replacement."

It was true, we didn't start out right. So I told them, "Let me do it *my* way," and they did. I put on my Western suits and cowboy boots and then went back to what the critics called my "plainsy, backwoodsy manner." Slowly but surely we found the right format, and through some continued confidence from the people at ABC we were able to pick up steam and finally satisfy with those rating service numbers.

I felt pretty good about the whole thing after a while—that is, when the critics started calling our folksy little show "a success" and we all finally relaxed, which made for better entertainment. The most flattering reviews said our show hit the bull's-eye and compared me with Bing Crosby and Arthur Godfrey at their best. One reviewer called me the "bright new TV swinger with the Will Rogers touch." Thanks, *I think*.

After the show was revamped, the writers didn't have much to do, since I ended up using my own humor. In fact, the only part of the show they actually wrote was for me and Rowlf, a puppet dog that appeared on our show every week. I would walk over and sit on a bench and he would appear from behind it for the skit. Not too many people know that Rowlf was the beginning of a long and successful career for Jim Henson, of Muppets fame.

Jim Henson and his cohort Frank Oznowicz (later Frank Oz) were Rowlf's operators. Henson, who both created him and did his voice, had his right hand in Rowlf's head and his left hand in the dog's left paw, with Frank Oz working Rowlf's right paw and handling props. Crouching down behind the bench, with Jim wearing a headset microphone and both of them watching a monitor, they would work Rowlf for the two- or three-minute segment, as the two of us traded comic banter. He was brilliantly done, with Rowlf mimicking human gestures and sometimes singing and even playing a ukulele.

It was Bob Banner who suggested that we have some sort of character on the show, one that I could interact with for a regular comedy skit. I suggested he check out a particular act on local television in Washington, DC, that I remembered doing Wilkins Coffee commercials. It turned out to be Jim Henson and his company of puppet characters, which included Rowlf and several other bizarre-looking animals.

Bob's idea was definitely a good one. The segment with Rowlf was one of the most popular parts of the show, and I still have people tell me that they remember him. I guess he *was* popular; he drew two thousand fan letters a week, which wasn't too bad for a pooch made of foam rubber, fake fur and eyes made from Ping-Pong balls.

I treated Rowlf like he was real, but he *was* real to me, and I think that's one of the reasons he made such an impression on everyone. Jim Henson himself said it was the reason Rowlf was such a hit. Rowlf's longtime crush on Lassie was legendary, and one of my favorite shows was when we finally had Lassie on the show. It was one of the sweetest things you ever saw.

Rehearsals with Rowlf and his handlers were done in my office, and we'd always have a lot of fun clowning around. My secretary Willie loved Rowlf and would come in regularly to watch us work with the writers. Sometimes Rowlf and I would act like we were fighting, and on one occasion when we were joking and having one of our scuffles, I smacked his head and one of his eyeballs flew off. Well, when I did that, Willie screamed and ran out of the office, and you'd have thought that I'd mortally wounded somebody.

Jim Henson and I not only had a good stage rapport with Rowlf but we enjoyed each other as friends too. One of my most prized possessions is a miniature Rowlf that he and Frank Oz made and gave me for Christmas one year. The puppet stands about twenty inches high, and when you lift him off of the stand, there's Jim Henson standing there with his hands straight up in the air. It really is a well-made piece, and I wouldn't take anything in the world for it.

Not long after our show had become successful, my manager, Al Bruno, said, "You know, Jimmy, I can get you forty percent of the Muppets." The idea that he would try to intimidate them into giving me a percentage of their future profits, just because I had them on my television show, really hit me wrong. I told him I didn't want 40 percent of the Muppets because I hadn't done anything to earn it. "They're an asset to *The Jimmy Dean Show* and they've done good things for us," I said, "and I won't take it."

Many people I've told this story to over the years have said, "Well, Jimmy, I'll bet you're sorry *now* that you didn't take forty percent of the Muppets," and I tell them, "No, because I still haven't done anything to earn it." That was only one of the many instances where I've been offered part of something I had nothing to do with, like when songwriters and publishers offered me partial credits on songs if I'd record them. I have to live with *me*, and my conscience won't let me do that sort of thing.

Our program became a great showcase for a lot of country music acts, and the great part about it was they were playing *my* kind of music, so I would stand in the wings and enjoy them as a fan. We had so many of my good buddies on the show: Minnie Pearl, Eddy Arnold, Ernest Tubb, Hank Snow, Roy Clark, Homer and Jethro, George Jones, Arthur Godfrey, Faron Young, Carl Smith, Charlie Rich, The Jordanaires, Joe Maphis and Rex Allen. One thing that really pleased me about the show was the overwhelming big city acceptance of the country and even bluegrass music acts we'd have as guests. I was always glad to see Flatt and Scruggs get as much applause from the studio audience as anybody else who appeared.

Being in New York City and dealing with people who didn't know a lot about country music could really be challenging at times. Once, when I told them to book Buck Owens on the show, they did just

Backstage with
Eddy Arnold

With Rowlf and his secret crush Lassie

that . . . but they didn't book Buck Owens and the Buckeroos—just Buck without his band. Nobody would have ever thought of having him without his Buckaroos and his invaluable sideman Don Rich. When I told the producers this, they said they couldn't book them because it would put the show over budget. But I simply couldn't let it happen, so I made sure The Buckeroos were there and paid for them out of my pocket.

We also gave new artists a place to showcase their talents, like the great Grand Ole Opry star Connie Smith. I remember the first time I ever heard her sing. While making an appearance in Wichita, Kansas, I was riding down the road with a disc jockey and promoter friend of mine named Mack Sanders, and this voice suddenly came out of the radio. The record playing was called "Once a Day," and the girl singing it totally knocked me out. I got her name and told the people on my show, "I don't know what she looks like, and I don't care if she weighs five hundred pounds and is ugly as homemade soap—she's gonna do our show." Connie turned out to be as cute as a bug and one of the sweetest ladies God ever put breath in, and she's been my favorite country girl singer ever since.

One of the most creative individuals we ever had on our show was Roger Miller. He had such a vivid imagination, and of course back during those days he stayed so high he could go duck hunting with a rake. Roger used to say, "Now, don't forget, Dean, a bird in the hand will s——t in your fist!" Now *those* are words to live by.

Roger always had a story to lay on you. One of my favorites was about a young rooster and an old rooster, where at daybreak the young rooster hopped up on the fence and said, "Yack-ack-a-doodle-cack-a-doo-dack-a-doodle-yack-a-doo!" And nothing happened. Then the old rooster hopped up on the fence and said, "Cock-a-doo-dle-doo!" And all the lights in the house came on and people began to stir. The old rooster just turned to the young rooster and said, "You just can't beat those old standards, can you?"

I introduced Roger Miller and his song "King of the Road" on our television show when that great record first came out. And I'll never forget what happened at rehearsal. It was one of the funniest bits I'd ever seen. Roger and I were sitting on two nail kegs as he was singing and playing his guitar. He began singing, "Trailers for sale or rent . . ."

Then he quickly stopped and said, "Wait a minute! Can somebody get a shot of my left hand? Cameraman, can you get a shot of my left hand?" Well, when they shot his left hand that was chording the neck of the guitar, a large fly was sitting on his thumb like it had been sent from Central Casting. Roger said, "Well now, ladies and gentlemen, this is a thumb fly, but he's not a thumb fly all the time, he's a thumb fly only because today is Wednesday." Then he said, "On Thursdays, he's an index finger fly, and on Friday, well . . . ," and sticking his middle finger out, he said, "we don't even talk about Friday!" Roger went on like that while that fly sat there, and I'm telling you I was on the floor. It came right off the top of his head and was totally unrehearsed, he was just so quick and clever. What's really sad is that there was no tape rolling at the time. They didn't tape rehearsals, even though I'd asked them to many times, and that was the kind of thing you'd miss. I'm sure if I had a tape of that bit it would be priceless.

Besides being a certifiable nut, Roger Miller was a kind, good-hearted old boy and one of the most thoughtful people in the business. To show his appreciation for my being instrumental in his career, he once presented me with a plaque called the Gold Doorknob Award. It was beautifully done on an eight-by-ten-inch piece of gold-trimmed walnut, with a gold doorknob mounted in the middle. Just underneath the doorknob was a gold plate with the inscription "To Jimmy Dean . . . For the one million doors you've opened for me, I'm forever grateful . . . Roger Miller."

I've never put much stock in awards, but Roger's has meant the most to me and I'm very proud of it. Only he would have thought to do something like that. I not only lost a good friend, but the world lost one of its most creative and brightest stars when Roger Miller left us, and I still miss him.

———•———

Our show on ABC also featured a lot of the popular singers of the day, like Eydie Gorme, Jack Jones, Della Reese, Julius LaRosa, the McGuire Sisters, Rosemary Clooney, Bobby Rydell, Martha Raye, Hoagy Carmichael and Kay Starr, as well as wonderful performers like Forrest Tucker, opera singer Eileen Farrell and the great Pearl Bailey. I remember the tune that Pearlie and I did together. She used

Pearl Bailey

Eydie Gorme

Molly Bee and
Roger Miller

Comedy was also a big part of our television show, featuring many of the popular comedians of the day. There was Norm Crosby, whom I just loved, and also George Kirby, Corbett Monica and George Carlin. Carlin used to do our show regularly, and back then he was always dressed in a suit and tie, with a neat haircut. He had a bizarre but fresh twist to his comedy and never said one foul word, and I used to love it when he did his "hippy dippy weatherman."

Don Adams of *Get Smart* fame was also a regular on our show, and what a funny, funny man. Each time in his comedy skits, he would play off the same punch line and destroy everyone with his "Would you believe . . . ?" That was his whole bit—the same one he would later use in his hit television show.

When people ask me who were some of my personal favorites that were on the show I have to say The Mills Brothers, especially big ol' Harry. He was the singingest, swingingest son of a gun I'd ever heard in my life, and I loved to watch him perform. There was something about the way he'd pat his hands together when he sang and really get into a song.

I also loved Sam Cooke. What a great singer and delightful human being he was. Sam and I enjoyed hanging out together and would sometimes go out for a bite to eat after the show. Other favorites were Les Paul and Mary Ford; they were always fun to have on the show, and Les could totally crack me up with his dry sense of humor.

In our first season, *The Jimmy Dean Show* was taped at the ABC Studios on 77th Street in New York, and then moved over to the Colonial Theater on Broadway. Occasionally we would broadcast on location from places like Carnegie Hall and the Jackie Gleason Theater in Miami, Florida, and near the end of our second season we went to Lakeland, Florida, to do the show. I remember our guests were Kay Starr and Eddy Arnold that week, and that I did the introduction for the show while water-skiing.

It was because of this television show that I had the opportunity to have many adventures and meet lots of interesting people from all fields of entertainment. One time the network sent us for three weeks

Don Adams and Molly Bee

to the ABC studios in Los Angeles where they produced most all of their variety shows, including *The Lawrence Welk Show*. I remember finishing rehearsal one evening and going into our hotel's lounge to have a drink, and this young fellow walked over to me and said, "I wanted to meet you. My name is Don Shula, and I'm the coach of the Baltimore Colts."

Well, being a huge football fan, I was really excited to meet the renowned coach, and also to be invited to one of their workouts and to one of their games, where they let me sit on the bench. In fact, I've had quite a few thrills over the years, and can proudly say that I've caught passes from some of the greatest football players of all time, including Johnny Unitas, Joe Namath and Don Meredith.

Speaking of thrills, once for a publicity stunt ABC sent me to Akron, Ohio, to compete in the annual Soap Box Derby. The regular race is run by kids, who are required to build their own cars with no outside help, and it's one of the sweetest things you'll ever see in your life. I was to compete in their annual celebrity race against two others: my good buddy Art Carney and the great movie actor Wendell Corey. We were to race for their "oil can trophy," and also to provide some comic relief, I'm sure.

Since our cars were supplied by the track, I figured they were all basically the same, so I got this idea to ask one of the kids who was racing that day what I should do to win the race. He said, "Well, sir, get a crescent wrench and loosen all the wheel nuts one half turn, and then put a drop of oil by each wheel and spin them." He said that would allow the car to align itself, and by golly he was right—because I did what he said and I won!

Presenting the trophy that day was none other than Vice President Richard Nixon, and when he handed it to me, Art Carney announced, "If the race wasn't fixed, how come his name is on the trophy?" It really wasn't, but it made everybody look anyway, and we all got a big laugh out of it.

With Vice President
Richard Nixon,
Art Carney and
Wendell Corey
at the Soapbox
Derby

The biggest compliment our ABC show ever received came from one of the masters in show business. Once, while in Hollywood, I was invited to attend one of Frank Sinatra's recording sessions. It was interesting not only because it was held at night, but because he was the only artist I'd ever seen record with a live audience in the studio. There was actually a set of bleachers that held a small group of people that he would sing to. I guess it was more comfortable for him than singing to thin air. It was such a good idea too. I should have worked like that, because I enjoyed working to people and he obviously did too.

Sinatra was very, very nice to me that night, and I was delighted when he told me I had a good television show. Flattered and humbled, I said, "Aw, c'mon now . . ." and brusquely he said, "Hey! I said you've got a good show!" I caught myself and thanked him, and quickly learned that you didn't argue with the "Chairman of the Board."

It was in 1965, during our third season, that the network moved the show from Thursdays at 9 P.M. to Friday nights at 10, and I was pretty happy about landing such a good time slot. It was also in '65 that we took the show to Nashville to broadcast the Country Music Awards for the very first time. I enjoyed hosting the show at the Ryman Auditorium, the home of the Grand Ole Opry at the time, but with no air-conditioning it was hotter than a depot stove in that place. In fact, it got so hot that we burned out two television cameras during the live show.

Taking our television show to Nashville was fun, but there was another reason it was a treat for me. Joining our orchestra and making the show extra special was what I considered the "A Team" of country music's greatest musicians: Floyd Cramer on piano, Boots Randolph on saxophone, Charlie McCoy on harmonica, Grady Martin and Chet Atkins on guitars and Buddy Harman on drums. Now *that's* a band!

I was really proud that our show had the opportunity to expose the Country Music Awards to a national audience for the first time on network TV, and felt it gave a little boost to country music. The awards presentation deserved to be broadcast and seen by fans all over the country, and I was glad when the Country Music Association began to televise it nationally three years later.

Our television show certainly gave my career the biggest boost it ever had, and its closing came unexpectedly. I was told that the powers that be at ABC didn't feel the ratings were quite high enough and that the third season would be our last, though I later found out that we were a victim of the networks' canceling of all the rural shows. It seemed they were concerned about getting a "hokey" image with shows like *The Beverly Hillbillies, Green Acres* and *Petticoat Junction,* so when ABC decided to cancel any show that had a smidgen of "country" in it, we became one of their casualties.

When our show was canceled, I immediately called the head of American Broadcasting Companies, Inc., Leonard Goldenson. But I had no ax to grind, I was simply grateful. I told him, "I know you think I want to ask you for something, but I don't. I called you to thank you for three great years, and to tell you that going off the network is leaving me much better off than I was three years ago." And then I said, "Naturally, I feel that ABC is making a mistake, but I'm not bitter . . . as a result of this television show I can now go out and make a lot of money."

Well, he was the nicest! He tried to explain about the ratings, but I said I wasn't complaining. I told him that he and I were good friends and I hoped it would stay that way, and I meant that.

The final show was very emotional. I cried, as a lot of us did. And even though I was set for a five-month tour after the show ended, I would miss the hectic bustle of getting a show on the air, and all the friends I'd made doing it.

I worked with a good group of people on the ABC show, and I'd become attached to a lot of them. The worst part was that I didn't have a job to offer them, and I worried about their futures in such an uncertain business. Though there was one thing I *could* be certain of: After being canceled by CBS and ABC, I was the only person I knew that had been fired by two major networks.

9

OTHER STAGES
OF MY CAREER

HAVING THE ABC show was an ideal situation for me because it kept me at home with the family, although it never did pay as much as touring and doing stage shows. And since performing live was always my favorite thing to do, it was the natural choice for keeping groceries on the table after my TV show was canceled. Traveling and being gone a lot was not an idea I relished, however, but sometimes a man has to do what a man has to do. So I made a five-year plan: I would work the road and make all the money I could, and then retire to the farm property I owned in Virginia.

"The road" turned out to be a superhighway, one with many twists and turns. I covered a lot of territory and took a lot of different directions over the years, but somehow always managed to keep going forward. I was always willing to try something new; if it looked like it might be fun, and make money too, then I was game. My many tours included countless performances on a lot of different stages, including the deck of a battleship, on water skis, on horseback and on an elephant's back. I also rode in a jillion parades all around the country in a variety of vehicles, including the usual convertibles, floats, in a tractor trailer, and once even in a hovercraft.

Many of the shows I worked over the years were package shows, where several performers would group up to ensure a decent-sized audience. They were big back in the fifties and sixties, and some of the first I ever played were booked by my old manager Connie B. Gay. It must have been about 1957 when he booked my band The Texas Wildcats and me on one of my most memorable tours. It featured some pretty big stars too—Ernest Tubb, Minnie Pearl and Andy Griffith—and it took us to three cities—Washington, DC; Richmond, Virginia; and Baltimore, Maryland. The Wildcats provided the music for all of the musical acts, while I acted as master of ceremonies.

Ernest Tubb was by far the biggest star of that show, and Minnie Pearl was a popular comedienne and star of the Grand Ole Opry by this time. Andy Griffith was just getting started in the business as a country comedian, and I remember he only had two pieces of material to use on the show. One was called "A Good Man Is Hard to Find," which he preached like a sermon, and the other was one he'd had a hit record with called "What It Was Was Football." Andy used to come to me before each show and say, "Jimmy, which one should I do tonight?" and every time I'd tell him I thought he ought to do both of them.

This of course was long before Andy Griffith's success in movies with *No Time for Sergeants* and on television with *The Andy Griffith Show* and *Matlock*. In fact, I recall him saying to me back then, "Jimmy, there's a book I just read called *No Time for Sergeants,* and if they ever do that thing on Broadway, one way or the other I'm gonna read for it 'cause I want to play that part." He did indeed play the part of the lead character, Will Stockdale, on Broadway as well as in the movie production of *Sergeants,* and was perfect for the part. Of course it was the beginning of a stellar career for Andy, and as we all know the rest is show business history.

———•———

In the beginning I paid my dues in the crummiest dives and joints around, but as a result of having hit records and a television show, this time the road would take our band and show to some of the nicest places in the country. From the Circle Star Theater near San Francisco to Blinstrub's club in Boston and places in between—you name it and we played it.

Our little five-piece band was joined by local musicians in each town to make a full orchestra, so it made for a pretty big show. We had some really talented opening acts too: Kay Starr, the Lennon Sisters, Jerry Reed, Dottie West, Molly Bee, Boots Randolph, the Chuck Cassey Singers and even my old TV hound dog buddy Rowlf the Muppet.

I played "theater in the round" a lot during the late 1960s, each one usually for a week at a time. There were a lot of them around the country back then, including the ones we played near Buffalo, in San Francisco, Anaheim, Salt Lake City, Phoenix, and one out on Long Island.

Theater in the round is exactly what it sounds like, with a big circle as the stage in the middle of the theater and the audience sitting all the way around it. The band or orchestra was usually in the orchestra pit down on one side of the stage, and each theater usually held around two thousand people. Sometimes the theaters would have a rotating stage, and I once told an audience, "I want you to know that this is the first time I've ever worked on a *spit*."

But no matter how much you moved around to entertain the audience and give them a better view, a lot of times people were still looking at your back. I used to tell my audience, "Now, a lot of the time some of you will be looking at my backside . . . but now that I think about it, that may be the best view you'll ever have of me!"

The theater in Salt Lake City was one I used to enjoy playing a lot. It was such a great place to have fun with the audience. I would pick on the Mormons there mercilessly and kid them about being as good a Mormon as I was a Baptist, and they would love it. I got away with it, because I think you can say things to people like that if you let them know that it's done with love.

Our audience always seemed to have a good time too, especially when we'd ask them to participate. There was this one bit we used to do with the song "Mame," where we'd get a lady up from the audience on stage with us and dress her up for the number. And I never understood it: We'd get some little old lady up there and she'd say, "Oh God, Jimmy! I wish I'd had another drink before I got up here. I'm so nervous and afraid, 'cause I've never been on a stage before!" Then we'd dress her up as Mame with a big floppy hat and a feather boa, and all of a sudden her inhibitions were out the window. As the

Boots Randolph, Grandpa Jones
and Molly Bee

Kay Starr

Imperials and I would sing to her, she'd be bumping and grinding to the music and having a helluva time while we guided her through the steps of the routine. Those ladies always loved that bit, and it really was cute, especially the big finish with them in the middle and us kneeling, arms extended.

It was about 1968 that the road took us to theater in the round in Anaheim, California, with our show featuring an eight-man vocal group called the Cimarron Singers. My opening act there was the wonderful singing group, the Lennon Sisters, who had worked with me several times throughout the years. The Lennons were consummate professionals and the sweetest girls you'd ever want to meet, and ladies all—you just couldn't ask for nicer people.

I have always loved the Lennons' old boss Lawrence Welk and his television show, and have said many times that I thought he was the smartest man in show business. His show focused on pure entertainment and was always done with class, great singers, the best musicians in the business and everyone impeccably attired. Lawrence Welk always tailored his music for the people, as it should be. One night the Lennons talked Welk into coming out to see our show, and afterward he paid me a helluva compliment backstage when he kept saying to me, "What a showman, what a showman!"

The Phoenix Star Theater was a favorite venue of mine too, one I would play many times. Appearing with our show in Phoenix for one performance was a singing trio that included the popular actress Jane Russell. The other two singers, Connie Haines and Beryl Davis were really good, but Jane Russell was the obvious draw, as she was already a big movie star.

It was in that theater in Phoenix that I saw for the last time my dad's second cousin, the great baseball player Dizzy Dean. He and his wife, Ruth, used to spend their winters in Phoenix and I was thrilled they had come out to see our show. Diz was such a colorful character, and I always loved his down-home "you bet your boots" phraseology. We got him up on stage that night because I knew he liked to sing from hearing him warble an occasional tune as a sports commentator on television. His favorite song was "The Wabash Cannonball," so I said, "Diz, why don't you sing that for us?" Reluctantly he said, "But, Jimmy, I don't know what key I do it in." I assured him, "Just start singing, Diz, and the band will find you." So he did, and they did—and when he finished that song, you never heard such a roar from a crowd. Those people loved that old man to death, and I don't know if I've ever felt that much love in a theater for one person as I did for him that night.

It was also when I was working theater in the round at the Phoenix Star Theater that someone threatened my life. The police in Phoenix said that somebody had called them and said, "We're gonna shoot Jimmy Dean on stage tonight." Now, *there's* a sobering thought. I remember the police telling me, "This place is loaded with cops Jimmy, so if he tries anything he'll never get out of here." Great! In other words, *if he blows your head off we've got him.*

The police in that theater felt they had the situation under control and I guess they did all they could do, but I'll tell you what . . . you can rationalize all you want, but when you're seated there in the middle of that stage with one spotlight on you while you're singing a ballad, the thought of that sniper out there in the crowd *will* cross your mind. It was obviously a hoax because nothing happened, but I promise you one thing: I had an extremely fast-moving act that night.

It was after the threat on my life that my friend Elvis Presley gave me a gun. I had opened in Vegas the following week, and after my second show one night he came flying into my dressing room. I'll never forget it: He had on this big wine-colored cape, and after he said hello and hugged my neck, he reached down into the pocket of that cape and pulled out a thirty-eight snub-nose, complete with holster and ammunition. Obviously aware of my death threat, Elvis handed it to me and said, "J.D., if they've got a right to shoot at us, we've got a right to shoot back." And then he said, "Be sure you know how to use it."

Actually, that wasn't the only time someone threatened my life. I once got a letter from a kid in Boston who was evidently a fan of the late actor James Dean. "If you don't stop using his name," she wrote, "we're gonna get a gang together and kill you." Hey, kids, I was here *first*!

Speaking of James Dean, there was always considerable confusion between him and me. I believe there were times when he was known as Jimmy Dean, but I've never used the name James Dean, the reason being it isn't my name. When I was born my mother named me Jimmy and not James.

Then there are some people who actually think James Dean and I were the same person. One time in an airport this lady—and I use the term loosely—walked up to me and said, "I thought you were dead!" "I am," I told her, "they just dug me up to play one more date."

I suppose for every dumb remark I've heard there have been a thousand that were complimentary, the nicest being from the great Ted Lewis. It was in the famous showroom the Blue Room at the Roosevelt Hotel in New Orleans that I met the entertainer of "Me And My Shadow" fame. His show had closed there the night before, and he'd stayed over to see my opening show the next night. Afterward, Lewis came back to my dressing room and said to me, "Young man, I worked with Will Rogers, and I never saw anybody that I thought could step into his boots, but I think maybe you could."

I must have done *something* right at that performance, because even the newspaper reviewers called me a "modern-day Will Rogers." Being compared to him was the highest compliment I've ever been paid in all my years of performing. Mr. Rogers was once quoted as saying he never met a man he didn't like, and I can truthfully say I never met an *audience* I didn't like. I surely hope it was obvious.

10

COUNTRY FRIENDS
AND RURAL PLACES

THE RURAL HUMOR and style of Will Rogers was never something I ever tried to emulate, but his down-to-earth common sense was one thing I could always relate to. I guess once a country boy, always a country boy. And though some of my recordings occasionally crossed over onto the pop charts, I'm sure I'll forever be known as a country singer—which suits the hell out of me.

In fact, at one time I was invited to join the "mother church" of country music, the Grand Ole Opry. But because of their mandatory number of appearances a month and the fact that I lived in New Jersey, back then I could never afford to go to Nashville and join their roster of stars. I guess the truth is, I just didn't want to get down there and get mixed up in all that talent.

Being from the country, I have to say that rural folks are my favorite people mainly because they're *real*, and I've found that for the most part, country music entertainers are the most sincere and authentic people in all of show business. It's impossible to include the many stories I have about them, but I'll share with you a few of my favorites.

Some country folks are just so real that they can be downright adorable. Years ago I was appearing at a Columbia Records convention in Miami along with Grand Ole Opry star Stonewall Jackson of the hit record "Waterloo" fame, and the next morning Stonewall and his wife came down to the hotel coffee shop, where I asked them to join me. When they sat down, I said, "Boy, this is some fancy hotel, isn't it?" And in a sweet Southern drawl, Stone's wife said, "Yeah, it is, Jimmy, but last night something bit me on my foot. I think it was a flea. Probably came out of one of those big old thick carpets." Then she said, "You know them big fancy carpets is all right for them that likes 'em, but you just give me something I can *mop*."

Many of my best friends were and still are Grand Ole Opry stars, and I go back a lot of years with most of them. In fact, it was Grandpa Jones who took my place when I left the *Town and Country Time* show in Washington, DC, in the late fifties. Grandpa was one of the funniest human beings I ever knew. I could just look at him and get tickled. When he took over the show in Washington, I remember asking him, "How do ya think you're going to do, Grandpa?" He said, "Well, I don't know, Jimmy, you're a fairly quick-witted boy, and my wit is slower than smoke off of s——t."

If I had one real close friend when I first started going to Nashville back in the sixties, it was Carl Smith, the country music star who had introduced me for my first appearance at the Grand Ole Opry. He

Out fishing with a couple of my Grand Ole Opry buddies—Country Music Hall of Famers Little Jimmy Dickens (left) and Bill Anderson

had some great horses and we used to enjoy riding together, and I liked Carl because he was brutally frank and you could always count on him to tell you the truth. Whenever I was in town, I would stay with him and his wife, Goldie Hill, a terrific lady and a singing star in her own right. Carl and I hung out a lot together for a long time and were such close friends that he and Goldie even named their son Dean after me.

Another good friend whose company I enjoy from time to time is Whisperin' Bill Anderson. Bill of course is the soft-spoken host of country music radio and television programs, but he's probably known best for his songwriting and hit records. We've had some great times deep-sea fishing when he and Little Jimmy Dickens visited on our boat up in New England, and although we don't see each other that often, we talk on the phone nearly every week and swap jokes.

Whisperin' Bill takes a lot of kidding about his soft voice, and good-naturedly I might add. A few years ago we were playing golf in Nashville and both of us were having a bad day. In fact, I don't think either of us could have found our butts with both hands if every finger had've been a flashlight. Bill hit a lousy drive and then reached for a three iron, took a cut at the ball and dribbled it about five yards. Completely exasperated, I cracked up when he leaned up on the club and said, "Permit me to say at this time, 'whisperin' s——t'!"

Minnie Pearl and I also became great friends after working together on many occasions. Minnie was not only a wonderful comedienne and entertainer, but she was an elegant and brilliant lady. She was also one of the most perceptive human beings I've ever known. Once I was expounding on the virtues of a very well-known radio and TV personality, on how knowledgeable he was of country music and what an authority he was. Minnie said to me, "He truly is that. If there is an authority on country music, he is one. But, Jimmy, he is a small man." Well, when she said that, I got kind of ticked off. After all, we were appearing on his show that night, and besides, I considered him a good friend. Then she said it again, "Jimmy, he's a small man, and you're a big man." So I asked Minnie what she meant by it and she said, "You just watch. You'll see one of these days." Later on I found out how right Minnie was, when my friend let some petty disagreement end our longtime friendship.

Minnie's husband, Henry Cannon, was one of my favorite people too, and a really good airplane pilot who flew Minnie and a lot of country stars to their dates. He also had a wonderful sense of humor, and even Minnie herself told me Henry was the funniest man she ever knew. Once, when Tammy Wynette was getting married for about the fifth time, they had received an invitation to the wedding, which was being held in Florida. Henry told Minnie, "You go ahead if you want to, but I'll just stay here in Nashville and wait around for one of her *summer* weddings."

The last time I saw Minnie Pearl was at her home a few months after her debilitating stroke. It had paralyzed one side of her body and left her confined to a wheelchair, but it hadn't dampened her spirits or her sense of humor. She rattled off stories and jokes like she always did and then had Henry bring in her usual cocktail for the evening. I don't think I'll ever forget that picture of Minnie sitting there in that wheelchair, with her head to one side and a soda straw in her mouth sipping on a tall glass of Maker's Mark whiskey—straight. What a gal!

The great singing cowboy Roy Rogers was another good friend who had a wonderful sense of humor. Truly one of the "good guys," Roy was a sweet and gentle man. While I was living in New Jersey, I got a call from him saying he needed to come to the Big Apple to fire a guy who was working for him, and that he'd like to get together with me while he was in town. When I met him at his hotel, he told me he needed to go fire the guy but he'd be back shortly. But after a while I looked up and there was Roy hollering as he came through the lobby of the hotel, so happy that he literally picked me up and swung me around. I've often wondered if anyone witnessed that scene and what they must have thought. I said, "Roy, what's the matter with you?" And he said, "Jimmy, I hate to fire people, and I'm so glad I didn't have to fire the guy. We worked things out after all!"

To celebrate that night Roy and I decided to go out for a bite to eat at a famous steak house in New York City, and while we were there it snowed. After dinner and a couple of drinks we were both in a rare mood, and as we went outside to leave, we got into a rather spirited snowball fight and played like a couple of little kids.

Through the years there have been many stories related to me by my country music friends, and one of the funniest I ever heard came

One of my many appearances
on the Grand Ole Opry

Backstage at the Grand Ole
Opry with old friends George
Hamilton IV and Roy Clark

Backstage
at the Grand Ole
Opry with Minnie
Pearl, Roy Clark,
and Dottie West

from the "Singing Sheriff," Faron Young. It seemed that Faron was paying fellow country singer Webb Pierce a visit at his home in the exclusive Franklin Road area of suburban Nashville, where his neighbors included Minnie Pearl and the governor of Tennessee. Faron said while the two of them were shooting pool they had a few drinks, too many in fact, and they both ended up getting bombed.

After a while, Faron said, he told Webb he was going home, and he went out and got into his brand-new Lincoln that was parked in front of the house. Well, in his stupor Webb followed him outside and said, "Sheriff, you're too drunk to drive home. Get out of the car!" Faron said, "Okay," and got out and slammed the door. But when he did, the car was in gear, and because it was brand-new, the idle was set up too fast. So the two of them stood there and watched as Faron's car drove slowly down the street all by itself. It even took a bank in the road like somebody was steering it. And what was so funny about the whole thing was that Faron said Webb just stood there looking at the car and then at him, as if to say, "How the hell are you doing that?"

Faron said he and Webb stood there watching the brand-new Lincoln turn a banked curve and then go out of sight, when they began to hear . . . click . . . click . . . click . . . and then boom! And every light in the neighborhood went out, including the governor's mansion. The "clicks," they later found out, were mailboxes, and the "boom" was when Faron's brand-new car wound up around a light pole.

Hank Snow was another funny human being, but most of the time it was accidental. One time, when Hank and I were doing a show together, we were backstage in the dressing room just sitting around shooting the bull. Hank would have a few drinks with you, but he would never want you to think he was the least bit inebriated. He also enjoyed smoking a pipe, and this night he pulled one out and began loading it from his pouch of tobacco. As he sat there, I watched him fumble as he tried to hit the bowl of the pipe with each pinch of tobacco, but got ten times as much down the front of his beautiful white suit than he did in his pipe. When Hank was finally satisfied with his loaded pipe, he tried to put the mouthpiece in his mouth, but he kept missing it. I watched him stab it first into his cheek, his chin, his forehead and finally his mouth. Well, by this time I was hysterical, and when he caught me laughing at him, he looked at me as if he had done it all on purpose and said, "Did you see that? Wasn't that funny?"

There have been so many of my entertainer friends that have passed on and I miss them terribly, especially Roger Miller. I've said many times that Roger was the most spontaneous and creative person I ever knew, and maybe even the funniest. He was a wonderful guy too, but like most everyone, I miss his crazy songs and dry sense of humor.

The most poignant moment I ever witnessed with Roger was during an interview we did when he was a guest on my syndicated television show in the seventies. I asked him, "Roger, how do you do it? How can you be so quick and funny and so 'up' all the time?" He looked rather serious and replied, "Well, I was always afraid if I didn't make people laugh that they would go away and leave me alone."

One of my favorite times with Roger was about two years before he passed away. I was in Nashville to tape a Statler Brothers television show for the Nashville Network, and after the taping my wife Donna and I went back to our hotel to have a nightcap in the cocktail lounge. The lounge of the Music City Sheridan was in the middle of the lobby, and because it was late we were the only patrons there. Just as we were ready to call it a night, Donna said, "Isn't that Roger Miller coming through the lobby?" I looked up and motioned for him to come join us and then ordered him a beer.

After sitting and chatting for a few minutes, we all looked up and saw Jimmy Fortune of the Statler Brothers coming in the lounge. Jimmy joined us too, and it was only a matter of time before we all moved over to the piano and began singing together and swapping songs. It was a great time, and I'll never forget when Roger turned to me and said, "We don't do this kind of thing anymore. We just don't get together anymore and we should do this more often." Roger was right, and we all agreed to make more time in our busy lives to enjoy each other. How I wish we could have made that promise a lot sooner.

The saddest memory I have of Roger was the very last time I saw him. Donna and I were appearing on a Minnie Pearl tribute show that was being taped at the Grand Ole Opry House, and we shared a dressing room with Roger. He said, "Jimmy, let me show y'all where they're gonna zap me next." He was obviously talking about where his next cancer treatment would be on his body, because he took off his shirt to show us his back. Down his spine there was an X drawn on his skin about every three inches. In spite of his cancer, his sense of humor was still intact, because about that time the wardrobe lady opened the door, looked at Donna's evening gown hanging on the rack and said, "Who's wearing the red dress?" Quick as ever, Roger said, "I am." That was Roger Miller . . . an entertainer until the very end.

———•———

My country music friends and I worked together not only on television shows, but many times on package shows and at state and county fairs. The fact is, I worked so many that the press dubbed me "The King of the County Fairs." We played numerous state fairs, in New York, Michigan, Illinois, Minnesota and Kansas to name a few, holding the record at the Ohio State Fair for a long time over people like Jack Benny and Perry Como. We did quite well at all of them, especially in '61 at the West Texas Fair in Abilene, where our show drew the largest opening-night crowd they'd ever seen.

There were times we would work along with other musical acts, and certainly one of the most exciting times I ever had was at the New York State Fair. They booked just me and my conductor to work with the Duke Ellington Orchestra, and boy, was it a blast! I just loved singing with those guys.

It was at the Kentucky State Fair that I had my first encounter with my friend Rosemary Clooney, who was originally from the Bluegrass State. The William Morris Agency had booked us on the show, where we were to share equal billing. It was supposed to be "The Rosemary Clooney and Jimmy Dean Show," but Joe Higgins, the agent who booked it, had my name on the marquee as being a featured part of Rosie's show. Needless to say, I was ticked off royally at Joe, and was ready to pinch his head off.

There was also another little act on this "Rosie Clooney Show" named Fabian, that nobody had ever heard of except the teeny boppers. After the show, these teenagers were coming around to me asking, "Where's Fabian? Where's Fabian?" And I'd tell them, "Hell, I don't know where Fabian is!" And then an idea hit me. That little pinhead of an agent Joe Higgins was staying at our hotel and I remember his room number, 428, to this day. So I started telling these young girls, "Look, I don't know where Fabian is right now, but I do know that after the last show tonight he's having a little Coca-Cola party at the hotel in room four-twenty-eight." Then I said, "Now, you can tell a few of your friends about it, but don't tell too many."

The next morning as I was sitting in the hotel restaurant having breakfast, here came Joe Higgins down the stairs with bags under his eyes that could've carried golf balls. He really did look terrible. As he walked over to me, he said, "You son of a bitch . . . " And I said, "Well, Joe, what's the matter?" And he said, "What's the *matter*? Have you ever been called a lying mother f——ker by a twelve-year-old girl?" Paybacks are hell, Joe.

Along with state fairs, I also played many rodeos. They were located mostly in the Southwest, in Texas, New Mexico, Oklahoma and Arkansas, and beginning in the late 1950s, I worked a lot of them at least two or three times over a period of about fifteen to twenty years. It was a rough and tough business and I loved it, and because I was born and raised in cowboy country, it was like going home . . . I fit like socks on a rooster.

Each rodeo would schedule the entertainers' segment at different times during the event, but most of the time we went on somewhere in the middle of the rodeo. For our part of the show, they'd have a tractor pull a stage into the arena that would already have the band set up on it, ready to go. The rodeos would also furnish me with a horse for each show, since I always thought it made for good showmanship to ride one when making my entrance and exit. The music would start and the announcer would introduce me as I made my entrance, barreling in wide open. I'd make the circle around the arena and then ride up to the stage, dismount and do the show. Then my horse would be waiting for me when the show was finished, and I'd ride him going slowly around the arena while shaking hands with people in the crowd. After that I'd barrel-ass to the exit door, stop, turn around and doff my hat to the crowd as I backed the horse out of the arena. I always backed out, because I never thought it looked very nice to go riding out leaving the audience with a lasting impression of *two* horses' asses.

The Houston Astrodome was an incredible place, and one of the most exciting experiences I ever had was working the first rodeo held there. One of the best rodeo cowboys that ever lived was my friend Jim Shoulders, and as we were standing behind the shoots at the rodeo one day, Jim turned to me and said, "Jimmy, the only thing bigger than this is *outside!*"

As you might imagine, a rodeo arena can be a pretty dangerous place. It was during our show in the Astrodome that I once came close to a real disaster. Horses had been slipping and falling on the baseball dugouts, where plywood and about three inches of dirt had been put in an effort to cover them. It was a real hazard, and the people in charge should have fixed them, but they didn't. For my show, I went barreling out into the arena like I always did, but with seven big spotlights hitting me in my eyes, I couldn't see much at all. As my horse and I tried to make the turn at third base, he fell in front of the dugout, taking me with him. Luckily, I cleared the stirrups just in time, but then he rolled over on my left foot and mashed it.

Greeting the crowd at one of
my many rodeo appearances

After the fall, as I stood up, the audience jumped to their feet in applause, which had to be the first time I ever got a standing ovation just for being alive. We went right ahead with the show, even though the fall had burst the side of my cowboy boot, and I could feel the blood squishing around inside as I walked around the stage. The horse had survived unscathed, so I got back on him and rode him out of the arena after the show was over. Then when I got to the backstage area, some smart-ass just *had* to say, "Hey, Jimmy, that was one hell of an opener!"

The medical personnel promptly tended to me, cutting my boot off as my foot had swelled up like a melon and the blood oozed from under my toenails. And though it had been mashed, somehow it wasn't broken, thank God, and I opened the next week in Las Vegas wearing a soft cast.

Another memorable rodeo experience happened in Blue Earth, Minnesota. In the middle of my act, I looked up and saw where seven Brahma bulls had gotten loose and wandered into the arena. As I slowly backed off the stage I told the audience, "Staying here with those guys is against my religion . . . I'm a devout coward!" I told them, "And as soon as they leave, I'll come back," as the rodeo cowboys rushed in to wrangle them back into their pen.

I made a lot of friends in the rodeo business, and always had a deep respect for rodeo cowboys, especially bull riders. I always loved watching them, and the feeling seemed to be mutual. In fact, I shared a distinction with the great country and western entertainer Rex Allen. I was told we were the only performers that the rodeo cowboys would come out from behind their shoots to watch.

We'd have a lot of fun with the audience during our show too, one time in particular when we were at the Idaho Snake River Stampede. We always did a bit with a song called "Honey," where I'd get some woman out of the audience to help me sing. I'd sing the line, "I'm in love with you," and she'd sing "honey" . . . and on it would go, with her answering each of my lines by singing "honey." It was always a lot of fun, but this one particular time, for my "victim" I happened to get a real live wire. Before we sang the song, I asked her what her name was and where she was from, and so on, and then I asked what her husband did. She replied, "He's in the same business as you." I said, "Oh, is he an entertainer?" And she said, "No . . . he sells manure spreaders." Well, I got tickled and so did the audience, and we never got over it for the rest of the show. Right in the middle of a sentimental ballad, I'd get tickled all over again, and then the audience would lose it too. That lady completely destroyed our show.

There was even a prison rodeo that I worked a couple of times, an annual event at the Texas State Penitentiary in Huntsville. The participants were the actual prisoners themselves, and I always thought that it was kind of cruel to put those guys through the rigors of a rodeo. It's a dangerous business, especially if you don't know what you're doing, and none of those guys were rodeo people, just inmates. Actually, I think some of them had hoped they'd get hurt just to get a little time off from prison life.

Just visiting the prison was a disturbing experience for me. When you first go in, they take all of your valuables, including your watch, your jewelry and your money. Then once inside, you walk through these long halls and then down to an electric gate. That gate was probably the most disturbing part, because when it closes behind you it has the most permanent sound you've ever heard in your life. *Clunk!!!*

Seeing men in cages bothered me a lot too, although the inmates were free to walk around in certain places. There were always a few hanging around wanting to chat when we were rehearsing for the show, and they were usually pretty interesting to talk to. Most of them had kept their sense of humor too. One inmate told me that whenever a new inmate would first arrive, the other prisoners would always ask, "Yeah, we know you didn't do it, but what did they *say* you did?"

And then once, as I was walking through the prison yard, I heard a voice yell out, "Hey, Jimmy! We watch your show every week . . . but I don't guess we do a whole helluva lot for your ratings!"

I remember the prisoners had these three inmates that they wanted me to hear sing, and who had written some lyrics to a song with a familiar melody. One of them told me, "We wrote these lyrics but we stole the melody," and another turned to him and said, "*borrowed*. Did you forget why the hell we're here?!"

I don't know if it's true, but I once heard that the majority of jokes people tell originate in prisons, and I can understand why. I would imagine that keeping your sense of humor would be essential, especially during one of those prison rodeos, as a damned Brahma bull tromped around on your head. And while they might not have been professionals, some of those inmates did indeed make some pretty good cowboys.

If there was ever one rodeo performer who made the biggest impression on me, it would have to be a cowboy named Freckles Brown. Freckles was a bull rider and one of the greatest. He'd come out of the shoot on some of the biggest and baddest bulls in the business, looking like he was made of rubber from the waist up.

In a profession where youth prevails, Freck rode until he was over fifty years old, which is virtually unheard of. I had seen him ride many times throughout the years and figured he would just keep going until some Brahma did him in out there in that arena, but he eventually left the rodeo circuit and ended up at the University of Oklahoma teaching rodeo. Before Freckles passed away, I had the opportunity to recite a piece of material to him that I had written, one for which he was my inspiration.

Freckles Brown

His aging hands were gnarled by the tugging of a rope
And he walked with a limp but he stood erect and his eyes were
*   keen with hope*
The stands were full at the rodeo as he walked behind the shoots
And he said he wanted just one more ride as he plopped down his
*   entry loot*
Now, there was a time when old Freckles was right at the top of the
*   heap*
But years took their toll and he made few shows and the ones he
*   made were cheap*
But like all of us from time to time he got a feeling in his bones
He'd ride once more and stand tall again and pay off past due loans.
The bull he drew was a spinner, big tough and fast, and he smiled at
*   me as he rosined his glove and said, "If I ride him, it'll be my last"*
The bull, he spun, but old Freckles stayed like he'd been glued or
*   tied*

*And the shoot boss said, "That's the way it's done . . . just look at
that old man ride!"*
*The buzzer sounded and Freck stepped down with a grin you could
see a mile*
*And we all knew then that we'd seen a ride like we wouldn't see for
a while*
*As he started to leave the crowd went wild . . . how well he knew
that sound*
*But ten feet from the shoots he grabbed his chest and he crumpled
to the ground*
*Oh, his spirit was strong but his heart was weak, and there in the
dirt he died*
*But those who saw it won't soon forget when old Freckles took his
last ride.*

Traveling the country and performing at the many rodeos and
fairs with me was a wonderful four-man vocal group called the
Imperials. For years the Imps and I worked together, playing everywhere from Podunk, Idaho, to the showrooms in Las Vegas, and for
a short period of time one of their members was a young singer
named Larry Gatlin.

Also singing backup for me at one time was the popular vocal
group the Oak Ridge Boys. They were an exciting act and great
showmen that gave 110 percent on stage. The Oaks traveled with me
for four years just before they hit it big with their own careers as
country music superstars. I remember when they had just recorded a
song called "Y'all Come Back Saloon." They said, "J.D., we want to
play something for you," and when I heard it, I told them I thought
it was a smash hit. It was, of course, along with a jillion other songs
they would record.

One thing about the Oak Ridge Boys I'll always remember is their
fairness and integrity. They were still working for me and had some
contract dates to fulfill when their records hit big, and they were
surely pulling in much bigger money for their own personal appearances than they were with me. But they never balked at having to
work my dates for less money, nor did they ever try to charge me a
dime more. The night they were leaving my show, they said, "You

wanted us when nobody wanted us, and if you ever need us we'll be there for free."

The Oak Ridge Boys proved it some time later when I asked them to play a benefit show in Dallas. They were road weary and dog tired, but they were there. Quality people and good guys, those Oaks. They make me proud of my country roots, and show business could use a lot more folks like them.

11

CASINO
SHOWROOMS

OVER THE YEARS I've had the good fortune of entertaining many different audiences, from the *Grand Ole Opry* and rodeos and fairs, to theaters, television and coliseums. People everywhere are basically the same though. They're looking for fun and to escape their everyday troubles and woes. And the audiences in casino showrooms are no different. I played a lot of those rooms, which were actually a nice change of pace for me. After coming off a string of one-nighters or performing at a week-long rodeo, I was able to settle down for a three- to four-week-long stint at a club in Reno, Sparks or Las Vegas, Nevada.

I had a lot of fun with the audiences there and used to tell them, "Now, I'm gonna pick on everybody, and I assure you I'll get to you before the night's out. But it's done with love and I don't mean a thing by it." Radio and TV personality Ralph Emery once called me the "country Don Rickles" because my humor is sometimes infused with insults to others. But I just feel like when we can get to where we can pick on all races, creeds or colors—what have you—and do it with love and not mean anything by it, that this would be a better place in which to live. So I'd tell my audience, "If your feelings are easily hurt, now would be a wonderful time to leave, because I *will* get you."

Of course, my secretary Willie Bruffy would be there with me at all of my shows and was accommodated for as stipulated in my contract. Each night after my first show, she'd do what we called the "rest room review," where she'd go into the ladies' room to hear what they were saying about our show. In Vegas the press didn't mean a damn thing; it was what the people and the taxi drivers said about your show that could make you or break you.

I liked playing the showrooms in Reno and Sparks because they were more family oriented, but I really didn't care much for Las Vegas. I think what really bothered me about Vegas was that you'd see people there losing money that they should have been using to buy groceries and shoes and clothes for their kids. I didn't mind seeing big spenders lose money in those casinos, but you'd see the others everywhere and that bothered me a lot.

You see it all in Las Vegas. People come from everywhere trying to hit the jackpot, but go home exhausted and exasperated most of the time. And the one line you overhear most often with a hundred different names is "Now, Ethel, give me that money I told you not to give me!" Then there was the most comical scene I ever witnessed in a casino, which involved a man so drunk he could hardly stand. He stumbled out into the middle of the room with two hands full of quarters, threw them back over his head and said, "Now, that saves me the trouble of pulling all those f——kin' handles!"

Harrah's was where I worked many times in Reno during the sixties and seventies. It was a big, beautiful place that was the most popular casino there during that time. And while most of the casinos supplied a suite for their performers, Harrah's put us in a beautiful spacious home out by the country club. It was in their showroom that we recorded the album *Live at Harrah's,* with Chet Atkins producing. We had supplemented our orchestra that week with extra musicians, and used the best cuts from several nights of taping for the record.

Jerry Reed, the talented musician, singer and actor, was my opening act at Harrah's for a while. Jerry was just starting out in show business and was a cute kid back then, but nervous as a cat. The audiences loved him and gave him plenty of applause, but he would nevertheless come off the stage saying, "They hated me! They hated me!"

I have to say my favorite casino showroom to work was John Ascuaga's Golden Nugget in Sparks. It was the largest casino in the Reno area at the time and featured performers like Liberace, Robert Goulet, Buck Owens, Red Skelton, Danny Thomas and Debbie Reynolds for three-week stints. It also had seven of the best restaurants in the world, which didn't hurt my feelings at all. How I'd love to go back and get that pan roast just one more time, with a good cold beer.

Also featured at the Golden Nugget was a pair of trained elephants that appeared there as the opening act throughout the entire season. They were billed as "Bertha and Tina—The World's Most Amazing Performing Elephants," and they were really good. Once, during one of my cocktail shows, I was in a squirrelly mood, and instead of the usual opening monologue and jokes, I started out by saying, "You know, this is the first time that I ever got dressed with elephants, and I'll tell you, sometimes it gets a little bit rank back there." Then I said, "They really are wonderful, though, and I just think the world of them. But I think that Tina really kind of digs me, and she gives good trunk." Well, I never heard such a reaction in my life. There was a huge roar, and then it got quiet, and then the roar started up all over again. We never did get straightened out during that whole show; even the musicians couldn't keep from laughing and had a hard time playing.

One time some public relations people in Reno came up with a crazy idea to use one of those elephants for a publicity photo with me. They wanted to take a picture of me sitting on Bertha with my golf bag over my shoulder, so we all went to a location they had chosen out by a big lake. Because the hair on an elephant's back is really stiff and wiry, they take a blowtorch and burn the hair down on its back before you ride one. (It doesn't hurt them a bit because their skin is so thick.) After they had singed Bertha's back, I climbed on and we posed for the shoot. But when I got off, there were these little red spots all over the butt of my britches. Evidently they hadn't singed off all the hairs, and I had bled in a lot of different places where the remaining elephant hairs stuck me.

Before then I didn't know it, but elephants just love water. After we finished shooting that day, we all looked around and saw Bertha heading for the lake. She went right out in the middle of it, and many times all you could see out there was her trunk sticking up and her trainer in a rowboat trying to get her out. He was hitting her trunk with a boat oar and calling her every name in the book, but she wasn't about to give up a good time. I don't know if Bertha could hear him through the water or not, but it took him about four hours to get her out of that lake.

In Las Vegas they call the main drag that goes through town the "strip," which is where the biggest and most popular showrooms and casinos are located. I was the first country artist to play the Las Vegas strip, and the Flamingo was the first place I ever worked there. The guy that owned it came to the airport to pick me up, and I'll never forget what he said as he drove me to the hotel. "Jimmy, you see all these fancy hotels?" he asked. "Those weren't built by people tryin' to win; they were built by people tryin' to get even." Then he told me, "Basically we have three big gamblers here; we have Texans, Jews and Orientals." And considering what he said, I've often thought if you were a Chinese Jew from Ft. Worth, it would *not* be wise for you to go to Vegas.

The entertainers' contracts in Vegas were usually for four weeks at a time, and even though we worked two shows a night, seven nights a week, we still had time for recreation. Golf was a favorite pastime, and some of us also enjoyed boating and skiing on Lake Mead. For a while Jim Henson and his Muppet Rowlf were appearing nightly as part of our show, and it was on Lake Mead that I taught Jim how to water-ski. It's a picture I'll never forget: Jim back there skiing with his long hair and beard waving in the breeze. And with that skinny frame and spindly legs, I couldn't help but think how much he looked like Jesus on water skis.

Another of the showrooms in Las Vegas that we played was in the Landmark Hotel. It was a tall structure, that reminded me a lot of the revolving Space Needle restaurant in Seattle. It's gone now, but in its heyday the Landmark was a rather posh place on the strip, and I thought I was tall hog at the trough when I worked there. The country singer Dottie West opened for me a lot when we played the Landmark. She and I had recorded an album of songs together, some of which we would sing in the show.

The Desert Inn was where I performed most of the time when I worked in Las Vegas. Howard Hughes, the eccentric entrepreneur, owned the D.I. along with many other hotels and showrooms in town. I had a long-term contract with Hughes, whom I never saw, by the way.

The Desert Inn's showroom was perfect for entertaining and I loved working there, besides the fact that the hotel treated their star like a king. For accommodations they supplied a big, beautiful home that was situated right behind the theater. Plus the golf course was nearby, and every morning they would have my golf cart and clubs parked at my door, ready and waiting for me and my usual ten o'clock tee time. Sweet.

The pay at the Desert Inn was also pretty good, I thought. To me sixty-five thousand dollars a week seemed like all the money in the world back in the late sixties, especially for a country boy. Nowadays they've probably got lounge acts making that much, but as they say, everything is relative.

Our show would draw the occasional celebrity in the audience, and I once had a rather startling experience on stage. I used to sing "Alabama Jubilee" as the opening song in our show, and there's a line in it that says, "You ought to see Deacon Jones when he rattles his bones." This one night when I had just finished singing the song, I turned around to the band for a couple of seconds, and when I turned back to the audience there was the biggest, blackest guy you ever saw standing right in front of me. Serious and unsmiling, he said to me, "*I'm* Deacon Jones . . . ," and it was the athlete Deacon Jones of the Los Angeles Rams football team. There he stood big as a wall, wearing a big fur coat and looking real mean, but then he smiled, as it was all in fun, thank God. A friend of mine had brought him by the show to pull the gag on me, and the audience got a huge charge out of it.

One night the popular singer and actress Debbie Reynolds came to see our show at the Desert Inn and was seated in a booth all by herself. She took a bow when I acknowledged her from the stage, and then after the show she came backstage for a visit. I told her how honored and flattered we were that she was there and how appreciative of the fact that she would come to see our show. Then she said, "I must tell you truthfully, Jimmy, my mother is the reason I'm here." She said her mother had told her that if she wanted to learn how to work a show in Vegas, she should go and watch Jimmy Dean perform.

A couple of years later, I went to see Debbie's show—at the Desert Inn incidentally—and she was really good. She was funny and picked on herself a lot, and she had indeed picked up a few tips from the farmer that she'd embellished for her own act, especially while mingling with the audience. In fact, a lot of entertainers copied my act, though I'll refrain from mentioning names. But I don't know why they'd want to do that anyway, because I wasn't that good.

———•———

Elvis played Vegas regularly back in the late sixties, and there were many times he would drop in and visit our show at the D.I. Afterward he would usually end up backstage, where he'd hug my neck and always flatter me with "You country genius son of a bitch . . . you country genius son of a bitch!"

During one stint at the D.I. when Dottie West was my opening act, Elvis came in to watch our show and she acknowledged him, introducing him from the stage. Of course the audience went bananas, but she caught pure *hell* from the stage manager. He told her in no uncertain terms that if there was a celebrity in the house, it was the star of the show who introduced them and *not* the opening act.

Sometimes I'd look over and Elvis would be standing in the wings while we were finishing up our show, but one particular night he came in without me knowing it. While at the Desert Inn I would use a wireless microphone when I performed, and that night there was obviously something wrong with the one I had. It kept cutting out, so I said to the sound engineer, "Can you get me another microphone out here?" I tried continuing with the show while I waited, but no new microphone showed up. I asked again for a replacement, but still no mike. Finally, as I was getting ready to blow a fuse, the audience erupted with gasps and cheers of delight. Unbeknownst to me, Elvis was coming out of the wings and across the stage to deliver my microphone. He said, "Is this the item you were looking for, sir?" Well, needless to say, the rest my show that evening was shot to hell—Elvis Presley was in the house.

I guess it's no secret that Elvis had a passion for acting and movies, and when the movie *Patton* with George C. Scott came out, he couldn't wait to tell me about it. He said, "Dean, you've got to go see this movie." I told him I didn't want to go see it, that I happened to be a big fan of General Patton's and I didn't want to see anybody tear him down for some of the things he did. But I finally did go see it, and it turned out to be one of my favorite films of all time.

After I saw *Patton,* Elvis was visiting backstage again one night, and as we were talking about it, he went into this monologue from the movie that must have lasted for ten minutes. It was the entire opening scene that George C. Scott performed in front of a huge American flag, and Elvis knew it by heart. He did it well too. I got the feeling it was that kind of role he would have liked to have sunk his teeth into if he'd had the chance.

I remember that Elvis would sometimes call us before the last show of the night and say, "Hey, Dean, would you and the guys hang around after the show?" He loved to come over to our gig at the end of the evening and sing with my backup vocal group, the Imperials. And anybody who says Elvis couldn't go anywhere without an entourage of bodyguards doesn't know what they're talking about. He'd show up at our dressing room door and it would just be him and a driver.

A lot of times Elvis would cut his show by a couple of numbers and come watch the last part of ours, and then afterward we'd go down to my dressing room. Our piano player Joe Moscheo would sit down at the piano, and Elvis and the Imperials would start singing—nothing but gospel songs and spirituals.

To me Elvis was a person with multiple personalities, because he was somebody one day and somebody different the next. But I used to watch him there with that wonderful look on his face—with no gyrations and no put-on—and I'd say to myself, *I don't really know if I know Elvis Presley, but I think that's him, that one there singing those gospel songs.*

It was during one of those jam sessions that I told Elvis I was having

With Robert Goulet
at his show in Vegas

Some of my Vegas duds

With Elvis backstage at the
Desert Inn in Las Vegas

a helluva time getting "up" for that second show. And it was true, especially during that last week of the month-long contract. My energy level began to wane every night, and I would try to keep going by eating four or five tablespoons of raw honey before each show. I knew that honey was instant energy because it's predigested and the sugar goes right to the bloodstream.

I told Elvis that, in spite of eating all that honey, I was still having a hard time, and he said, "Tell me about it, Jimmy, I know just what you mean. I'll have my doctor call you tomorrow." Sure enough, his doctor called the next day and I explained to him what my problem was. I remember his words to this day. He said, "Jimmy, what you have is the old Las Vegas 'blahs.' I'll send you over some pills. Just take one about a half an hour before the first show, and then another one before the second show, and you'll be fine."

So true to his word, the doctor sent over these little bitty yellow pills, and that night I took one thirty minutes before showtime. I remember just sailing right through that first show; then I took another pill about a half hour before the second show. Same thing— I was just flying and having a high old time. In fact, the show ran over that night I was having so much fun.

It was usually an every night thing that a few of us guys would go somewhere and have a bite to eat, so after our show ended around one o'clock that night, we set out for breakfast. I used to order things like a bowl of chili with three scrambled eggs in it and a stack of toast with a glass of whole milk, but I noticed that particular night I wasn't very hungry. I had also noticed during the show that I was sweating a lot more than I ordinarily did.

Some of us also had a tee time every morning at ten o'clock, and that meant getting to bed so I could get up the next day for our golf game. But when I lay down to go to sleep that night, my heart was beating really hard and my eyes wouldn't close. It was then I said to myself, *Dean, you are on drugs!* So I got up and found that bottle of little yellow pills, walked over to the john and dumped them in. I really don't know how strong they were, but I would bet that the lid blew off the city septic tank somewhere in downtown Las Vegas.

I'm sure Elvis and his doctor meant well by me, because they obviously thought that pill business was okay, since it worked for EP. I remember he always had a small box filled with pills that he carried around with him—pills of all colors, shapes and sizes—and I really think Elvis thought they could do no harm. And you know, I could understand how people could get hooked on them, because they made you feel so good . . . but not for very long. I'll admit to a fondness for wine or a cocktail, but I've had the good sense to stay away from cocaine and all the drugs that have been the bane of many a performer. As a matter of fact, the only thing I'd put up my nose is my finger.

———•———

One of the most memorable and emotional shows I ever played was in the showroom at the Golden Nugget. While we were there for one of our month-long stints, I read an article in the newspaper about an eleven-year-old boy who had leukemia and was not expected to live. The story was about his dying request to ride in a helicopter, and his nurses in the hospital had put together the funds to pay for it. I also read how much his folks were in debt from his enormous medical bills, and that they had no more collateral because their house was in hock as far as it would go. I suggested we play a benefit for the boy and at least try get his folks out of debt, and I began putting it together by calling my entertainer friends working in the area to ask for their help.

The first person I called was Larry Gatlin, who was working in Vegas with his Gatlin Brothers show at the time, and he agreed to come over and perform for us. Also in town was my old friend Roy Clark, who was playing at Harrah's, and when I called him and asked if he would appear, he said, "You betcha, I'll be there." Roy even brought his entire troupe for the show, but the thing I loved most about Roy that day was when he came into my dressing room and said, "I am here, and I am on time!" Roy put on his usual top-notch show that day and donated five thousand dollars to boot.

I had also donated five thousand dollars to the cause, but the most generous contribution made that day was from the Nugget and its owner, Johnny Ascuaga himself. Johnny donated all the sales from the liquor that day, which must have cost him a pretty penny for the packed house crowd. He also had his chefs bake a huge cake for the occasion.

At the end of the show, the boy and his family joined us on stage, and after they lit the candles on the cake, they wheeled out the reddest moped you ever saw. I had gone down and bought it for him, and when they started it up and he saw that bright red moped, that kid wrapped his arms around my legs and hugged me as tight as he could. It was an emotional moment for everyone, with not a dry eye in the house. We raised enough money that day to save the family's home, and I remember his daddy telling me after the show, "Well, Jimmy, that's one miracle down and one to go."

I don't think I ever witnessed more love and compassion from a gathering of people than I did the day of that benefit show, and if there was ever proof that prayer is an effective tool, then this was it for me. That boy was supposed to die, but just a couple of months later he was out delivering papers on his new moped, and the last I heard he was alive and well and cancer free. Miracle number two.

Spending so much time around those casinos, it's a damn good thing I didn't have a gambling habit, or I'd be broke today. Sometimes I'd have a little fun and drop a few thousand at the blackjack tables, but I had a certain amount I would spend and then I'd stop at that. I'd spent a lot of years working hard in those casino showrooms and I'd made a pile of money too. Thank God I had the good sense not to blow it.

12

GUEST SHOTS

INTERACTING WITH AUDIENCES, being able to see the smiles you put on people's faces, was the best part about working stage shows. In that respect, they were a lot more gratifying than working on television, and I got to where I really didn't miss having my own TV show. Besides, I would make plenty of appearances on the different television variety shows in between my road dates.

I had become somewhat of a regular on a TV show called *The Hollywood Palace,* a popular weekly prime time show that was actually taped in Hollywood and ran for many years in the 1960s. Along with a different celebrity host each week, it featured a different lineup of popular performers of the day. Besides appearing on the show from time to time, I would also be asked occasionally to host it.

A favorite memory of mine from the *Palace* show was the time I appeared along with the wonderful singer Kate Smith. She and I used to play cards on the set while we were waiting to tape the show, and I would always beat her at the game of gin. We had a lot of fun together, and she even made me a crown out of playing cards that was really kind of cute and nicely done.

Kate had a great sense of humor and I loved to kid her. Once while she was performing her number during rehearsal, she was nearly knocking the rear wall out of the building with her powerful voice.

Afterward I said, "You're not going to hold back like that on the show are you, Kate?" And when Kate Smith got tickled, her whole body laughed.

Guesting along with Lawrence Welk, I once played *The Hollywood Palace* when Bing Crosby was the host. Trying to be respectful but dying to talk to him, I said, "Mr. Crosby, I sure don't want to bother you, but I just may be the biggest fan you ever had," and he said in his low and easy, casual voice, "Jimmy, my boy, sit down and have some coffee." We talked for the longest time, and I'll not ever forget the wonderful chat I had with one of my all-time heroes.

Another time, I worked the *Palace* with the great star and wonderful man Jack Benny. I always loved his radio show and reminded him of one of his comedy bits that was a favorite of mine. He remembered it too, and amazingly repeated a lot of it back to me.

Benny also told me a great story about his old buddy George Burns. It was an established fact that George loved to play tricks on Jack, but Jack loved it when he did. George would walk up to him and dump his cigar ashes in the pocket of Jack's beautiful suit jacket, and Jack would simply laugh.

One time, Benny said, when he was out walking, George Burns pulled up beside him and said, "We're having our usual Tuesday night poker game at so and so's house, but it's going to be black tie." Benny said he thought the idea was kind of dumb but went along with it anyway. "So, Jimmy," Jack told me, "I had on my tuxedo when I went over to this fancy house and rang the doorbell, and the butler said, 'Oh yes, Mr. Benny, they've been expecting you.'" Benny said when he walked into the card room, all six guys were sitting around the card table buck naked, laughing hysterically as he stood there all dressed up in his tux.

I made plenty of other TV show appearances over the years, on shows such as *Fantasy Island* and *Murder She Wrote*. There was also *The Glen Campbell Goodtime Hour*, *The Andy Williams Show*, *The Steve Allen Show*, *The Perry Como Show*, *The Vic Damone Show*, *Rowan & Martin's Laugh-In*, *The Tennessee Ernie Ford Show*, *The Joey Bishop Show*, *Hee Haw* and Regis Philbin's local show in San Diego. Variety shows were definitely the big thing during the sixties, not only in prime time but in the afternoons as well. There were the

Appearing with
Bing Crosby and
Lawrence Welk
on The Hollywood
Palace

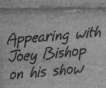

Appearing with
Joey Bishop
on his show

daily musical/variety/chat shows like *The Merv Griffin Show,* on which I would sometimes cohost or fill in as guest host. There was also *The Mike Douglas Show,* which had basically the same format, but unlike the other shows it was taped in Philadelphia.

When you cohosted *The Mike Douglas Show* for the week, you could have anybody you wanted on there as a guest. You would just give them a list of the people you wanted to have on the show and the staff would book them.

This one week when I cohosted, I gave them country singer Mel Tillis's name. Mel was well known in country music circles as a hit songwriter, but he was just getting his start as an entertainer and wasn't very well known by the masses. He had a wonderful singing voice, but Mel stuttered when he talked, and about midweek all hell broke loose when the show's producers found out about it. They said, "Jimmy, we can't do that. We *cannot* have somebody on here with a speech impediment. *We just can't do it,* and that's all there is to it." So I told them, "But if you'll just leave it to me, I'll take the curse off of it. Just let me introduce him and I promise, you'll love him." So I fought them tooth and nail, and they finally agreed to let Mel perform on the show.

I remember he was scared to death, probably because this was Mel's first appearance on national television. Obviously excited and wanting to make a good impression, he had gone out and bought a brand-new Martin guitar just before he came to Philadelphia to do the show. When he arrived at rehearsal that day, Mel opened the case and took out his beautiful new guitar, but it didn't have the first string on it—and there were no strings anywhere in the case. He had forgotten to have strings put on it in the store. Mel went ahead and rehearsed without his guitar, but boy, was he nervous. When it came time for me to introduce him on the show, I said, "Now, folks, before he comes out here, I want to tell those of you who don't know that Mel Tillis stutters." I continued, "Now, when he sings he doesn't stutter; it's only when he talks. But it's shows like this that have been the greatest therapy in the world for him, because each time he does a show like this he gets a little better."

Well, Mel came out there and knocked them dead. He was just great! He was so funny, he literally destroyed Mike Douglas and the audience, and just wiped everybody out. Mel was back on the show many times after that, and as a result of *The Mike Douglas Show,* he went on to star on *The Glen Campbell Goodtime Hour.* That was just the beginning for Mel, and as we all know, the rest is show business history.

Besides being one of the best songwriters and entertainers in the business, Mel Tillis has done more than anyone I know to help tear down the barriers for people with speech impediments. He gives me a lot of credit for giving him his "first break into big-time television," as he puts it, but it was Mel's talents that put him on the road to success, and it was his courage that forged the way.

I'm not sure what year *The Tonight Show* began on NBC, but long before there was Johnny Carson, there were other hosts, like Jerry Lester, Steve Allen and Jack Paar. I had been a guest on the show when Jack Paar was host, and later on they invited me back to host the show for a week. It was during a period of twenty-nine weeks in 1962 that *The Tonight Show* was on a rotating emcee basis between Jack Paar's and Johnny Carson's tenures. Jerry Lewis had been hosting the show for two weeks when I took over, and I was pretty excited to learn that when the ratings came in, they said I had the highest ever, with the exception of one night when Lewis had hosted. The newspaper reviewers said that "having to follow Lewis was a tough spot," and they lauded the fact that I had held my own, saying I'd topped guest hosts like Art Linkletter, Joey Bishop, Merv Griffin, Steve Lawrence and Groucho Marx.

One thing I really enjoyed about hosting *The Tonight Show* was being able to have a few of my friends on the show, giving some of them their national debut. I was glad to have my buddies Roger Miller and Roy Clark on there, as the show had been known to kick-start many a career and their appearances would definitely give them some major exposure. Roger sung some of his funky tunes, like "Dang Me" and "You Can't Roller Skate in a Buffalo Herd," and was funny and entertaining as always. And I remember introducing Roy Clark as "the most talented musician I ever fired." He knocked them dead as only he knows how, and was asked to come back many times, including as guest host.

Sharing a laugh with Archie Campbell on Hee Haw

With Mel Tillis on The Mike Douglas Show

I remember the night my friend Stuart Hamblen was on the show too. He was just great. He sang two of my favorite songs that he'd written, "It Is No Secret (What God Can Do)" and "This Old House." I loved it when he turned to Skitch Henderson, the musical director, and told him, "For the tempo, I want you to play it 'happy Baptist,' but not *too* happy."

After Johnny Carson had taken over *The Tonight Show,* the network booked me again to fill in for him in January of '63, making me the first guest host he ever had. And when the ratings came in for that show, I had not only topped all of the other guest hosts, but I had also outrated Johnny Carson himself.

Johnny took a lot of "vacations" back then too, or it could have been that he'd just have one of his little snits that he was so famous for and refuse to show up. To me Carson was kind of a weird duck anyway, and I never thought he liked me to begin with. All the time I was around him when we were being managed by the Sheils and Bruno Agency, I never knew him to be the same way twice. I actually filled in for him on his show at least a half dozen times when he would get mad about something and refuse to do it, and NBC would call and say, "Jimmy, we need you."

Probably the most interesting television appearance I ever made was on Dick Clark's *American Bandstand.* The show was live, with an audience of teenagers who danced to the latest records while Dick acted as host, and on each show he would feature a recording star who would lip-synch their hit record. Dick made my introduction and then the record started playing, except it wasn't mine; it was somebody else's song instead of "Big Bad John." So there I was, acting like I was singing, and all the while this hoppin' little rhythm-and-blues song was going on, I was singing "Amazing Grace" to myself.

Well, when the record mercifully finished playing, Dick Clark came over to me for our on-air interview and apologized profusely, saying they had mistakenly played a record by an artist named Dee Clark. "I was pretty sure it wasn't mine," I said, and then I asked Dick if Dee Clark was a relative of his. Well, the look on his face was sheer horror, and after the next song started playing and the camera left us, I found out why. He turned to me and said, "You SOB, you know Dee Clark is black!" But I didn't. Sorry about that, Dick . . . and you too, Dee.

The *Bandstand* appearance may have been interesting, but the most exciting guest shots I did were on an ABC show called *American Sportsman*. Hunting was a hobby of mine for many years, and when I appeared on *American Sportsman*, I had the opportunity to stalk big game in Alaska. I still have the trophy polar bear rug in our recreation room, made from the twelfth largest polar bear ever killed in Alaska at the time. I just loved Alaska and especially being out on Wild Man Lake, near which I got my Kodiak bear. Alaska has to be one of the most magnificent states in the nation. There is a solitude and freedom about it that I just love—and there's nothing like waking up in the morning to see a Kodiak bear or a herd of caribou meandering about.

Getting to the remote parts of Alaska wasn't always easy and could be downright tricky. Flying into camp one time, I'll never forget how our bush plane bounced all over the place when we landed. I turned to our guide and said, "Ron, I've got an idea. Why don't you see if you can't get that damned moose in the plane?" He looked puzzled, then I said, "That way we won't have to shoot him, we'll just scare him to death!" Those *American Sportsman* shows were always a lot of fun, and I'm forever grateful to ABC for some great times.

Then there was the ever popular *Ed Sullivan Show*, on which I appeared many times. The producer of the Sullivan show would book an act to perform for a certain amount of time, and because they used to overbook their shows, they were notorious for cutting a performer's time. Bob Precht, Ed Sullivan's son-in-law, happened to produce the show, and invariably he would come knocking on my dressing room door. It would be a little bit before showtime that I'd hear him knock and I'd say, "*No*, Bob. I'm not cutting a *damn thing*, Bob!"

One time my friend Jerry Vale told me, "Ed Sullivan loves you. If you'd invite him over to your house for dinner, he'd have you on his show all the time." I told Jerry I liked Sullivan all right, but he wasn't my friend, and if someone came to my house for dinner it was because they're my friend, not for what they could do for me.

Throughout the years I did indeed make a lot of good friends in show business, and none whose company I enjoyed more than the great "Schnoz," Jimmy Durante. We worked on several television shows together, and I always loved the old man's sense of humor and just hanging out with him. We liked to kid each other a lot, and I think he must have enjoyed my company too, because after rehearsals he'd always look at me and say, "Boy, let's go get some clams," and how he did love them.

Jimmy was extremely nearsighted—blind as a bat really—but he was also extremely vain and refused to wear his glasses while on TV. We all used cue cards, but because of Durante's poor eyesight he would have them print the words on his cue cards so big they couldn't get more than three or four words on each card. Durante would still stomp all over his lines on occasion, and I would tease him by saying, "Jimmy, if you can't cut it, let me up there. The card says 'JD,' and that could mean Jimmy Dean, Jimmy Dickens—it could mean anybody. So I can do it if you can't cut it!" Durante would just turn to me and say in that gravelly voice, "Boy, I've had about all of you I can take!"

I'll tell you something about Jimmy Durante you may not know. He told me not to tell this to anyone because it would reveal a part of his act that he wanted to remain a mystery, but since he's been gone for a long time, I really don't feel I'm violating a confidence.

Durante used to always end every performance with the line " . . . and good night, Mrs. Calabash, wherever you are." Once, when I asked him who she was and what the line meant, he related this story to me. He said one time when he was working at the Copa in New York, a bunch of his buddies invited him to go to the horse races. So he went, but had nothing but miserable luck all day long. Finally, just as a lark, on the last race he decided to gamble on a horse that had odds of winning of about forty to one. Her name? Mrs. Calabash. Durante told me, "I put a few bucks on her nose and she ran like she was trying to balance it." The horse ended up dead last and Jimmy, of course, lost all his money.

That night, Jimmy said, his buddies from the racetrack came back to see his show, and at the end as he went to walk off the stage, he paused and came back to the microphone. Durante took off his hat, looked skyward, and as an inside joke to his buddies, he said, " . . . and good night, Mrs. Calabash, wherever you are." For years people have attached a sentimental meaning to that line, thinking Mrs. Calabash must have been a long-lost love or the one

With one of my favorite people,
Jimmy Durante

Ed Sullivan and Rowlf

that got away. But in reality she was a damned racehorse—and a dismal loser at that.

I had a ton of respect for Jimmy Durante and his talents and loved to watch him perform, especially when he'd sing a ballad. He could put more heart in a song than any singer around. There's no wonder he was so beloved. Once, as we were getting ready to do a TV show together and having a conversation about the business, I confided in him that no matter how many times I'd appeared on television or how many shows I had worked, I would still get a little nervous about it. And it was true; after all those years of performing, no matter where it was, I would always have a case of the butterflies.

So during my chat with him, I asked, "Jimmy, how long do you have to be in this business before you stop getting butterflies?" He looked me straight in the eye and answered gruffly, "If you ever do boy, quit, 'cause you won't be worth a s———t." And *that* my friend, was some of the best show business advice I ever received.

⚛ 13 ⚛

BRANDO I AIN'T

A **LOT OF** things I am and a lot of things I am not, but I think I'm as good an American as there is. I love this country a lot. It's been very, very good to me, and I consider myself extremely fortunate to have been paid so well for something that I've had such a ball doing. Whether it was on radio and records, or in television, theater or movies, I'm grateful to have been free and able to do what I love, and that's to entertain people.

But there's one thing about this country that has never made sense to me. In my industry—the entertainment business—why should a guy have to belong to *five* different unions to pursue one profession? First there was the AFM—the American Federation of Musicians. This I had to join to be able to play a musical instrument and perform on a nightclub stage. Then there was AFTRA—the American Federation of Television and Radio Artists—of which I had to be a member to perform on radio or on a television stage. Then to perform at rodeos I had to join the RCA—the Rodeo Cowboy's Association—or at least I was *advised* to join. There was also SAG—the Screen Actors Guild—this one for performing on a movie or TV. And finally there was AGVA—the American Guild of Variety Artists—of which I've never been quite sure, but I think I was required to join if I ever wanted to play a pay toilet in Podunk, Iowa.

Appearing in the theatrical production of Destry Rides Again

Never having had too many pleasant experiences with unions, I don't suppose the guy at the Screen Actors Guild in New York City will ever forget the day I joined. One morning I received a phone call in my office from someone at SAG saying, "We have your first check here for *The Daniel Boone Show*. Would you like to come pay your dues and get it?" My first thought was, *What the hell are they doing with my check over there? I don't work for them.* My answer was a definite no, and I sent my secretary Willie to take them my membership fee and to pick up my paycheck. But then a little while later Willie came back saying they wouldn't accept my check or give her my paycheck, and that a union official said I had to come there in person to join.

Well, the thought of having to go out into a very rainy and wet New York City just to pacify some union jerkwad started my none too slow burn. Standing on a street corner with the wind in my face, I tried flagging down a taxi, but then a passing car sped by and splashed me, soaking my cowboy boots and my jeans up to the knees. The burn was getting considerably worse, and by the time I got to that union office, I was ready to pinch somebody's head off.

When I entered the SAG office, I went straight over to the girl behind the reception desk and said, "I want to talk to the boss man." And she said, "What?" "The head honcho," I said, "the guy with the big fuzzy balls! The boss—I want to talk to *the boss*!" Obviously startled, she said, "Just a minute, sir!" and quickly left the room.

And then, there he was. Appearing from out of the back room was Mr. Out-of-Work-Actor-Turned-Union-Official, Harvey Hasbeen himself. This big, tall lunkhead came walking toward me grinning like we were old friends and stuck his hand out to shake, but when he did, I put my dues check in his hand. "Here, take this," I said, "and that's the very last time I ever want to see you or hear from you, because God forbid I should ever have to depend on the likes of you for anything in this world." Then I told him, "The only thing I ask of you is that you stay the hell out of my way, and don't prevent me from doing for myself!" And then, being the sweet little buckaroo I am, I said, "Have a good day."

My acting career actually started with plays, and though I was a novice, the audiences seemed to accept me and treat me as if I were a seasoned performer. It was in 1961 that I was offered my first role, in the summer stock production of a Western called *Destry Rides Again*. For ten weeks I played the title role of Destry and traveled what was called the "strawhat circuit," to Washington, DC; Baltimore, Maryland; Springfield, Massachusetts; Camden, New Jersey; Valley Forge, Pennsylvania; and Long Island, New York. Also in the play was John Mento, my inspiration for "Big Bad John," as well as an actor named Earl Hammond and the popular actress Monique Van Vooren.

I enjoyed acting and had fun with it, and I guess that's why I had such an easy time learning my lines and remembering them. But it was also easy to have *too* much fun on stage and really screw up the play. As a matter of fact, our stage manager Billy Rollo said we were the worst disciplined company of actors he'd ever seen. Practically every night we'd get tickled and screw up, and I could break up

Monique Van Vooren every night if I chose to. Backstage after almost every show Billy Rollo would come to us exasperated and grumbling, "What is this s——t?!!!"

After *Destry Rides Again,* I had the opportunity to star in my first non-singing role, as Will Stockdale, the lead in the play *No Time for Sergeants.* It was only for a one-week stint in Canton, Ohio, but I came to understand why Andy Griffith wanted so much to play that role. It was an awful lot of fun to do.

Acting in plays didn't pay much money—about seven hundred dollars a week as I recall—but it turned out to be an invaluable learning experience for me. In the mid-1960s *Daniel Boone* starring Fess Parker was one of the most popular Westerns on television, and after it had been on for a while I was offered a role as Daniel Boone's sidekick. From 1967 until 1970 I played a character named Josh Clements, not the sharpest knife in the drawer, but a good ole boy. I enjoyed the job and especially working with Fess Parker, one of the nicest, most genuine people God ever put breath in, and the epitome of the word *gentleman.* In fact, he was so nice it took me two years before I believed him. Also on the show were regulars Ed Ames of the Ames Brothers, a popular singing group of the fifties, and Rosie Greer, the ex–football player from the Los Angeles Rams. With Rosie Greer at six-foot-five- and Fess at six-foot-seven-inches tall, I felt like a midget at six-foot-three.

Fess had a major interest in *Daniel Boone* and actually owned half of it. He also directed several of the episodes and I think was more interested in directing than acting, but he was pretty darn good at both. Fess was understandably serious about the show, but he was still fun and pleasant to work with. He gave me my first acting experience on film and I owe a lot to him for taking a chance on me.

Ed Ames played another of Daniel Boone's sidekicks, a character named Mingo, and appeared on only a few of the same shows as I did. This one time when we worked together, he said to me, "Jimmy, I want you to hear a record I made." I said, "Okay" and went with him to his dressing room to listen to it. The record was called "My Cup Runneth Over with Love," and it was a really good song. After I'd heard it, he asked me what I thought about it, so I told him, "Ed, I think it's a helluva record, but you're not out front enough. The music is too loud and it's covering up your voice. You need to get that thing remixed." He said, "You know, Jimmy, I believe you're right." Ed took my advice and had the record remixed with his voice louder than before, and it turned out to be a huge hit record for him.

I worked with Rosie Greer a lot, a real sweetheart of a guy, and I can attest to the fact that the rumors you may have heard were true. Indeed this big, macho football-playing son of a gun enjoyed doing needlepoint. He would bring his sewing materials to the set and needlepoint some of the most beautiful stuff you ever saw in your life.

The first time I worked with Rosie, he had sprained his ankle while filming on location, and he leaned on me for that entire week of taping. I don't know when I've ever supported as much weight on my two-hundred-pound frame as I did when I supported his two hundred and fifty pounds, but I didn't mind helping him out. It ended up forging what I considered to be a pretty good relationship, and a friendship that has sustained to this day.

A lot of times *Daniel Boone* would feature guest stars, and once I remember working with a nine-year-old actress named Jodie Foster. In the episode she played an orphan girl with a little brother who ended up in my care. Jodie was a great little actress back then and a complete professional, even at that young age.

Also starring as a guest on the show was the hysterical Foster Brooks. It was the first time I'd ever met Brooks, who was without a doubt one of the funniest characters in show business. He did the best drunk act I ever saw anybody do, and the funny thing about it was that he never touched the stuff; he was a real teetotaler.

On one of the episodes, Brooks and I did a scene together in a barroom, and I had one helluva time keeping control and trying not to laugh. With his teeth out and dressed in shabby skid row attire, Brooks played a drunk who was standing at the bar when Daniel Boone and I came into the tavern. When we got to the bar, Foster turned to me and slurred, "You want to buy me a drink?" I said, "Okay, what'll you have?" "I'll have mulled wine," he said. So I told him, "Well, that sounds good. Bartender . . . three mulled wines!" That was when Foster belched and said, "That's great. What are *you* gonna drink?"

My favorite Foster Brooks story was about the time he was staying at the Hollywood Roosevelt Hotel during an earthquake. "My

The Daniel Boone
show cast . . .
Fess Parker,
Jimmy, and
Ed Ames

Hey Jimmy
Long time no see!
Best wishes!
Jodie Foster
2000

Posing with a
young Jodie Foster
and friend, guests
on the Daniel
Boone show

wife and I were involved in this marvelous sexual experience when the earthquake hit," he said. "It knocked me completely out of bed, and it damned near woke up my wife!"

Another great memory I have from *Daniel Boone* was the time I was on my way to a shoot on location and I already had on my frontier outfit for the show, when the car I was riding in pulled up at a light and stopped by a car being driven by my friend, the comedian Bill Cosby. Bill was dressed as a soldier in a Confederate uniform, obviously on his way to location too, and when he saw me we both jumped out the car and hugged each other in the middle of the highway. Cars all around us were honking for us to get out of the way, but I've often wondered what those people who witnessed that scene must have thought was going on.

One of the most delightful encounters I've ever had was when I was on my way home to New Jersey after taping *Daniel Boone*. It was on a flight from L.A. to New York when I looked across the aisle of the first-class section and there was Red Skelton. We had known each other for a long time, and when he saw me he said, "Jimmy, come over and sit down." So we sat together on the flight. I told him, "You know, my youngest son is the biggest fan you ever had and he loves you to death. I was wondering if you could sign something for him." "I'd be happy to," he said.

Well, as most everybody knows, Red Skelton was one of the greatest comedians of our time, but few people know what a wonderful artist he was. Clowns were his specialty, and a painting of one of his clowns is priceless today. As we talked, he took out a legal pad and began to sketch. Then he asked, "What's your son's name?" I told him, and before we landed in New York, he had drawn a pencil sketch of one of his clowns and signed it for my son Robert. Today it must surely be a true collector's item.

Another little known fact about Red Skelton was that he cheerfully gave of himself and his talents, even though he was in constant pain and wore leg braces. You never saw him without that wonderful smile, but that's really the kind of guy he was, a genuine sweetheart of a man.

Being a part of *Daniel Boone* was truly a wonderful experience for me, and now forty years later it's still being aired on the cable TV networks, along with a lot of other shows from the fifties and six-ties. It's kind of fun to be channel surfing and run across one of those old episodes. I remember that the first one I ever did had a glitch in it that nobody, including the director, noticed until it was too late. Keep in mind that this show was set in the eighteenth century: At the end of the last scene, I was leaving Daniel Boone's rural homestead and walking off into the sunset, when the camera panned back and there, across the sky, was a huge vapor trail left by a jet airplane.

I don't see any of those folks from the Boone show anymore, although I do talk to Fess Parker on occasion. A few years ago, Donna and I were dining at a fine restaurant and were surprised and delighted to see a Fess Parker merlot on their wine list. Since we enjoy a little red wine with dinner, we ordered a bottle and loved it so much that it became our favorite. It turned out that Fess had been in the business for many years and had built quite a reputation with his vineyards. His winery, which is located in Santa Barbara, California, also features a big, beautiful hotel and a shop where you can buy souvenirs, including wine bottle toppers made like adorable little Daniel Boone coonskin hats.

———————

My acting in television also included some made for TV movies. In the late sixties and seventies I did several of them, working with an impressive list of actors, like Lee Majors and Joey Heatherton in *The Ballad of Andy Crocker,* an Aaron Spelling production. I also worked with Jerry Reed in *The Alamo* and with Don Johnson and Mark Hamill in *The City.* The latter was a horror/suspense story where Mark Hamill played my psychotic son who stalked me and terrorized our family. He was a wonderful actor and a very pleasant young man, but the interesting thing about Mark was that he had just finished filming the movie *Star Wars.* It had yet to be released, but he told me all about it on the set and showed me some still pic-tures from the movie. Looking at them and seeing all those weird characters, I remember saying to myself, *What in the hell is this?* Little did I know it would be such a smash.

One movie that made a significant difference in my life was a James Bond film. In 1971 I had the opportunity to play a starring role along with Sean Connery in the action suspense thriller *Diamonds Are Forever*. I played a Howard Hughes–like character named Willard Whyte, an eccentric multimillionaire who was being stalked by God only knows who, but was safe under the protection of Secret Agent 007, James Bond.

The movie also starred Jill St. John, Bruce Cabot, Charles Gray and two voluptuous young ladies in the roles of my nemeses Bambi and Thumper. *Diamonds* was shot in several different locations including London, Las Vegas, Long Beach, and Palm Desert, California, and was filmed regularly over a period of several months. Every now and then they would let me go home for a few days, so I didn't have to be away from my home and family the entire time.

I liked Sean Connery. He was a most enjoyable dude, with a good sense of humor, who liked referring to me as the "noisy American," my wife Donna's favorite nickname for me. Being a golf enthusiast, Sean had a net behind each set, where he and I would practice hitting golf balls, with him giving me pointers whenever I would hit. He was a good golf teacher too, and somewhat patient—that is until I'd do something wrong, then he'd give me a playful whack on the wrist with the handle of his club.

One thing I couldn't get used to while working on this film was the producers' colossal waste of time and money. I was accustomed to doing shows like *Daniel Boone* where you didn't film just a half of a page of script a day, but four or five pages of script or even more. When we were filming *Diamonds* in London for six weeks, I sat there in that Dorchester Hotel, sometimes for days, doing absolutely nothing. I had an expensive and gorgeous suite too, with everything paid for, including my food, but they didn't seem to care or worry about the expense. I guess since those pictures make the kind of money they do, the producers didn't have to worry about it.

An odd thing I noticed while in England: I have the tendency to pick up accents from wherever I am or from people I'm with. And after being in London for all that time, my British accent had gotten so thick that if I'd stayed there for two more weeks, I don't even think Winston Churchill could've understood me.

During my stay in England, I enjoyed the British people, especially their sense of humor. I remember on one gorgeous Sunday afternoon when my friends Bill and Barbara McDavid were visiting from Ft. Worth, Texas, we decided we would have a little lunch, but we wanted to get out of the city and away from the tourist attractions. We got into a taxi and told the driver to take us where the Britishers go, so he drove us to a little sidewalk cafe somewhere out of town.

During our lunch, Bill ordered a bottle of wine, and as we were enjoying the lovely setting we noticed that seated off to our right was the most handsome old British man you ever saw. This guy looked like the epitome of an English gentleman with his shock of white hair and little white mustache, attired in a beautiful tweed suit complete with vest and a gold pocket watch chain. He really was as handsome as could be. Just then, a gal came walking by wearing a pair of the shortest shorts any of us had ever seen, and with her butt hanging out of both sides. We all watched in amazement as she walked by, and I remember Barbara saying, "Now, that's vulgar!" Bill and I also made a comment, but when we glanced around at the little old Britisher, he looked at us with a twinkle in his eye and said simply, "A bit cheeky, wouldn't you say?"

There was an interesting thing about filming this movie. After *Diamonds Are Forever,* I was working for Howard Hughes at one of his hotels—the Desert Inn—with him paying me about a half million dollars a year. Since he was the one who started the producers of the James Bond movies in the business, as a courtesy to Hughes they would send him the first sixteen-millimeter copy of every James Bond movie. And it occurred to me: Wouldn't it be something if when they sent him *Diamonds* and he saw me playing him, he wouldn't be happy about it and say, "That son of a bitch is playing me and I don't like it—fire him!" I would have lost a great-paying job over an acting part that had only paid about twelve thousand dollars. Thankfully, I never heard a word from him.

Another thing I remember about filming this movie, and I don't even know if it made it to the film, was a very sexy scene where Sean Connery and Jill St. John were lying on a waterbed. The mattress itself was completely transparent, and you could see the water inside of it, where live exotic fish were swimming. The crew would spend a lot of time getting ready to shoot the scene, but then every time they would get the cameras rolling, one of those exotic fish would die and float to

Filming the
James Bond
film Diamonds
Are Forever
with
Sean Connery

On the set of Murder, She Wrote
with Angela Lansbury

the top of the mattress. No sooner would they all get into the scene than a fish would go belly-up. The fish-in-the-mattress idea was a clever one, I suppose, but I don't know if they *ever* got that scene shot.

It's amazing how popular those James Bond movies still are and what a cult following they have after all these years. So many times someone has walked up to me and said, "I really enjoyed you as Willard Whyte," or they'll quote one of my lines from the movie. But the question that's asked most often, and especially by the guys, is "What was it like to work with Bambi and Thumper?" I see the disappointment on their faces every time when I have to tell them I never laid eyes on those girls. They were a real popular part of the film, but we were never on location together; we filmed our parts at different times and never saw each other.

It's also true that I never saw the movie until many years later, when my son Robert had to hog-tie me to watch the video. I'd never watched it because I could never bear to see myself on film. Not only do I hate to hear myself sing, but I don't like to watch myself act either.

Since the Bond movie, I've made some guest appearances on different television shows, with the most recent being *Murder, She Wrote* with Angela Lansbury. It was a lot of fun being the "murderee" on the popular TV show, and I especially enjoyed working with Miss Lansbury, a very lovely person.

While I was in Los Angeles to tape *Murder, She Wrote,* my old friend and TV producer Bob Banner set up an interview for me with the producers of *Matlock,* the Andy Griffith detective show. I had told Bob that I wouldn't mind doing a little more acting, and I didn't mind going all the way out to L.A. if I could get a good role in a good show. But it seems there's a lackadaisical attitude prevalent in L.A., where no one seems to be in a hurry, or hardly ever on time. Donna and I arrived at the *Matlock* offices about fifteen minutes early that morning for my 10 A.M. appointment, and found absolutely no one around. Ten o'clock in the morning and no one's there! We hung around outside the office park buildings expecting someone to arrive any minute, but they didn't, and with punctuality being my one pet peeve in life, I didn't care to hang around and talk to someone who would waste my time anyway. No one had arrived by five minutes after ten, so we left without seeing or talking to anyone. Thank goodness I didn't need the work and could be as independent as crap on a doorknob.

Sometimes I think I'd like to get back into acting, because I enjoyed it. Most of the time it was fun, and I'll forever cherish the experiences I had and the friendships I made.

Actually, as I look back upon my entire life as an entertainer, I can truthfully say I enjoyed every part of it. Being on stage was always exciting, whether it was in a honky-tonk in Washington, DC, or on a movie set in London.

Most people would say that my life as an entertainer was charmed, but it wasn't *all* wonderful.

I've always considered the entertainment business merely a vehicle anyway, one that has carried me from Plainview, Texas, to where I am today. A means to an end that was extremely fragile and totally unpredictable, but an industry that has treated me very, very well, and to which I'll always be grateful.

PART TWO

THE SAUSAGE MAN

14

THE JIMMY DEAN MEAT COMPANY: THE BEGINNING

IN THIS BOOK I've shared with you the many facets of the entertainment business that I was fortunate enough to be a part of and enjoy. I don't think you can succeed to the extent that I did and *not* enjoy it. But I knew it wouldn't last forever, and I'm ever so glad that when I made a dollar or two I was careful to use it wisely.

I've had a lot of friends in the entertainment industry and have known many of them who have made a fortune and ended up broke. You hear about them all the time, and I *swore* I'd never be one of them. Though I was fortunate to have a mother who taught me to save my money ("Always put some away for a rainy day, Jimmy"), there was another experience in my life that made a big impression on me. It was during my days in Washington, DC, that I witnessed firsthand the pathetic results of a squandered career.

Elton Britt was a huge recording star during World War II who had made a lot of money with his yodeling and a big hit called "There's a Star Spangled Banner." After a long career, Elton lost his money and got so sick that some local musicians had to throw a benefit show to bail him out of his medical bills. I went to help out that day, and when they brought him on stage in his wheelchair with that blanket on his lap, I saw the embarrassment on his face and on the faces of his family members. As I stood there feeling great pity for him, I never lost that picture, and that day I made myself a promise: If I could help it, nobody would *ever* have to play a benefit show for Jimmy Dean. By the grace of God, *that* would never happen to *me*.

I worked long and hard in the entertainment business, and I always tried to put some of my money where it would work for me. Over the years, I invested in a variety of businesses: banks, limousine companies, a lime grove, a Christmas tree farm, restaurants, real estate, music publishing and racehorses, just to name a few.

A lot of times my accountant would make recommendations or I would use the help of investment brokers. My contention has always been that one of the greatest assets a man can have is an awareness of and the willingness to admit his own shortcomings. I know where I'm dumb—which is damn near everywhere—but I've tried in the places where I'm dumb to hire the smartest people I could find. Though I figured I'm *still* smarter than them, because *they're* working for *me*.

By far the most lucrative business I ever got involved in was the meat business. It was during the Christmas holidays in 1965, while visiting my mother in Plainview, that my cousin-in-law told me about his business venture into hog farming. Troy Pritchard was married to my cousin Lucy Kay, daughter of Aunt Julia and Uncle Roy on my mother's side, and along with Troy's brother they owned a hog farm in Edmonson, just outside of Plainview.

On Christmas Day, Troy drove me out to see his operation, and though pork prices were down and the place was losing money and had deteriorated somewhat, it still looked interesting to me. Looking back to my roots, an investment in hog farming felt like the right thing to do, so before I flew back home to New Jersey I bought Troy's brother's half of the business. The Edmonson Stock Farm was a new and exciting experience for me. It was a big operation and big business. I was ready for the challenge of making it even bigger and better, and to capitalize on my celebrity status, we changed the name to the Jimmy Dean Pig Parlor.

Troy Pritchard had been in the hog business for several years when I got involved, and since I had a rather sizable investment in his stock farm, I was also able to bring in my brother Don for a piece of the action. Together, the three of us formed the JDT Products Corporation, for Jimmy, Don and Troy. At no cost to Don, I gave him a third of the business, as well as the job of assisting Troy in operations.

The business was as interesting as it was involved. Troy and his foreman were almost as particular with their animals as doctors and nurses are with babies in a hospital nursery. The hogs were raised in a controlled, disease-free environment called SPF, or "specific pathogen free." First they were started from litters that were delivered by cesarean, and then raised for three months in pens with totally germ-free slatted oak floors. That meant that the hogs' feet never touched the ground. Their pens were suspended over a lagoon waste-disposal system made of concrete—a trough that emptied into a field and was washed down daily. To maintain the sanitary conditions, you had to change into shoes or boots that hadn't touched other ground before entering a gate that led into the pens, plus you had to cover your clothes with coveralls that hadn't been worn anywhere other than in the yard where the pens were.

Paying a visit to the Jimmy Dean Pig Parlor

All of this sounds wonderful and good, but in fact it was done for monetary reasons. An animal that had no virus of any kind to fight was healthier and got fatter sooner, therefore it was ready for market about a month sooner than one raised under ordinary conditions. Also, the litters usually numbered two or three more pigs than the average. Our hogs were beautiful animals and extremely healthy, and it paid off too. Out of our six to seven thousand hogs a year, we never had a diseased pig, sow or boar.

By 1967, I was managing several investments including the pig farm in Texas, and after pumping some money into the operation, I saw it double in size. Things were going along really fine. In fact, after pork prices began to improve, the company even started to show a modest profit.

Things didn't go well for long, however, because it was during that year that all of a sudden the bottom dropped out of the hog market. I learned a lot about the hog business when the prices of hogs took a nosedive. Basically, I was losing about twenty dollars an animal each time I sold one. It was like attaching a twenty-dollar bill to his tail and saying, "Bye." I knew I couldn't go on like that forever, but what the hell was I going to do?

There's an old saying that goes, "When a door closes, a window opens somewhere," and I believe it's true. I guess it's kind of like trying to find the silver lining in whatever adversity you might be going through. The hog business had turned out to be a bust, but it wasn't too long before I would have a revelation.

One day while I was visiting in Plainview, Don and I were sitting in a local diner having sausage and eggs. I always did love sausage and still do, but as I was chewing my food, I reached in my mouth and pulled out a piece of gristle about the size of the tip of your little finger. I said to Don, "You know, there's got to be room in this country for a good quality sausage." It didn't take a rocket scientist to figure out what my next business venture should be. After all . . . when life hands you lemons, you make lemonade.

So many times people have asked me how and why I got started in the sausage business, and most of the time I kid them by saying, "If you had ever seen my act, you would have realized that diversification was imperative." People don't usually buy that, and I don't expect them to, but I do think diversification is a good idea.

Actually, the "sausage story" has a simple beginning, although the entire saga spans thirty years of my life. It was a complex series of ups and downs, as you'll read about in the next few chapters. But as I said, the beginning is pretty straightforward: I had a failing hog farm and something had to give with this money-losing operation, so discussions were held with my partners, Troy Pritchard and my brother Don.

The idea I had for a sausage company seemed like a good way to rectify the problem, and I didn't meet with much opposition from either of them, probably because I was the only one who would be investing any money. In effect, the sausage company would merely be a continuation of the hog farm and would provide a ready market for the pigs—virtually a win-win situation.

Actually, the idea of making sausage came naturally for me, since it was commonplace among my family when I was growing up in West Texas. Sausage was usually the only meat we'd have to eat, and every year Mom would buy a piglet that we would fatten up for slaughtering. We'd feed it and take care of it until it weighed about two hundred pounds, and because it was a lot like having a pet, we'd have to be careful not to get attached to the little booger.

It was in the fall of the year when we'd butcher our hog, and Mom, Don and I would always handle the gory job ourselves. We didn't have the money to pay somebody else to slaughter it, and if we asked someone to help they'd be entitled to part of the meat, and we couldn't afford that either. Mom would cook the liver on butchering day because we didn't have any refrigeration to keep it, then she'd use most of the meat for making sausage. Don and I would grind the meat on an old hand grinder, and Mom would season it and make sausage, something she no doubt learned from my granddaddy. It was then put up in jars, and after having to eat sausage all winter long, by springtime I'd be pretty sick of it.

Come slaughtering time I'd also help my granddaddy make sausage. I can still see Papa Taylor out there on the porch with his number three washtub. He'd clean it out real good, and then mix up the meat and spices in it with his hands—no gloves. I'd grind the meat in the kitchen, and he'd stir up the mixture in that washtub with his hairy old arm. And *man*, if we did anything like that today they would jack up the jail and throw us under it. After a while Papa would pat out a little patty in his hand and give it to Grandma Ludie to fry up. He'd give it a little taste and then add a little more spice if need be, and then do it all over again until he was satisfied with the flavor.

So now the sausage making torch had been passed on to me. I began the research and decided to build a sausage plant in my hometown of Plainview, Texas, then I had Don set up the initial marketing network. Our new venture would be known as the Jimmy Dean Meat Company.

Since neither my brother Don nor Troy Pritchard invested any money to build the sausage plant, I had to put up all I had, as well as borrow from everyone and everywhere. I got a little from the banks, some from friends, and along with a loan from the Small Business Administration, I mortgaged everything from my home to my boots and my jockstrap.

One special friend, my buddy Mack Sanders, who owned a radio station in Wichita, Kansas, loaned me twenty-five thousand dollars with no questions asked—no collateral, no nothing. I was extremely grateful that he had that kind of confidence in me 'cause that was a lot of money back then, and without him our company might not have gotten off the ground. I'll always remember that. *Thanks, Mack.*

Work on the two-story, twenty-seven-thousand-square-foot packing plant started in March of 1968. It was originally projected to cost five hundred thousand dollars to build, but ended up costing around six hundred thousand. It would house the offices of Jimmy Dean Enterprises, and include sausage storage and carcass holding facilities in addition to the slaughter and packing facilities. Later on we would add on another sixty-five-hundred-square-foot extension, as our aim was to become a national company, and our expansion was to take that goal into consideration. We also constructed a new 160-ton-per-day feed mill about a mile from the packing plant, that milled grain we bought from the local farmers. There we added supplements and specialized in mixing rations for our company, as well as for some of the other hog feeders in the area too.

Our sausage plant would produce one of the few pure pork sausages available. Some of the others that were advertised as "pure pork" sausage contained a lot of gristle and fat and even other ingredients besides pork, but we were sure we would be putting out the highest-quality product available for about the same amount of money. We used the whole hog and could have made a lot more money by not using the more expensive parts, but it would have cheapened the quality of the product. For almost a year we experimented with various recipes, adding and deleting certain ingredients, until we felt like we had come up with "the perfect sausage."

My aim in business is the same as in entertaining: Appeal to the people with quality and honesty and you'll win their confidence. *Maintain* quality and honesty, and you'll keep it. We were sure our product would be superior to any on the market because it was made from top hogs, younger and leaner than the sows used by the rest of the industry. Our sausage was also packaged warm rather than chilled, the way most other companies did theirs. Plus, we were the first plant to bone, grind and package pork while it was still warm. A pig became sausage in little more than an hour, then the sausage was quick-chilled to forty degrees before being shipped out in refrigerated trucks.

There was no way for me to know if this venture was going to work, and I had no guarantee my investment would pay off. All I had was a theory—that if you make a quality product, keep the quality and promote it well, then you can't go wrong. But there was something else that would see me through the most difficult times, and that was a belief in myself. I never lost sight of Mom's advice to *never give up*, and I was convinced I could succeed at anything I believed in and set out to do. I never thought about failure. I can tell you an awful lot about temporary setbacks, but the word failure is *not* in my vocabulary.

———•———

There was quite the buzz about our new sausage plant in Plainview, with many festivities surrounding its grand opening on May 25, 1969. The day before, dubbed Jimmy Dean Day, there were literally thousands of people at the Hale County airport to welcome our plane. On opening day, the press dubbed the occasion "the biggest thing to hit the Texas Panhandle since irrigation," and more than a thousand people jammed into the plant for the ceremonies. Texas Governor Preston Smith made proclamations and presentations at the dedication, and I remember distinctly shaking hands with so many people that my hand was actually sore.

Tours of the plant were also open to the public that day, and there was a ribbon cutting ceremony that afternoon. Governor Smith handled the cutting of the ribbon, and instead of using scissors, we asked him to use a more appropriate cutting tool—a butcher knife. The people of Plainview seemed to be extra proud of their hometown boy who was bringing back jobs and revenue. They even paid tribute by painting "Home of Jimmy Dean" in big black letters on the Plainview water tower. Now *that* will make you puff up with pride!

The Jimmy Dean Meat Company began producing sausage in May of 1969 and was the only venture of its kind in the world: a self-contained plant that could process four hundred hogs a day. We started out producing one- and two-pound packages that were sold only in the Texas Panhandle and the South Plains area, but it wasn't long before we expanded to Houston and then throughout Texas, Louisiana and Oklahoma.

When we first opened, our company employed sixty people, including my brother Don Dean as vice president of marketing and distribution and Troy Pritchard as secretary-treasurer. I served as president and chairman of the board, and because I wouldn't accept a salary, I was the only one at the company who never received a paycheck.

Our product looked a lot different from the others in the supermarket, mostly because of the colors I had chosen for the packaging. When Don and Troy asked me for my opinion, I told them I thought the colors black and gold stood for quality, so we agreed on a gold package with black lettering. I was taken aback, however, when the grocery and food brokers first saw the package and said, "Are you crazy? You can't sell meat packaged in *gold*!" Well, I wasn't about to change anything. I liked it and thought it was handsome. And it never seemed to hurt a thing, so I guess it goes to show you that they don't know everything either.

I was also responsible for our red-and-black JD company logo, where the J was made like a cowboy boot and the D was attached to the boot. I had actually designed it many years ago as a shirt monogram and someone suggested it would go well on the package. One day, after having been in business for over three years, we were all in a board meeting when somebody said, "Did anyone ever register that trademark?" That was when everybody started looking around the room at each other like deer in the headlights, and as it turned out, nobody had. That evening there was a guy from our company on a plane, and when the trademark offices opened in Washington, DC, the next morning, he was there to register our JD logo. We had dodged a bullet that time, and were extremely lucky that no one had ever tried to use it.

Our first slogan was "Have a good breakfast, have a good day," and from almost the beginning we used an advertising agency from out of Little Rock, Arkansas, called Holland and Associates. It was headed up by a wonderful guy named Bill Holland who was a real dapper and handsome dude. Bill and I became great friends and partners when I bought into his business, and we worked together a lot promoting the sausage company.

A favorite memory of mine was one day when Bill and I were doing a media blitz in Washington, DC. Our schedule was really tight that day, with radio, television and newspaper interviews, so we hired a limousine to drive us around, since the driver knew the city. We were actually so busy we didn't have time for lunch, so we bought a pound of bologna, a loaf of bread and a quart of milk at the grocery store.

Since it was a nice day, we had the windows down in the limo on our way to the next stop, and as we were eating, we pulled up at a stoplight next to this old boy in a pickup truck. "Must be nice," he said, looking over at us. "It ain't bad," I said. "You want a slice of bologna?" And he took it. Bill and I just laughed and went on down the road.

It was unfortunate that we lost Bill Holland much too soon. He liked to smoke those nonfiltered Camel cigarettes and died in his thirties of lung cancer. After Bill passed away, for a long time our company used a media buying service out of Memphis to place our television commercials.

Wearing a different hat

Our first sausage plant
in Plainview, Texas

The Story of Jimmy Dean
Pure Pork Sausage

To promote our product, we would sometimes use newspaper ads, and though television commercials were more expensive, they were our best selling tools. When we wanted to break into an area, the first thing we would do was run the TV commercials, which would create a demand. Then consumers would ask their grocer for the product and we'd sell to the distributors that supplied the grocers. I think my celebrity status must have certainly helped, but I knew it would only take the product off the shelf one time. If the quality wasn't there, it wouldn't take it off a second time.

A lot of celebrities have attached their names to products, and they've learned it takes more than just a name, it takes work and know-how. As my longtime friend in the advertising business, Bob Berry, once said, "The marketing graveyard is filled with many headstones of celebrity products that never made it." Most of them just lent their name to the product and knew nothing about it. However, I was a lot closer to this operation than most people thought, and fighting off their ideas that the meat company was a franchise was one of the toughest things I had to do. The product wasn't just something I lent my name to; I was *definitely* up to my neck in the sausage business.

After six months in operation, the Jimmy Dean Meat Company was in the black, and I guess you could say we were an instant success. Indeed, when we first started out, the company took off faster than we thought it would—way *too* fast, in fact—and that can leave you worse off than if it takes off too slowly. Expanding too quickly left us undercapitalized, because we had to pay the farmers for their hogs up front when they delivered them, but the buyers for our products had six weeks to pay us. There was a pretty hefty lapse there, so that meant I needed to find a way to borrow more money.

So here I was again trying to find money anywhere and looking to friends like country star Porter Wagoner. I considered Porter a rather astute businessman and offered him a pretty good deal if he would loan me a million dollars, but he wouldn't do it. I couldn't really blame him, because it seemed like *every* country act had *some* way to get rich. I would later read in several interviews that Porter said he did indeed loan me the money, which was not true.

When I couldn't get another loan from the Small Business Association, I was at the end of my rope and was forced to refinance my home. And I'll tell you something: When your house is on the block, you *will* get out there and hustle. That was when I hit the road, with my secretary Willie Bruffy in tow, and sometimes my brother Don. We traveled all over the country doing promotions, meeting and greeting meat buyers, grocery people and anybody else who even *looked* like they would buy a pound of sausage.

————•————

After a little more than two years in the business, our company had become the number one seller of breakfast sausage in America, and we only covered a third of the country. The factory in Plainview was humming like a well-oiled machine, and eventually we employed about a hundred and fifty people with an annual payroll of more than three million dollars.

Everybody seemed pretty happy, and our employees considered theirs the best job in town. Not only because they were being paid fifty cents to a dollar above minimum wage an hour, but they also had a profit sharing program. Bonuses were given for increased production, and there was also plenty of overtime work if they wanted it. As a result, production records were topped time and time again, and morale was high among the employees.

It really was like working for one big happy family. Every now and then I would put on a hard hat and white coat and walk through the plant shaking hands, thanking the workers for the terrific job they were doing. I remember the first time we turned out a million pounds of sausage in a week's time. To express my thanks, I flew in food and champagne for an appreciation party for all the employees.

It's a funny thing, though, during all these years of being associated with rural humor and sausage, I've only heard one good sausage joke. It was about a guy who owned a sausage plant that was doing very well, and he had a son who was a long-haired hippie complete with ragged jeans and dirty sneakers. The boy couldn't have cared less about the sausage business, and all he wanted to do was smoke those funny cigarettes, drink beer and party all the time on Daddy's money.

But one day the old man grabbed the boy by the collar and said, "Son, one of these days you're gonna own this sausage business, so you're damned well gonna learn something about it." And the son said, "Hey, Pops, I can dig it. I can handle that." So the old man took him down to the sausage plant, shuffling him from the kill floor to packaging. Somewhere along the way, they came upon a beautiful, huge, stainless steel machine that was gleaming and shiny, and as the old man puffed up with pride, he said, "Son, do you see that machine? That is my invention. That is *my* innovation into the sausage industry." Then he said, "Son, I'll have you know, that you can put a pig in one end of that machine and out the other end comes a sausage." Sarcastically the boy said, "Well, whoopee, Pops. Big deal. You show me a machine where you can put in a *sausage* and out comes a *pig*, then you'll have a machine." The old man replied, "Well, son, I haven't got a machine like that, but your mama has!"

Three years after our company had begun, I was still excited and enthusiastic about the business. I felt good about the fact that we had started a hog boom in the Texas Panhandle, an area that had always been known for its cotton fields and cattle. But it had gotten to the point where West Texas hog raisers weren't increasing their production fast enough to keep up with our company's demands. That was when we started talking about branching out, and as our company vice president, Duane Getty, told the press at the time, "We were simply outgrowing the facility in Plainview."

To get ahead, we would have to go where our production could grow, so we looked to a little town in the heart of swine country, Osceola, Iowa. Since my role with the company was mostly in promotion and sales, Don and Troy handled the business negotiations with the state of Iowa. The town of Osceola pushed hard for the second factory, assisting us in every way possible. They donated land for the plant and promised adequate water, power and sewer services.

After five years in business, the Jimmy Dean Meat Company opened its second plant in Osceola, a giant in capability compared to the Plainview plant, mainly because the animals were more readily available there. But not long after it opened, our sales leveled off and we couldn't run both plants at capacity. After an eight-year run, our plant in Plainview closed its doors in March of 1978. It hurt me to see it close down, because I really wanted to do something for my hometown, but unfortunately the circumstances were beyond my control.

Another thing that was beyond my control was the Food and Drug Administration. I found that with most of my dealings with them I'd wind up exasperated, saying, "*What?!!*" and "*Why?!!*" a lot. So, if for no other reason than to let you know how foolishly some of your tax dollars are being spent, I'll relate a story to you.

It's a funny thing that a lot of people still call our product Jimmy Dean Pure Pork Sausage, even though that name hasn't been on the label since 1969. When we first started out, it was called "pure pork," but not long afterward we got a call from the truth in labeling division of the FDA. They said we couldn't call it "pure pork" sausage, and I said, "*Why?!!*" And are you ready for this? They said it was because it had seasoning in it. Can you believe that? Just because it had salt and pepper and sage, etc., we had to change the name to simply Jimmy Dean Sausage. That meant of course having to change all of our packaging and television commercials—all at our expense.

That wasn't the only time I would tangle with the FDA. I remember our star salesman Dewey Bishop coming to me, saying the reason we weren't selling as much sausage in the South was because it wasn't *seasoned* for the South. So we started the research and brought in every brand of popular Southern sausage we could find. We tasted it and tested it over and over, and found that basically all we needed to do to our sausage was put in a little more sage and a little less pepper to suit Southern tastes.

Our new product was to be called Jimmy Dean's Southern Style Sausage . . . At least that's what we *thought* we were going to call it. That was when we got a call from a Dr. Dumbass in Washington, DC, saying we couldn't call it "Southern style" sausage. Again I asked, "*Why?!!*" And he said, "Because it wasn't made in the South." "*What?!!*" I exclaimed. "I didn't say it was Southern sausage, I said it was *Southern style*!" He then informed me that it *wasn't* Southern style sausage because it was made in Iowa. So I asked him, "Are you telling me that all Kentucky Fried Chicken comes out of Kentucky? That all Spanish peanuts come from Spain? And that all Polish sausage comes from Poland?" I told him we'd spent about a half million dollars and a lot of man-hours to create this product and felt it was authentic. "Well," he replied, "you can't call it that unless you call it Jimmy Dean's Southern Style Sausage and print in the same size letters 'Made in Iowa.' "

Well, by this time I was totally irritated with this jerkwad, so I said, "Doctor, you're nitpicking me, and all in the world you're doing is trying to justify your job and create problems." I told him, "I'm not doing anything wrong, *haven't* done anything wrong, and have no *intention* of doing anything wrong." Then I said, "And I'll tell you what I'm going to do. I'm going to call it Jimmy Dean Southern Style Sausage whether you like it or not!" "Fine," he said. "Now let me tell you what *I'm* going to do. I'm going to fine you ten thousand dollars, and then I'm going to put you in jail for ten years." Well, that was when I said, "I think I'd like to give this matter some more consideration."

We ended up calling our product "Jimmy Dean's Special Recipe," but when I think about it, not going ahead with the original name may have been one of the most monumental mistakes of my life. I could have afforded the ten-thousand-dollar fine, but I was too busy for the ten years in jail. But then they wouldn't have dared keep me in jail after I'd told the press why I was there. Plus, we would have sold more sausage than we could've possibly made.

It just frosts me, though—the kind of shenanigans that go on with the federal government, and the fact that we're paying tax dollars for some guy to nitpick people like me to justify his job. That doctor seemed to be enjoying himself too, and I'd bet money he bragged to somebody, "I'll bet you can't guess who *I* ticked off today!"

If I've said it once I've said it a jillion times: I've never seen a federal intervention of any kind dealing with the law of supply and demand when something didn't get screwed up. Ninety-five percent of the time it does. The federal government has slowed down, delayed or completely stopped some wonderful efforts on the part of many people and businesses. And as far as I'm concerned, if they're that good at running a business, why do they operate at the deficits they do per annum? When you get your business in great shape, then you can come and tell me how to run mine.

Shortly after moving our sausage plant to Iowa in '72, Don and I decided that we didn't like the way Troy Pritchard was handling things. The decision was made to buy Troy out of his part of the business, so I raked up the money to pay him for his part and then gave Don half of it. Now the meat company was strictly a brother act, with Don and me each owning 50 percent.

Unfortunately, it was about this time that pork prices were rising sharply and the economy was dealing with the mid-1970s recession. Faced with these two elements and manning the helm full-time by himself, Don definitely had his hands full. People were simply not buying as much sausage, and it wasn't long before our company's sales began to decline.

Another problem that was coming to the surface was Don's arrogance. Don was, by all accounts, a great first-meeting salesman. He'd go in with his usual "Hi, I'm Jimmy Dean's brother and I'd like to sell you our sausage!" But since our product had been a hot item on the market, its extreme popularity had evidently gone to Don's head. He began to alienate the meat buyers and was turning people off left and right, and the decline in our sales reflected that.

One instance was with the head meat buyer for the Winn-Dixie stores in Montgomery, Alabama. When Don went to the buyer's office to discuss putting our product in his stores, I was told that Don sat down, propped his feet up on the man's desk and said, "Well, I know you've gotta have it, so when do you want it?" Obviously irritated, the meat buyer said, "What?" and Don repeated himself. The buyer then told Don he didn't have to have our product, didn't want it, and that it would *never* be in his stores.

Don was obviously trying to take advantage of our popularity, playing the big wheel he'd always wanted to be. But as I've always maintained, *most big wheels only go around in circles.* If he had only heeded Mom's advice when she said, "You can get more bees with honey than you can with vinegar."

The combination of economic events and Don's arrogance was leading to increasing financial problems within our company, so Don decided to recruit the help of a man whom he felt was an experienced food executive and businessman. As my brother's advisor, Al Holton was to oversee all areas of operation and bring the company back under control. But after Holton came aboard as executive vice president in 1974, things at the Jimmy Dean Meat Company would never again be the same.

15

THE JIMMY DEAN MEAT COMPANY: THE DECLINE

I GUESS MOST businesses have their problems, especially when first starting out, and ours was certainly no different. Most of the problems were minor, however, and it was fairly smooth sailing, that is until I gave my brother complete control of the company. Nevertheless, I continued to have faith and trust in Don to do the best he could for the business, and to protect the name and quality of our product.

By the time we entered our fifth year of operation, we were in financial trouble, so to get our company back on track, Don and his new executive vice president Al Holton had big plans. Part of their strategy was to borrow heavily from Dallas banks and cut operating expenses, which was no easy task.

One of the dumbest moves they made was to cut advertising costs, which meant cutting back on television commercials—our most effective sales tool. They also kept raising the price of our sausage and setting the retail price higher than all the other brands. As a result, our sales continued to take a nosedive. Our product was going out of date just sitting on the shelves in the stores, and the returns from the grocers to the distributors were enormous.

It didn't take long for me to realize that this Holton guy didn't know his butt from first base, because that year our profits continued to plummet. We had one of our worst years ever, and after years of success, our company showed an operating loss for the first time.

Still, Don thought Al Holton could do no wrong. In the meantime, the two of them made the decision to move our corporate offices from Plainview to Dallas, Texas—which didn't set well with me. I preferred to remain loyal to my hometown, but since our accountants and banks were in Dallas, I reluctantly agreed.

It was when Don and Al Holton decided they were going to start messing with the quality of our product that I hit the roof. I was royally ticked off when they changed our sausage packages in many of our markets from the one-pound to a twelve-ounce size. I believed that this would cheat and bamboozle our customers, especially the American housewife. People had been good to me and had fed me a pretty fair brand of groceries for a long, long time, and I wasn't about to start lying to them and cheating them now.

Though I didn't know it at the time, it was the general consensus among our employees that Don was running the company into the ground, and that he just didn't know what the hell he was doing. And he certainly wouldn't listen to me; anything I'd say was just tossed out the window. His grandiose ideas and arrogance, combined with our sales going down and spoils going up, caused a complete change in the marketplace for us. I had also gotten a few tips from people in the industry that something was rotten in Denmark, but all I knew for sure was that the company wasn't operating right and sales were dropping like a rocket.

It was when I found out that our annual sales had gone from fifty-five million to thirty-three million dollars a year that I *knew* we were in serious trouble. I personally couldn't get any straight answers from Don, and would eventually learn he was keeping the truth of what was happening from me. Our company was being destroyed by management or the lack thereof, and not only did we have a bunch of arrogant big wheels with huge egos, we now had some serious financial problems.

I take full responsibility for the problems with our company at the time, the main reason being that I didn't take as active a role in the business as I should have. I had left things entirely up to Don, giving him full rein to hire people like Al Holton, and now together they had brought the company down to ruins. In my opinion there was only one way to turn things around, so I decided to fire Al Holton.

Much to my disappointment, my brother Don wouldn't allow me to fire Holton and he sided with his friend and cohort. With Don owning 50 percent of the business and Al Holton as executive vice president, they said I didn't have the power—and it turned out they were right. The two of them even slapped me with a lawsuit and got a court order to keep me from entering company doors. They actually barred me from my own office, not wanting me to interfere in the day-to-day operations of the business. Sadly, this was the beginning of the end of my relationship with my brother Don.

When Don filed the lawsuit against me in July of '77, I felt the need to break the news to Mom as gently as possible. I told her the press would be saying some things that wouldn't be very nice, but not to pay any attention to it, that it didn't mean anything. That was when Mom said, "Don's cheating you, isn't he?" She asked, "Don did you wrong, didn't he?" Not wanting to say anything against my brother, I hemmed and hawed and finally said, "Well . . . not really . . . it's all right." Then she said, "I *know* he's doing you wrong, and I could have *told* you he was doing you wrong." So I asked her, "Well, if you could have told me, then why didn't you?" She said simply, "Well, I just hoped it would work itself out."

Mom's intuition was right on target—the only way she could have known what was going on with Don and me. I hadn't told her about our dispute for not wanting to upset her, and he certainly wasn't going to tell her himself. I'd known her mother's intuition was pretty well honed anyway, especially when she told me how much she despised Al Holton and that she thought he was a crook.

Indeed, the lawsuit Don had against me got pretty sticky, and the press was having a field day. So there was only one thing I could do, and that was to buy Don out of the company and try to settle out of court. It made me feel pretty stupid too, because I was the only one that had a monetary investment in the company; it was all my capital that had started it.

To settle, I told Don I'd give him half of what the company was worth. And though he had all but destroyed it, his lawyers had somehow determined the company's worth to be much more than it actually was. The court ruled that I owed Don half of its proven worth through our agreement in DonJim, Inc. So in the end, I had to buy back what I had made my brother a present of, just so I could try to straighten out what he'd screwed up.

I think this had to be the most difficult time in my life. If anybody had ever told me I was going to go through a nightmare like this, I would have never started this sausage company. Financially I was fixed pretty good and didn't need the headaches that came with the company, much less the heartaches. It destroyed friendships, my relationship with my only sibling and his family, and it almost destroyed me financially. Even my integrity and credibility as a businessman were at stake, and it seemed as though the Jimmy Dean Meat Company was coming to an end.

I was devastated professionally and personally, particularly by friends who could have testified on my behalf but wouldn't for fear of losing Don's friendship. There's one thing you can say about somebody who straddles a fence: They'll usually wind up with a sore crotch.

After the lawsuit with Don was settled, my problems were still not over. I went through a myriad of emotions at the time, and as anyone who knows me can tell you, I have a real hard time keeping them hidden. Shortly after the dispute with Don, I was accused of bad-mouthing him to the Dallas media by saying, "It's a terrible thing when the biggest mistake you ever made in your life was trusting in your own brother."

I also got into trouble by writing a piece of material about our dispute. The idea came from so many people saying things to me like "Jimmy, don't you know any better than to go into business with kinfolks?" And then they'd say, "Let me tell you what happened between me and my cousin . . . " or "Let me tell you what happened with me and my sister . . ." They inspired me to write a piece of material called "Don't Go into Business with Kinfolks," and I thought since so many people could relate to it, that they might even buy a record of it. It wasn't long after the lawsuit that I made an appearance on *The Mike Douglas Show* and decided to recite "Kinfolks" on national TV.

"Don't Go into Business with Kinfolks"

*Don't go into business with kinfolks, an old saying you'll find to be
    true
'Cause if you go into business with kinfolks, they'll soon give the
    business to you.
Relatives just don't make good partners, with their fine cars, cigars
    and dames
They'll go through your money like water and behind your back
    they'll be calling you names.*

*Credit cards usually start the erosion, at best they're a hell of a mess.
My ex-partner now owns half of Dallas, all charged to American
    Express.
So don't make your brother your partner, it starts ills for which
    there are no cures.
You'll find he'll develop eye trouble and can't tell his money from
    yours.*

*So just send your relatives money, oh it sounds like I'm out of my
    mind.
It's a pain in the neck but just send them a check, at least this way
    they can't steal you blind.*

Well, you can probably guess what happened next. Yep, another lawsuit. This time Don sued me for 4.3 million dollars, for libel, slander and defamation of character. The case was basically laughed out of the courtroom, however, when the judge dismissed it and threw it out of court.

———•———

It wasn't long after the lawsuits with Don that a most unusual phone call came into the office. It was from a very polite and well-educated man who wanted to relate a story to me, of when he and his parents and family came to see me perform in Las Vegas. He told me his mom and dad were celebrating their fiftieth wedding anniversary that evening, and that I made their night when I came to their table and sang a song called "When Your Old Wedding Ring Was New." He said he told himself at the time, "I owe that man something." And then he said, "I hear you have some problems . . . Can I take care of anyone for you?" Taken aback I asked, "What do you mean by that?" And he said, "*You* know what I mean, Jimmy." Stuttering and stammering, I thanked him kindly but politely declined his offer.

In retrospect, I feel sorry for my brother because he turned on the best friend he ever had. Although I think now I understand the reasons for his resentment toward me, and that his living in my shadow had to be a pretty lonely place.

It's funny, when we were kids, Don was always the fair-haired boy. He was smarter than me in school, he could pull more bolls in the cotton fields, and everything he tried to do he could do better than me. He was also the first of us to have a bicycle and a car. He wanted so badly to beat me in every way, and took great joy in doing it. But Don also wanted to be able to do the things *I* did and have the things *I* had, whether it was the talent to entertain people or the confidence to take care of business.

After the dispute over the company, Don and I were totally and completely estranged and never saw each other again except at Mom's funeral. For fifteen years we didn't speak or have any contact whatsoever. It broke my heart that I never saw my brother again after that. Don died of lung cancer at the age of sixty-four on November 2, 1994.

I can't imagine how Don must have felt, realizing that the only thing he ever did successfully was screw his own brother. My only hope is that he somehow found peace within and was able to look at himself in the mirror.

These days when I look at *myself*, I see a head so wrinkled that it looks like twelve minutes of bad reception. But I can shave my face

Visiting Don in Germany about 1951

and honestly say, "I like you. You may have lost a few battles, but you won the war fair and square." I'm reminded of a favorite poem of mine that I'd like to share with you, written by Dale Wimbrow . . .

The Guy in the Glass

When you get what you want in your struggle for self,
And the world makes you King for a day,
Then go to the mirror and look at yourself,
And see what that guy has to say.

For it isn't your Father, or Mother, or Wife,
Whose judgement upon you must pass.
The feller whose verdict counts most in your life
Is the one staring back from the glass.

He's the feller to please, never mind all the rest,
For he's with you clear up to the end,
And you've passed your most dangerous, difficult test
If the man in the glass is your friend.

You may be like Jack Horner and "chisel" a plum,
And think you're a wonderful guy,
But the man in the glass says you're only a bum
If you can't look him straight in the eye.

You can fool the whole world down the pathway of years,
And get pats on the back as you pass,
But your final reward will be heartaches and tears
If you've cheated the guy in the glass.

16

THE JIMMY DEAN MEAT COMPANY: THE RESURRECTION

IF YOU'VE EVER smoked cigarettes and tried to quit, then you know the effect a stressful situation can have on you. After having quit five years before, I picked the habit back up again when this thing with my brother Don happened. I was in a meeting with several of us from the company, sweating bullets trying to get it back on its feet, when somebody had a cigarette burning. It looked too good to me at the time so I bummed one. I remember it so well, because after I took the first puff I was as drunk as I'd ever been in my life for about two minutes, and about half-sick. The next day, having had just one cigarette the day before, I thought, I can have one anytime I want. Wrong, Dean. I tried smoking just one and went right back to three packs a day.

Even though we were in the middle of a lawsuit, I went to work as soon as possible to try and put the sausage company back together. It wasn't easy, mainly because I was still barred from my office and was having to straighten it out from a hotel room across the street. And what a mess it was! Forget having to build a business up from the ground floor—this time I had to start from the basement.

The first thing I had to do was fire about half the people that Don had hired. I found myself in a den of thieves, having to weed them out one by one. One guy, I discovered, had gone down to a clothing store and charged about four thousand dollars' worth of clothes to the company. I told him, "You've got a problem. You have Rolls-Royce taste and a Volkswagen budget, and I'm afraid I can't use you anymore." Another, I noticed, was flying to North Carolina an awful lot, and I didn't think we were doing that much business there. I played detective, checking his phone bills, and found out he was flying there on the company's expense to visit some woman while he was supposed to be working.

After getting rid of some of the riffraff in the company, I then went about reestablishing our credibility, beginning with reinstituting our one-pound package of sausage. And when I reassumed control of the company, I discovered more reasons why our sales had taken a nose-dive in recent years. First of all, the media buying service that Don had been using was placing most of our commercials on TV from midnight to sign-off. We were getting ripped off with the least desirable time slot, and either Don or Al Holton didn't care or they didn't know any better. That was when I went looking for an ad agency to help the company get back on track, and someone in Dallas recommended a man named Bob Berry.

Following their rather shaky presentation in my hotel room, I hired Bob Berry and his partner Don Sumner to handle our TV commercials, even though their Sumner-Berry Advertising had only been in business for a few months. I remember Bob saying, "Well, this train is going downhill, and it's a tough enough job to get it stopped, but if you're lucky enough to get it stopped, it's virtually impossible to push it back up that hill." The two of them seemed to have a genuine desire to help me, though, so I decided to put my complete faith in them.

The relationship with our new advertising agency turned out to be a good one, and their strategies worked out well. At first, we put out only newspaper ads because we didn't have much money to spend, and then Bob Berry worked out a joint coupon deal with the Quaker Oats and Aunt Jemima companies to run in color newspaper inserts. I was still losing distribution at the time from the bad deals made by Don and Al Holton, so being associated with the two other companies helped to restore some of our credibility.

The next thing I had to do was to try and mend a lot of torn-down fences. I knew it would take personal involvement on my part, so I flew all around the country, to Ohio, Indiana, Michigan, Louisiana, Oklahoma or wherever it was necessary to apologize for all that Don and Al had said and done. My secretary Willie and I would get into a car and drive around the countryside making sales calls, telling the meat buyers how sorry I was, and asking them what I could do to make amends. We'd go into the grocery stores and spend time with the meat managers and talk to the ladies who were shopping. And if we passed a radio station, big or small, I would go in and get on the air and chat with the DJ to promote our product.

There were times when I didn't know if I was going to be able to pull this company back or not. When I told one particular distributor on the West Coast that I was trying to rebuild it, he told me, "You'd better look at it, Jimmy, and make sure it's worth rebuilding." All I knew was that my name and reputation were on the line, as well as a lot of people's jobs.

Over a period of several months we practically covered every corner of the United States, going into meat buyers' offices with my hat in my hand and apologizing for what my brother had done. In fact it took several years of saying, "I'm sorry . . . We'll be fair and ethical this time . . . We'll do it right and it won't happen again." It was an extra long time before we got our products back into the segment of Winn-Dixie stores Don had insulted, and only then after I had gone down and talked to the head honcho himself.

Rebuilding the sausage company was a slow and painful process, a task more difficult than building it originally, but eventually I was well accepted at the grocery chains again. I have to believe that a lot of it was the result of my apologizing to a bunch of people who had been wronged, and looking them in the eye and telling them the truth about what happened. As time went on, our sales began to pick up, and it seemed as though we had indeed gotten the train stopped and headed back up the hill.

———•———

From that point on, I stayed involved with the business as president of the company and chairman of the board, making the decisions in product and market selection. But because I was still active in the entertainment business, I had to leave the day-to-day operations up to three vice presidents. Music was still a very big part of my life during this time. I was doing a thirty-minute syndicated television show based in Nashville and I also spent a lot of time writing songs. But about a third of my time was now being spent in Dallas so that I could oversee the sausage business and make sure we would keep on growing.

After I got things going well with the company, I received a call one morning from my friend Ted Strauss who headed up First City Bank in Dallas. He said, "Jimmy, you've got this six-million-dollar line of credit here and you're not using it. Are you mad at us, or have we done something wrong?" I thought, *How ironic.* Not too long ago I couldn't *buy* a loan from his bank. I said, "No, Ted, I just don't happen to need it right now." Our company president Duane Getty was in the office at the time, and I turned to him and said, "Isn't that the way it is? Prove to the world you can walk on water, and some son of a bitch will give you a boat." I never have been able to understand why you can get all the money in the world you want, only if you can prove you don't need it.

The steady growth of our company's success was also largely attributable to the television commercials I was producing with the help of Bob Berry's ad agency. I never wanted our commercials to appear staged, so I would simply go in and sit down on a stool with a pound of sausage, look into the camera and tell the truth about it.

Our commercials were all totally ad-lib and off the cuff, and to me there's something honest about not having any scripts—just a guy talking about a product he knows very well. If we were introducing a new product, Bob would have an outline written of certain key factors, to give me the general idea of what the commercial was about, and then I would put it into my own words. I wasn't about to have anyone from an ad agency standing over me telling me exactly what to say and how to say it. That's what I liked best about working with Bob: He was smart enough to stay the hell out of my way.

Bob Berry and I got along not only professionally, but personally as well, and we're still great friends today. He and I just always seemed to read from the same sheet of music, and not only were our commercials effective sales tools but they were also cost-effective.

The two of us working together could crank out an unheard of number of commercials in a short amount of time, actually breaking our own record one day when we cut thirteen in one session.

On this one particular day we had a little time left over on the videotape when Bob turned to me and asked, "Have we got anything we can do in ten seconds?" I thought for a minute, and then sat back down on the set and said, "Yeah, Bob, roll the camera." I proceeded to cut a ten-second commercial that said, "A lot of people will ask you to do things for them and you do it, and they forget to say thank you. I asked you to buy Jimmy Dean Sausage and you did that, and I just wanted to say thank you." To this day that particular commercial has received more positive response than any we've ever done.

I guess the most fun I ever had with my commercials was with some radio spots we did back then. They were short little poems I had written that I would recite with only a country-style guitar playing in the background. Each one was about whatever was eating me at the time, and ended with just a blip about the sausage company at the end, along with a disclaimer. Actually they were commentaries in a way, with my comedic take on a controversial subject such as taxes, lawyers, gasoline prices, welfare chiselers, weathermen or the U.S. Mail . . .

> *Funny thing that letter I mailed*
> *Somewhere the Postal Service failed*
> *I think about it and it makes me sore*
> *The service gets worse and the stamps cost more*
> *Ain't that a mess? I'll take Pony Express . . .*
> *(This message is brought to you by Jimmy Dean Sausage*
> *and does not necessarily reflect the opinion of this station.)*

The little ditties actually received a lot of positive feedback from the public. In fact, when they first came out, the manager of a Dallas TV station made an appearance on the evening news paying tribute to them, saying they were the best commercials on the air. Seems like I struck a nerve and that a lot of folks agreed with me.

When my office moved from New York to Dallas in the late seventies, my longtime secretary Willie Bruffy also made the move and continued to keep me organized in every way. Willie was a large woman with real long straight red hair, and was an extremely smart and well-liked lady.

They don't come along like Willie very often. She turned out to be the most loyal, dedicated and competent employee I ever had. I could always count on Willie to take care of the smallest detail with great aplomb. She was usually at least one step ahead of me, and by the time I would get around to asking her to do something, she had already done it. I'd say, "Willie, get me that file on so-and-so," and she'd already have it under her arm.

Besides working in my office and catering to my every need, Willie traveled with me most everywhere I went. She downright spoiled me, catering to my every whim, even carrying a miniature black pepper grinder in her bag, knowing how I liked to douse my food with fresh ground pepper.

Sometimes we'd go on promotional tours around the country that lasted four to five weeks, attending planned receptions, cocktail parties or dinners to entertain grocers, brokers and distributors. We'd go to towns for radio promotions, do cooking shows on local television, and stop at grocery stores making store calls. Willie and I would hang out in the meat department, where I would wrap "George Washington coupons" (one-dollar bills) around the rolls of sausage and hand them out to customers, while she took photographs of people there with me, and later making sure each one received a copy of their photo in the mail. Willie was the greatest.

In 1980, after working as my secretary for twenty-one years, Willie finally quit and moved back to New York City. She was extremely unhappy in Dallas; she really didn't have much of a life there, the main reason being she couldn't drive a car and wouldn't learn how to drive. I told her so many times, "Willie, if you'll learn how to drive, I'll *buy* you a car," but she never would.

Through the years, Willie and I kept in touch, and each Christmas I continued to send her a gift of a thousand dollars. Having never been married and being retired, I knew she could use the money because of her increasing health problems. Willie was always terribly obese and suffered for an awfully long time. Sadly, she passed away in a nursing home in May 2002.

About a year before Willie died, I was revamping my will, considering what and how much to leave to whom. When I mentioned to my wife Donna that I was leaving ten thousand dollars to Willie, she asked, "Why are you waiting to give it to her when you pass on? Maybe you should give her the money now since she can use it. That way you'll have the joy of giving it, and the benefit of seeing her enjoy it too." A great idea I thought, so I did that . . . and I'm ever so glad I did.

———•———

When she left my employ, I knew Willie would be difficult to replace, but I had no idea. I went through a number of secretaries, and believe me when I tell you some of them were real doozies—or maybe I should say *dizzies*. One I hired was not to be believed. She was supposed to be an executive secretary, mind you, but she was as dumb as a box of rocks. One day she came into my office and said, "Mr. Dean, you have an invitation from President and Mrs. Reagan to a State Dinner at the White House." I told her to check the book and if we were open we'd do it, and a few minutes later she came back saying our calendar was indeed open. I said, "Great. I'm assuming that it's formal, right?" She said, "No, it's not formal, but you have to wear a black tie." I couldn't believe it. Here I had an *executive secretary* that didn't know the meaning of "black tie" attire.

Despite my dilemma with secretaries, the stress levels around the office were considerably lower by this time, and in 1982 I finally quit smoking cigarettes for good. At the time I was smoking so much my complexion was just kind of gray, no doubt from not getting the proper amount of oxygen in my blood. My three packs a day had also drained me, and I didn't have enough energy to properly handle the business at hand. A group of us would be in a meeting in the latter part of the afternoon and I would let things pass that I knew were wrong. I'd tell myself I'd deal with it later, and the next morning I'd have to fix it when I got to the office.

When people asked me if I got irritable when I quit smoking, I would tell them, "Irritable, hell—I fired three people that didn't even work for me!" I don't know anything about cocaine or heroin, or any other drug, but I don't see how any of them could be more addictive than cigarettes. I always carried my cigarette pack in my left front shirt pocket, and for several weeks after quitting I nearly pounded my left tit off patting down my pocket looking for a pack of cigarettes that wasn't there.

With our company back on track, diversifying within the company was something that became lucrative for us as well. We began with what was known as "fringe" products, marketing the parts of the hog that we couldn't use for sausage. A lot of it was sold for fertilizer, and since we used a process at our plant that produced superior hides, companies like Wolverine would buy them to make Hush Puppies shoes. At one time we even tried to market a high-priced apparel line called Pigskin by Jimmy Dean. We also sold the inner skin (at our cost) to Phoenix's Burn Treatment Bank, which at that time served 4,700 hospitals nationwide. It was a good feeling to know that we might be helping to save people's lives.

With our plant in Iowa chugging right along, I would visit often to help keep up the employees' morale, shaking hands and patting backs. The annual Christmas party we had for them was something I never missed, and to the employees it was the event of the year. Everybody got dressed up to enjoy the free food and booze. And you never saw people who could go from stone-cold sober to knee-walking, commode-hugging drunk so fast in your life.

At one of our Christmas parties, I distinctly remember one guy and his wife who looked so nice all dressed up, coming to me and saying, "Mr. Dean, we really do want to thank you for these years of employment, because the job has enabled us to get all of our kids into college. We really appreciate the work and the job, and we both wanted to sincerely thank you before the party got under way." I thought, What a nice gesture, and I thanked them. But I promise you it wasn't an hour before that same guy came up to me again and slurred, "Jimmy, let me tell you what's wrong with your f——king plant . . ."

Another time at the Christmas party I was standing at the bar waiting to get a drink, when I felt someone's hands on both cheeks of my butt. I looked around and here was this old gal standing there with a cheek in each hand. She said, "I've wanted to do that all night long!" Completely stunned, I said, "Well, now you've done it!" We just smiled at each other and she walked away.

The Jimmy Dean Meat Company continued to grow and grow, with estimated sales reaching seventy-five million dollars per year. All the hard work and dedication had paid off, and by 1984 a national survey of consumers had named our product "America's #1 Breakfast Sausage."

I think I had proven beyond a shadow of a doubt that I knew what was best for the company, and that it was best left in my hands. After all, it was my own name I was trying to save, and there's no telling what would have happened to it had I left it to someone else. I didn't set out to work that hard, nor had I planned to spend so much time and energy on this particular business venture. And had I known it was going to cost me as much blood, sweat and tears, and my relationship with my brother, I would have never considered it in the first place.

17

NOBODY DOESN'T LIKE SARA LEE

MY MOTHER HAD told me many times that getting knocked down is a part of life, but getting up is also, and I think that philosophy was a big part of what helped me put my sausage company back together. Fifteen years after we had started the company, we were once again at the top, enjoying our success as number one in the country.

During this time, unbeknownst to me, my company was under a great deal of scrutiny, no doubt as a result of its success. One day while vacationing on my boat in Florida, I got a call from a guy in the meat business in Ft. Worth saying somebody was interested in buying the company. The caller, who was affiliated with Consolidated Foods, told me that their chief executive officer, John Bryan, wanted to talk to me, then he gave me John's number at their headquarters in Chicago.

This of course interested me very much because I was familiar with Consolidated Foods, who had numerous other products under their corporate umbrella, including Sara Lee, Coach Leather, Hanes panty hose, L'egg's stockings and Champion Sportswear. As CEO, John Bryan was in charge of acquisitions and was the guy with whom I would negotiate.

The next day I called their headquarters, and when John Bryan answered the phone, he said, "Jimmy, why don't you come up to

Chicago and talk to us?" I told him, "Well, Chicago's never been one of my favorite cities in the world. It's cold and it's very windy, and I'm here on my boat in Florida." I said, "Why don't you come down here and talk to me?" I was more or less feeling him out to see how much he really wanted to talk to me, and if he wanted to go to all that trouble. He said, "Okay, how about tomorrow morning?" We set up the meeting, and I knew he was indeed serious when I saw him walking down the dock the next day.

After coming aboard my boat and talking for a while, John Bryan finally got down to business and popped the question. "How much do you want for your company?" he asked. "I'm not going to tell you that," I said. "*You're* going to tell *me* how much you're going to give me for it." I knew John Bryan wouldn't have been interested in my company if he hadn't done the research, and that he knew just how much to offer me. So I told him, "You know what we do per annum and you know exactly what we're worth. So you go back to Chicago and figure it out, and when you've figured it out, give me a call and I'll come and talk to you."

When we concluded our meeting, I told John Bryan that when I came to Chicago I would be coming by myself, with no attorney, but I doubt if he believed that. I also told him that I didn't want the contract to be some long, drawn-out document. I didn't even comprehend *layman's* law, much less legal documents with all their "whereas-es" and "party of the first parts." I only wanted a simple document that I could understand.

It was several weeks before John Bryan called me saying they were ready to talk. I flew to Chicago, where I was met at the airport by a stretch limousine, a far cry from the treatment he'd gotten when he came to my boat in Florida. After arriving at the offices, I was shown to their conference room, where there was only three of us—John Bryan, a company financial officer and me, and not an attorney in sight. The entire agreement they produced had been written on one side of one piece of paper—simple, straight and to the point, just like I wanted. We talked briefly, and after reading over their document and asking a few questions, I said, "Gentlemen, I think it's going to be fun being in business with you. You just bought the Jimmy Dean Meat Company."

When my sausage company became a division of Consolidated Foods in June of 1984, I remained chairman of the board and company spokesperson, and to better reflect the diversification into non-meat breakfast items, the name of the company was changed to Jimmy Dean Foods.

Our employees at the meat company remained the same, but there was some concern that a big and impersonal corporation would change the family atmosphere of our company. Anytime a major corporation buys an entrepreneur's business, they buy it for its value and generally say, "You've got the secret and we're not going to change anything," but changes are always inevitable. Naturally, I was concerned about a change in the quality of our product because my name was still on it, and I didn't have the control I once had. Don't get me wrong—I'm not averse to change, because sometimes it's for the better—but I can't help but recall a story that was related to me by a man named Reese.

It was while dining at a restaurant somewhere in Canada that I met the son of the creator of Reese's Peanut Butter Cups, and he told me about the time he took over his father's company. The young Reese decided he was going to modernize the business, so instead of batch roasting the peanuts as they had been done for years, he put them on a conveyor to give them a more perfect roasting. After Reese Jr. had made the first batch of candy, his daddy took one bite and said, "My name will never go on that! That's not my product!" Others tasted it and agreed, but nobody could figure out what the problem was. The only difference was the roasting process of the peanuts, so they decided to get one of the batch roasters back out. After cooking a batch and separating the peanuts, they discovered that about 4 to 6 percent of them had been burned during the roasting process, hence the unique flavor of the peanuts and the candy. All they had to do then was make sure the new conveyor system burned the same amount of peanuts as the roasters. As the old saying goes, "It's hard to improve upon perfection."

With the Consolidated Foods merger, it was business as usual at our company in the beginning, with not many changes at all. They maintained our brand and then added new items to our line of products, some winners and some losers. Then about a year after I sold them my company, they decided that the name of one of their main products—Sara Lee—was more recognizable and would give them a higher profile. That was when Consolidated Foods changed their name to the Sara Lee Corporation.

All in all, corporate business seemed to suit me just fine, although the one part no one has ever explained to my satisfaction is the marketing department—something I had gotten along without just fine, up till this point in time.

The purpose of marketing has never made sense to me. I've always considered that department to be a bunch of textbook jockeys doing it by the numbers, wasting time, money and a lot of effort with all of their graphs and research. They're taught to sell a product with gimmickry, and I've always maintained that if you have a good product, you don't need gimmicks to sell it. And just how, when and why they became involved in the making of our television commercials I'll *never* know.

Thankfully, Bob Berry and his company stayed on as our advertising agency, so our TV commercials didn't change all that much. The problem was just trying to get them done with all the superfluous horse manure we had to contend with—courtesy of marketing. According to them, you had to have scripts and storyboards and everything done by the book, right down to the letter. And cue cards, for God's sake! I'd never *ever* used cue cards on my commercials, but the company insisted on paying to have them there every time.

That's another thing I could never get used to—the unnecessary spending by Sara Lee, or the "fat" as I called it. For instance, before when Bob Berry and I would cut our commercials, we would go into the studio with a great set he had built and knock out a bunch of ads in no time. But now, for each session, the company was paying dearly to rent an expensive house somewhere in an upscale neighborhood in Dallas—*more fat*—and their kitchens didn't look any better than Bob's sets. Camera equipment, huge lighting fixtures and television monitors had to be brought in, along with a producer, a director, lots of technicians, operators and their assistants—the place was literally crawling with people. To me it was just a lot of confusion that made the whole thing take more time, and me more than a little irritable.

As if each commercial shoot wasn't crowded enough, they would also bring in a lady to do my hair and makeup, and a wardrobe lady who brought several changes for me to wear, although in the past I would just wear whatever I thought looked nice. And to top it off, parked outside of the house they rented was a large motor home they had to rent for me to use as a dressing room.

One time they decided to cut one of our commercials on a farm with me leaning up against a fence. There I stood, waiting for them to roll tape, when the director got real excited and said, "Wait! Hey, Jimmy . . . if you'll move just a little bit to your right, we can get a shot of that windmill in the background. And maybe if that colt over there frolics this way, we can get a shot of him too." I said, "Wait a minute! If you do that, nobody's going to hear a word I'm saying 'cause they'll be looking at that colt. I haven't sold a horse in a long time, and I have no *intention* of trying to sell a windmill!" That was the problem with a lot of those advertising folks: They were trying to be creative and thought they had to rely on gimmicks, instead of telling the truth about the product. Sometimes they just didn't get it.

There were always lots of people in the marketing and advertising departments planning our commercials, and I suppose it was simply because there was so many of them on the payroll—still more "fat." And maybe they just wanted to get involved in the creative process, but it seemed to me they were only trying to justify their existence.

By 1998 Jimmy Dean Foods had grown to employing five hundred people and was indeed big business. At times, when people would ask, "How many people you got working for you, Jimmy?" I'd just kid them and say, "About half of 'em."

All in all, I really don't think I was that hard to work with, or for. My brother Don always *did* say that I was a nice guy usually, but that I could be as tough as the back of a shooting gallery. If you asked *some* of my employees what I was like to work for, they'd say, "He's the greatest guy in the world," and those were the people who were doing their jobs. But then others would say, "He's the most miserable son of a bitch alive," and those were the ones who *weren't* doing their jobs.

———•—

With our company now offering forty-one varieties of thirteen different products, our offices were moved to bigger and better locations throughout the years, and our processing plants were eventually moved to Tennessee and Alabama. Part of the company's success could most certainly be attributed to its brokers and distributors, and truthfully we could never have survived without them. To show our appreciation for selling a certain amount of product each year, we came up with an annual incentive trip that treated them and their spouses or guests to a weeklong vacation. The incentive program is still carried on, and since 1976 they've been rewarded with destinations such as Hawaii, Italy, Germany, France, Scotland and the Greek Isles, to name just a few.

For many years my wife, Donna, and I would also travel to the different markets around the country to show our appreciation to the brokers and distributors for their business. They enjoyed the fact that we would come to their town just to thank them, especially when we would entertain them with a special dinner and sing a few numbers. I guess I'm old-fashioned, but I'm firmly convinced that if someone is nice to you and you don't take the time to go by and shake hands and say thank you, they might forget to be nice in the future.

In all the years of having the company, I tried to instill that same philosophy into my employees. At most every meeting, I'd remind them of a favorite saying that went, "There's little we can't accomplish if it doesn't matter who gets the credit." Another favorite saying of mine was, "Perfection is almost good enough." But the most important thing I tried to instill in them was our motto at Jimmy Dean Foods: "Do what you say you're going to do, when you say you were going to do it, and try to do it a little better than you said you would."

Another adage that was applicable to my career was, "The harder I worked the luckier I got." Although I never worked hard in order to get rich . . . I just worked *hard*. I think part of it was I was scared, afraid I'd end up back in Plainview installing irrigation wells for the Peerless Pump Company again. I didn't like it when I was sixteen, and I knew I wouldn't like it when I was sixty.

People magazine once called me "a virtuoso at making a silk purse out of a sow's ear," but thanks to good loyal customers and a lot of hard work, our sausage has been number one in the country for a long time now. People have been good to me over the years and many have sent me their sausage recipes, which I appreciate, but I did want to share with you one of my favorites—from none other than the famous entertainer Liberace.

I had met "Lee" many years before and liked him, and if you never had a chance to see his show, then you missed something great. We both played the Nevada casinos regularly, and it's customary in most of the main showrooms for the incoming performer to attend the last dinner show of the outgoing performer. This one particular time Liberace's show was to follow mine at the Golden Nugget in Sparks.

I'll never forget how Lee came flying into my dressing room after the show. He was so excited you'd have thought he had just discovered gold. He said, "Jimmy, the show was great, but you've *got* to save the drippings from your hot sausage, and the next time you pop popcorn use those drippings instead of oil." Then he said, "And be sure to save the residue; that's the red pepper that gives it such a nice *zing*!" Lee loved to cook and he loved to eat too. And you know, he was right . . . I tried his recipe and it really *was* great.

With humor being one of the most important things in life to me, my being known for my sausage has also been the source of a few laughs over the years. I guess the question I get most often is "Hey, Jimmy, got any sausage on ya?" And my reply is usually "You really don't want me to answer that!" Some people ask if it bothers me that I'm more famous for my sausage these days than for my music, and I answer a resounding *no,* since the food business has certainly been more lucrative and reliable. I also tell them that "every day in my life is Groundhog Day" (ground hog . . . get it?). But the biggest chuckle I get from people is when I tell them, "You may knock my singing, but you can't beat my meat!"

In 2002 I was delighted and surprised to learn that I had been voted the number one meat spokesperson of all time by *Meat Marketing Magazine.* I was proud of the accolade, but I really didn't understand what the fuss was about, since all I ever did was tell the truth about a product that I knew and I believed in.

If the truth be known, I've never been in the meat business, or even in the entertainment business. I've always been in the *people* business. I learned a long time ago that before you can sell a product—whether it's sausage or a song—*you must first sell yourself.* That if people don't like you as a person, they won't want to buy anything you're trying to sell. If throughout my life I'd ever forgotten that one simple fact, I'd have surely been in a whole heckuva lot of trouble.

18

SOMEBODY DOESN'T LIKE SARA LEE

AS I DUG back into the history of the sausage company for this book, my having to relive it opened up a lot of old wounds, but without digging up so many bones, I had no other way to explain the development of our company and its many peaks and valleys.

Having Jimmy Dean Foods involved a lot of hard work, long hours and boot leather, and it furnished me with a combination of every emotion known to mankind, from euphoria to the depths of depression, and everything in between. But it was also an interesting, fun and extremely good ride, and all in all a tremendous learning experience.

What I wasn't prepared for, however, was the final blow I was dealt in 2002. After nearly a twenty-year relationship with Sara Lee, my agreement with them had turned into The Deal From Hell. The sausage company that I had devoted so much of my life to was taken away from me completely, and it was during this time that I endured some of the most painful days of my life.

The beginning of the end was actually around 1991 when my president, Duane Getty, left the company. I'm quite sure Sara Lee pressured him into leaving, as they did several of my key executives. When they initially bought the Jimmy Dean Meat Company, the big brass said the reason was because it was "lean, mean and making money." They told me my employees were doing a good job and that they didn't want to make any changes. But then I've seen it happen so many times: Corporations buy smaller businesses and eventually go in and clean house.

When Duane Getty left, they picked a couple of guys to interview for the position, and then they had Donna and me host each of them and their wives at our home for a few days. The Sara Lee brass said they wanted to get my opinion on them, but when I chose one over the other they completely ignored my choice and went with their own. Eventually they made the change to the guy I had wanted to be president in the first place, which shows they didn't have it all knowed up.

The deterioration of my relationship with Sara Lee continued gradually over the next several years, and I was left out of the decision-making process more and more. Like with some of their promotions, for instance. There was the Jimmy Dean race car they put together for the national circuit that they didn't consult with me about. I had turned down one race car deal after another for years, knowing it would cost more money than we could make out of it. The only way we could really make money was if we had the number one car, and that takes a bigger investment than Sara Lee was willing to make. Naturally their car was a very expensive flop.

I'll never forget one day while watching our car race on television, with it lagging behind miserably as usual, when my cousin Leon, a huge racing fan, called me from Tulia, Texas. "Jimmy," he said in his slow West Texas drawl, "you've either got to get a better driver or a faster car."

Another dismal failure was their Sara Lee Classic golf tournament that was held annually in Nashville for a few years. When they first thought about having it and mentioned it to me, I tried to tell them that if they could televise it on a network, it could be a highly successful promotional tool. But I guess what I said didn't mean anything to them. They didn't listen to me, so it fell by the wayside too.

It wasn't always like that. In the beginning Sara Lee would consult with me about new products and wanted my opinion and feedback, but that petered out completely after a few years. It eventually got to where new Jimmy Dean items that they hadn't even told me about would hit the market. I would see our new products in the stores or folks would ask me about them, and it was hard not to look shocked and embarrassed. I knew that changes were bound to take place when Sara Lee bought my company, but when they stopped consulting me on the issues of business, I should have read the writing on the wall.

As the corporate heads would change, each time more of my employees would be replaced. One of the most traumatic changes for me was when they got rid of Bob Berry and his advertising agency. They hired a new one, as well as a new marketing agency, and gradually pushed nearly all my people out and put new people in. I sat back and watched all these changes being made as they blatantly showed me they didn't trust my judgment. They were obviously going to show the country boy how it was done.

As time went on, I watched the distance that Sara Lee put between themselves and me grow much wider. They knew I was available to promote Jimmy Dean products, as I'd done all along, and I would let them know that regularly. It would involve flying around the country and spending a day or two in each different city visiting with brokers and distributors, but it always paid off in sales. I'd tell them, "Donna and I are ready to go out and shake some hands and entertain these people, so let us know when and where you need us to go." But they rarely took us up on it and our promoting eventually dwindled down to nothing. They just stopped sending us out there, saying it was "the old-fashioned way to sell" and it "doesn't work anymore."

Since I had been living in Richmond since 1990 and was hardly ever at our meat company office in Memphis, I kept a constant line of communication open with everyone by telephone each day. It didn't seem so important for me to be there, since everybody was so spread out anyway, with Sara Lee's corporate offices in Chicago and most of their other meat products' offices in Cincinnati. My administrative assistant and right arm Mary Moore, who was more or less my eyes and ears there, dealt with the administrative duties at my office in Memphis, along with our secretary JoAnn. I would chat with the meat company execs every so often on the telephone from

Richmond, but I was usually the one who initiated the calls, trying my damnedest to stay involved with the business.

There's just not a whole lot you can do when folks are determined to keep you in the dark, and more and more it became a constant battle to stay connected. In the last several years, Mary began to complain that the meat company execs were excluding our office from the day-to-day business and that she was rarely invited to meetings that concerned us. We had become victims of the mushroom syndrome—kept in the dark and fed horse manure.

Still I trudged along, determined to try to keep some control over the products that bore my name, to maintain their quality—and my integrity. If I was a thorn in their sides, so be it. I had a lot more at stake than all of them put together.

Stress, as we all know, can affect your health, and by the late 1990s my struggles with the meat company were beginning to take its toll. The doctor put me on sleeping pills because I was having such a hard time sleeping at night. I'd lay there with my wheels turning, worried about how I was going to keep a grasp on things.

Then one evening in July of 2001 I was sitting in my easy chair in the den watching the news, when all of a sudden I saw black for a few seconds. I sat there until my vision came back kind of blurred, and then it was okay again. I thought to myself, *What the hell was that?* About that time Donna called me into the kitchen to eat dinner, and I told her about it. "To the doctor," she said, but I said no, that we'd go in the morning if I wasn't better by then.

Later on that evening it happened again. As I got up out of my chair to go to bed something went wrong with my right eye. By this time it was too late to go to the doctor, and I didn't want to go to the emergency room. There was no pain involved, so I was thankful for that, but I was still kind of worried about it.

It turned out I'd had a "ministroke," or TIA, Transient Ischemic Attack. I had actually had a series of them, and permanently lost two-thirds of the sight in my right eye. The strokes also affected my walking and made me a little unsteady on my feet, and the physical therapy I had to go through didn't help at all.

As I've told you before, I don't give up, and come 2002 I thought I was seeing what might be the light at the end of the tunnel. In February I got the news that Sara Lee had decided to move the Jimmy Dean offices from Memphis to Cincinnati, where they would be housed along with other companies under the corporation's umbrella. I liked the idea and felt good about it, because it would put our meat company closer to the corporation and its operations, and it wouldn't be as alienated as it had been in the past. It would be good to have Mary and JoAnn where I thought they couldn't be ignored, and I decided I'd like to spend more time in our new office there.

The next thing I knew I got a call from Sara Lee saying that some of their brass was coming to visit me at my home in Virginia, and that they wanted to talk to me. Strange, I thought. What could they possibly want to fly all the way to Richmond, Virginia, to talk to me about? I soon discovered the answer: They were indeed moving the Jimmy Dean offices, but they weren't moving Jimmy Dean. I would have no office in Cincinnati.

Well, as you can imagine, that went over like a lead balloon. I was told there wasn't enough room for me to have an office in Cincinnati, but that I could keep the one in Memphis with Mary and JoAnn. I was royally ticked off, but what are you gonna do? They didn't want me in Cincinnati for some reason and my hands were tied. With the Jimmy Dean offices there and mine still in Memphis, my team and I would most *assuredly* be alienated and left out of the company business.

In the meantime, the meat company had hired a new head of advertising, who was wanting to come in and reinvent the wheel, so now I had to do battle with them over the commercials. They didn't want me and my usual sales pitch on camera. In fact, they didn't want me on camera at all. "It's time we go in a different direction," I was told, "because let's face it, Jimmy . . . you're not going to live forever." Great. In other words, "You're gonna die anyway, Jimmy, so we ought to start thinking of the future."

The new concept they had for our commercials turned out to be an entire marketing strategy planned around the dumbest idea I'd ever heard—Breakfast never sounded so good—and they wanted me to say that line at the end. It was a ridiculous commercial, showing sausage sizzling in the pan and skillets clanging in the breeze over the stove. Now, how believable was that? I thought, if there was that much wind in somebody's kitchen, they'd better run for the cellar, 'cause there was a helluva storm brewing. I kept telling them, "Breakfast doesn't *sound*. It tastes, looks and smells, but it doesn't sound, and I'm not going to say that stupid tag line."

I've always hated slogans and gimmicks anyway, but if this new concept had been a good one I might have gone along with it. After all, if you have a slogan like "Good to the last drop," who can argue with success? After I refused to say their ridiculous little tagline, they hired some guy to try and sound like me to say it, but they must have realized how bogus it sounded because they didn't use him for long.

It wasn't long after that commercial shoot that I got another call from the powers that be at the meat company. This time they said they wanted me and Donna to come to Cincinnati to meet, greet and entertain at a dinner for some Kroger grocery store people. That was another strange thing to me: that they would want us to do that when they thought it was such an old-fashioned way of selling product. But we flew up there and did just that, although the sound system was terrible and our presentation wasn't the best. I figure that Kroger dinner was only a pretense they used to get us to come to Cincinnati, because as I would later find out they had other plans for the farmer.

The night of the Kroger dinner, the Jimmy Dean execs invited us to come to their offices the next day for a luncheon before our flight back to Richmond. It was catered, and attended by a small group of people mostly unknown to us, and was complete with speeches from the various officers of the meat company. They had some awfully nice things to say about me and *to* me and Donna, and then they presented me with a JD company logo statuette etched in glass. A very nice welcome to Cincinnati, I thought, and somewhat of a consolation for them not allowing me to have an office in their building.

I knew things were not always what they seem, but I was still surprised to find out that Sara Lee had hired a woman to be the new president of Jimmy Dean Foods. I was shocked—not because she was a woman, but because no one at the company had even mentioned the fact that they were hiring a new president.

It wasn't long after the Kroger dinner that I was paid another visit at my home in Virginia—this time from that new woman president. She and her hatchet man sat at our kitchen table and told Donna and me that the company was going in a different direction, and that they were wanting to reach the younger housewife with their TV commercials. I tried to tell them that in doing so they were forgetting about the good, true, long established customers who were used to seeing ole JD with his products, but they said my commercials were not effective anymore. They told me I was no longer needed as company spokesman, and boom—the ax finally fell.

It took me and Donna a while to figure it out, but that luncheon we attended in Cincinnati had been my retirement party—a fact that everyone in the room knew except for us. I subsequently found out that the Jimmy Dean brand would be absorbed into the corporation as simply a line of products, and that our company would be dissolved. My life as the sausage man had come to a bitter end. No more Jimmy Dean Foods, no more chairman of the board, no more company spokesman and no more office in Memphis—all gone in one fell swoop.

I don't know exactly when the decision was made, but I think it was a while back that they decided to get rid of me. I learned that a lot of people whom I had trusted were anything but true friends. They turned into liars, turncoats, cutthroats. In short, a group of people I had trusted implicitly, very simply, stabbed me in the back.

Losing money is one thing, but losing faith in people hurts me the most. I'm pretty much a handshake-deal kind of guy, and when John Bryan first negotiated with me and shook my hand, saying I would always remain involved with my company, I believed him. I guess what we shook hands on never made it into the contract. But as I've said many times, no contract is any better than the people who signed it. I certainly figured that the brass at Sara Lee would honor the commitments of their predecessors, but I was wrong.

They told me my office would be closing in December of 2003, and since Mary Moore had been with our company for twenty-five years and JoAnn for twelve years, for them it was a real blow. The powers that be soon moved the closing date up to October and then again to August, which really had Mary and JoAnn scrambling around looking for jobs.

I sold all the stock I had in Sara Lee—all except one share, because I wanted to make sure I could attend the shareholders meetings and keep the stockholders better informed. I still receive a good chunk of money from them for using my name, but the fact remains that their termination of my contract has been demeaning and embarrassing. And now when people come up to me on the street and say, "I use your product all the time, Jimmy," it hurts me because I'm not associated or affiliated with it and I have no control over its quality.

So I would say to anyone in business not to trust verbal agreements and handshakes. They're no good anymore, so make sure you have a sound legal document with all the I's dotted and T's crossed. It's a cold, hard world out there in corporate America. I'm truly sorry, but that's the way it is.

❧ PART THREE ❧

FAMILY MATTERS

19

HOME AND FAMILY: PART ONE

I **TALKED A** lot about Mom in the beginning of this book, but I thought I'd share a little bit more about this most remarkable lady, along with some of my other kinfolks.

Like a lot of folks of her generation, Mom never strayed from her beginnings. She was born and raised near Waco, Texas, and grew up to be an unpretentious soul and a loyal member of the Baptist church. After I had accumulated a little fame and fortune and could afford to move her to a nicer part of town, Mom chose to stay in the poor little community of Seth Ward near Plainview. All of her friends were there and she was comfortable living among the mobile homes and housing projects where she'd moved thirty years earlier. And even though I had the means to buy her a new home, I had to be content with building her a new brick ranch on the same site as our old white frame house.

It was in my mom's kitchen that I learned many lessons when I was a kid, most of which were emphasized with a switch. Then, when I was older, it was also where she'd teach me one of life's most profound lessons: "It's nice to be important, but it's more important to be nice."

While visiting Mom at home one particular time, I could tell she had something on her mind, and I knew Ruth Dean well enough to know that I was going to hear about it. I'd had the one hit record on the country charts with "Bummin' Around" in 1953, and at the time I was hosting the morning variety show on CBS-TV. That wasn't a bad lick, though in most parts of the world it still didn't qualify me as being a big shot, but in Plainview, Texas, I was definitely "tall hog at the trough."

Obviously concerned about me getting a "big head," Mom said, "Jimmy, now that you're on that television and you're doing what you do, there's gonna be a lot of people looking at you and some of them might wanta be like you, so be nice." I've carried that with me ever since and have always thought it was great advice for anyone . . . *It makes no difference who you are or what you do, somebody may want to be like you, so be nice.*

Sometimes I've remembered Mom's advice and sometimes I've forgotten it, but I wish I had remembered it all along. There were times however, when it just wasn't possible to be nice, especially when I'd get mixed up with some of those television and recording officials. They just didn't understand "nice." The only way to deal with some of them was to be rude, crude and loud right along with them, because that's usually all they understood.

Mom certainly was a role model for me. She knew what was important in life and didn't hesitate to remind me. She just wanted the best for me, and I just wanted to do her proud.

In all my years in show business, the greatest reward I ever received was during a visit to Plainview sometime in the late fifties. One morning while I was at Mom's, the principal of the new Plainview High School called to ask her if I would come over and speak at an assembly later that day. I told her, "No way, I'm not going. They didn't want me when I wore bib overalls and they're not going to get me now." A little later on, the principal called back and persisted, and this time Mom asked me to go, with a sense of urgency I'd never heard from her before. I could tell it was important to her that I do it, so I agreed.

That afternoon, we got into the little Ford I'd bought her and drove over to the school for their special assembly, but this time instead of wearing brogan shoes, a homemade shirt and bib overalls, I was wearing a tailor-made suit, a nice shirt and tie, and shiny cowboy boots.

After my introduction, I walked out onto that stage and right into a standing ovation. Those kids were on their feet applauding and admiring me, but all I could think about was the times I'd been teased and taunted about the clothes I wore when I was a student. Then suddenly, like waking from a dream, there we were. It seemed like just the two of us in that big auditorium, with me up on stage and Mom seated in the first row positively beaming at the reception I was getting. In a matter of seconds I saw all the years of hurt and pain she'd held inside washed away and healed. She didn't speak, but she didn't have to. I could read her face like a book, as if she was saying, "Look at him; he's mine. And he's as good as anyone else."

The satisfaction on Mom's face was the greatest reward I've ever received, and I have to tell you, with all the hit records and awards that have been bestowed upon me, nothing even comes close to the feeling I had with my mama that day in that high school auditorium.

Mom was indeed a proud, tough and tenacious woman, and I really don't know how she dealt with all those years of adversity when I was a boy. It was especially hard on her when my old man was screwing around on her and leaving her for weeks on end. When he finally left us, Mom never remarried, she simply dedicated herself to raising my brother Don and me, working long, hard hours cutting people's hair for fifteen cents a head to support us.

Even though she didn't have to, Mom was still working well into her sixties, cutting hair three days a week. I tried to persuade her to stop, although I didn't insist too hard because I remembered my grand-daddy passing away soon after he'd retired. Besides, I think she need-ed something to do, and she *did* enjoy chatting with her customers.

It was Mom's family that supplied me with some of my fondest childhood memories, as they were all I really had when I was grow-ing up. My favorite aunt was Versie, possibly the best cook of all the Taylors and the one who would always stick up for me when I got into trouble. They just don't make 'em much like her anymore. There was also Aunt Ruby, who was married to my uncle Bob, and I guess everybody's got one like her—she was the ultra religious one in the family with the "holier than thou" attitude. And then there was my aunt Eva, a spinster lady who was a piece of work. I liked Eva a lot. She was known to have said the only thing she didn't like about having "Miss" on her tombstone was that she didn't miss a thing. And it was true. Aunt Eva definitely lived life to the fullest and did everything she wanted to do—and maybe several times. I can't think of her without remembering the story about the old lady who was asked if she'd ever been bedridden, to which she replied, "Lord yes . . . and a couple of times in a buggy!"

As I mentioned in my first chapter, my mom's dad, Papa Taylor, was the real father figure in my life, and as far as I'm concerned no finer man ever walked this earth. He was the most successful man I ever knew, but not by most people's standards. Papa probably never made more than ten thousand dollars a year in his life, but he had treasures that no amount of money could buy. He was the best farmer in Swisher County—his rows were straighter, his house was whiter and his barn was redder than anybody else's. He lived by the Farmer's Almanac and was endowed with more plain old common horse sense than anybody I've ever known in my life.

Papa also had a great relationship with The Man Upstairs. It gave him an inner peace like I'd never seen in anyone else, and if you want to talk wealth and success, well to me *that's it*. He seemed to have a direct line to God, and to hear Papa pray would always give me chill bumps.

One time in particular, I remember him sitting on the back porch with his dog Tige (short for Tiger), an ugly old bulldog with a hole in his tongue that a tooth stuck through when he panted. Papa Taylor's crops were heavy on his mind, and as I overheard him talking to God, he was explaining that there had just been too much rain and that it was too wet to get a combine out in the field to harvest. Papa was saying, "Now, listen, Lord, I've done all I can do, and if I don't get a combine in that field, I'm gonna lose all that wheat, so I need Your help Lord." As he sat there with his pocketknife digging the mud out of the bottom of his boots, Papa talked to the Lord just like He was you or me.

Not only was Papa a God-fearing man, but I remember Mom telling me a story once about how he could also be tough as nails. It seemed one time he had carried a wagonload of cotton to the gin that

My mother, Ruth Taylor Dean

At home with Mom at the piano

Papa and Ludie Taylor

was twenty miles away, and the gin's elevator had dropped and cut off two of his toes. The doctor just wanted to bandage up his foot and give him something for pain, but papa Taylor would hear nothing of it. He dumped those bloody toes from his boot out on the table and said, "No, sir, you just sew them back on!" So that's what the doctor did—with no anesthetic, no nothing, he literally sewed Papa's toes back on. Mom said they turned every color in the rainbow and then some, and everyone was sure he would lose them, but he didn't. Now, that's tough!

Papa Taylor and my grandma Ludie were an odd-looking couple, since she was much taller than him, and although they weren't very affectionate or demonstrative toward each other, their relationship was as solid as a rock. After all, they *did* raise nine good, healthy kids. And even though he only had a fourth-grade education, Papa Taylor was a brilliant man, and I always listened to what he had to say. That's probably why we were so close. I loved to sit and listen to him talk. Even his own children, my aunts and uncles would say to me, "I wish Papa loved us the way he loves you." My brother Don was always everyone else's favorite, but not to Papa. I was *his* fair-haired boy.

Papa Taylor's wisdom still guides me to this day, and one of the best pieces of advice he ever gave me was "Be yourself, boy, 'cause if people don't like you as you are, they're not going to like you as somebody you're trying to be." Papa was the wisest man I ever knew.

———•———

I learned a lot about life from my papa Taylor, but I guess it was from my real father that I learned the lesson of forgiveness. For a lot of years I carried around the pain of resentment I had toward him for leaving us when we were kids, along with the embarrassment of having to live down his bad name. I felt the poverty he'd left us in was unforgivable, and the folks he had borrowed money from and never paid back would never let me forget it.

It was said my father could charm people out of money who had never loaned a dime. I remember very well, when I was about eleven or twelve, a man who had obviously been bilked by my dad, sticking an angry finger in my face and saying, "You'll never amount to anything, because you're G. O. Dean's kid!" Such a sweetheart, that guy.

I rarely saw or heard from my dad through the years, but then after a silence of seventeen years he called me right out of the blue asking me for money to finance some crazy scheme of his. He called a few more times with various requests, but the conversations were always quick and brief—with a flat *no* from me. I guess he must have realized how bitter I was, because after a while he just gave up and stopped calling.

The next time I heard from my dad he was on his deathbed, and not being aware of it, I naturally bristled at hearing him on the phone. But this time, somehow his voice sounded different, because there was an urgency I'd never heard before. Then the words I thought I'd never hear came. "Jimmy," he said, "I haven't been much of a father and I'm sorry. Please, will you forgive me?" He paused and said, "I have cancer . . . My time is nearly all gone now."

It seemed like a lifetime before I could say anything, probably because my own life was flashing before my eyes, as I recalled every hardship he had left us. I suddenly felt small and tongue-tied, not knowing what to say to a man who was dying, the father I hardly knew. I knew I had to resolve a lot of years of resentment and anger and do it quickly.

It was at that moment that God may have given me a revelation, because as I pondered my father's words, I realized how futile and senseless it was to judge another. My father had told me he had made peace with the Lord, so I thought, *If the Lord has forgiven him, then who am I?* When I finally spoke and gave him my forgiveness, he said, "Thank you for that, Jimmy," and a few days later he was gone.

———•———

After suffering a stroke in 1978, my mother lived in a nursing home for the last few years of her life, since round-the-clock nursing care for her at home just wasn't available. During my many visits to the Heritage Home, it would break my heart to see her sitting in that wheelchair, especially when she'd ask, "Jimmy, when can I go home?" It was in a hospital in Plainview that Mom passed away at the age of eighty-five, on the first day of February in 1982.

The guilt feelings I've had since then have stayed with me, as I honestly do think I was partially responsible for her passing. I had

This is the last picture taken with Mom

stopped her from working completely when I told her, "You've worked hard enough for us, and now you're not going to have to do it anymore." Mom used to love to work in the yard, tending her flowers and pruning her rosebushes, and then I hired somebody to do it all, installing an irrigation system too. I only wanted to help, but I didn't realize it was probably good exercise for her, and when she didn't have anything to do, she simply became a couch potato.

There were so many people expected at Mom's funeral that instead of having her services at her beloved Seth Ward Baptist Church, they had to be held at the big downtown sanctuary of the First Baptist Church in Plainview. My brother Don and I both attended the service with our families, but we didn't sit together or even speak to each other since we were still estranged from the dispute over the sausage company.

Since I was paying for the entire funeral, I requested a short service, 'cause when those good old moss-backed Baptist preachers in West Texas get a funeral, they can go on and on, especially if they've got a big audience. And if the service is for someone with a little notoriety, well, look out—it can get longer, louder and even *more* dramatic.

I must say that losing my mother was the worst thing that has ever happened to me, and I still miss her every day that goes by. She was

20

HOME AND FAMILY: PART TWO

I **PROMISED I'D** tell you more about marrying Sue and having my children, so here goes. I have three children—two sons and a daughter. They're all grown now, with lives of their own, and I must say they've turned out to be some pretty fine folks. But before I get too far into the subject, I should probably start at the beginning—with my marriage to their mother, Sue.

Back in the late forties, when my military service took me from my home in West Texas to Washington, DC, my time was pretty much occupied with daily duties and playing music in the clubs at night. And though I was glad to get away from the hard life back home, I naturally missed my mom and family. I had my Air Force buddies to pal around with, but there was certainly one thing missing, and that was the company of a steady girlfriend. Most of the few dates I'd had were girls who would just hang out wherever I was playing music, having to watch me work at night.

It was while I was working with Dub Howington and his band that we were playing at one of the nicer places in town, the 400 Club. At the time we were backing up a singer named Dave Denny, who had done pretty well for himself, having landed a recording contract with RCA Records.

While on stage one night, I caught the glance of two girls in the club who were obviously coeds. They had come in carrying their roller skates with them, evidently killing time on their way to a skating party. Doing my duty as an entertainer, I casually stopped by their table during one of our breaks to make sure they were enjoying the music. The blonde was especially pretty, and I turned on the old charm a bit and asked her for her phone number so I could call and ask her for a date. Well, she must have liked me too, because not only did she give me her phone number, but we made a date right then and there. She told me that she lived in Takoma Park, Maryland, and I told her what day and time I'd pick her up.

The only problem with the date we made that night was that Mary Sue Wittauer was waiting patiently at the appointed day and hour, and Jimmy Ray Dean was nowhere to be found. I really can't remember what came up or what happened that evening . . . I just forgot all about it, and I lost her phone number to boot. *Way to go, Dean.* When I finally remembered our date, I felt like a big lug on a small wheel, and I simply wrote the whole thing off as a bad experience.

The next time I saw Sue was about a year later at the Dixie Pig, and a lot of things had changed by then. I had left the service and was playing music with the Texas Wildcats, and one night I looked down from the stage and spotted her sitting at a table with a nicely dressed gentleman, obviously her date. Sue was still as pretty as ever, and when she recognized me, she even managed to give me a little smile.

Thinking all was not lost with her, I moseyed over to their table during a break and struck up a conversation. I found out Sue's date was a country music fan who had wanted to check us out after hearing us advertised on the radio as the regular band at the club. Then finally the guy went to the bathroom and I had a chance to talk to her, and I did my best to apologize and say how sorry I was about standing her up.

Trying to cover fourteen months' time in less than a minute wasn't easy, so during the fastest conversation in history Sue told me she was still in college taking night classes, but had gotten a job working days as a secretary for the government. Then when I asked her for another date, she amazingly said *yes*. Again I asked her for her phone number, and she handed it to me just as her date was on his way back to the table.

When I called Sue the next day, she sounded pretty surprised. I guess because I hadn't lost her phone number again. With her schedule being so crazy, it wasn't easy for her to find an open night for a date with me, but the two of us finally settled on an evening.

Because I was an entertainer and not much for roller rinks or movie theaters, my first date with Sue was at the best place I knew to take her—the Dixie Pig. With her having to be satisfied with a barbecue sandwich and three sets of the Texas Wildcats, it's a wonder she would ever want to marry me, but six months later, on July 11, 1950, Mary Sue Wittauer said yes to becoming Mrs. Jimmy Dean.

The ceremony was held at the Presbyterian Church in Takoma Park, Maryland, with mostly her family in attendance since all of my relatives were so far away in Texas. Mom did make the trip, though, and I had several of my band members and musician buddies there.

Of course, in retrospect, it seems Sue and I were both too terribly young to be getting married. I was only twenty-one and Sue was twenty, but you couldn't tell us anything. I was in love, or at least I *thought* I was. I think I was more *impressed* with Sue than anything. Not only was she pretty and statuesque, but she was also college educated. I'd never even gone out with anyone who was in college before, and I had such admiration for someone with an education. It was especially flattering that she'd ever want anything to do with *me*, Mr. Ninth Grade.

In the beginning, we lived in a cramped, eighty-five-dollar-a-month one-bedroom apartment out in Seat Pleasant, Maryland. We struggled to get ahead, and I remember looking like a ghost on our wedding day after working two full-time jobs just to buy furniture for our new home. We furnished it piece by piece, but after a while, with both of us working, we were doing all right. In fact, we even managed to build a little savings account toward a down payment on a house.

It wasn't long before we would need the extra living space; just a short time after we were married, Sue discovered she was pregnant with our first child. The two of us had never discussed having children, but I remember we were both pretty excited about the news.

After finding out she was pregnant, Sue quit her job with the government and stayed home, keeping house and organizing my work schedule. She'd keep the calendar and the payroll, and basically handle the details of the music playing jobs that I'd book for the band.

On May 26, 1951, Sue gave birth to our first son, Garry Taylor Dean. The day he was born, I remember a friend of mine who was with me at the hospital said all I did was walk around with a dazed look, saying, "How about that? How *about* that?" When it came time to name him, I didn't want a "junior," and I liked the name Garry, as in my friend Garry Moore, the TV personality, so we spelled it the same way and gave him Mom's maiden name of Taylor for a middle name.

After Garry was born, Sue went back to work at the National Cotton Council to help pay the bills. We had to put off getting a home because our old clunker of a car had given out, and now we had the expense of having to buy a new car as well as another mouth to feed.

Having a child was a new experience and it totally changed our lives, but we had our day pretty much down to a science. At 6 A.M. Sue would crawl out of bed, change and feed the baby and then leave him in his playpen before leaving for work. Being a light sleeper, I would wake up if he made a peep, or whenever he would hurl his baby bottle across the linoleum floor. The little darlin' had a surefire way of getting me up in time for his next feeding.

While I was off at rehearsal in the afternoon, Sue's sister was usually around to watch Garry, but when she couldn't make it, I'd just pack him up and take him along. Jostling him around to studios and television stations may have taken its toll with colds and ear infections, but we had some good quality time together. I learned a lot about being a father in those days, and I loved being with my infant son.

When Sue would get home at around seven in the evening, we'd have about an hour to spend together with Garry, and then it was off to my job. Getting to the nightclubs from Seat Pleasant wasn't such a big deal for me, but the daily commute was murder for Sue. I was glad when we could finally pay off the loan on the new car so she could quit her job and stay home.

Sue and me on our
wedding day, July 1950

At home with Connie
and Garry, about 1957

Fatherhood didn't come so naturally for me at first. I remember driving our old two-door Plymouth one day with Garry in his car seat that was strapped safely to the front passenger seat of the car . . . or so I thought. Driving along, I had to slam the breaks on for some reason, and when I did, the front seat flung forward, catapulting Garry out of his car seat and into the floorboard of the car. Poor kid . . . he still has the scar on his forehead . . . but I think he cried harder that day not because he was hurt, but because he knew he was stuck with me for a father.

As Garry grew older, he was a real joy as a child. He did whatever he could to try to please me, like being my "gopher" if I wanted help when I was barbecuing. We enjoyed fishing and boating together, and he was especially wild for watching bull-riding, joining me on the road at rodeo shows when school was out. Garry wasn't any trouble at all as a little boy, but as a teenager later on that would change.

A few short years after Garry was born, Sue once again discovered she was pregnant. On March 29, 1954, at the Seventh Day Adventist Hospital in Takoma Park, Maryland, our daughter Connie Elizabeth Dean was born. We named her after my boss Connie B. Gay and his secretary Elizabeth Jane Trimner, although Sue maintains we chose Elizabeth because Elizabeth Taylor was her favorite actress.

Connie was truly the apple of my eye. She was a sweet baby and an affectionate child, and was most definitely "daddy's girl" right from the start. She was a stubborn little thing too. Connie was going to do what *she* wanted to do when *she* wanted to do it. She always got her butt spanked when she did wrong, though, but I remember this one time not having the heart to punish her. It was when we had a retired Navy guy as a neighbor, whose kids had all the vernacular of a sailor, and Connie played with them regularly. As she and I were saying her prayers in her bedroom one night, right in the middle of *"Now I lay me down to sleep, I pray the Lord my soul to keep . . . ,"* I heard this little voice say, "s——t!" for no obvious reason. I just froze. I really didn't know what to do, although I figured she probably didn't know what it meant. She was only about three years old at the time, so I just let it go and went on with the prayer.

Connie was always a pretty girl; in fact, she modeled fashions for several publications when she was about five years old. It was when she was that age that I was inspired to cowrite a song with my buddy Larry Marks called "To A Sleeping Beauty," and when I recorded it, I dedicated it to Connie.

To a Sleeping Beauty

Dear Daughter,

I tiptoed into your room tonight and I looked down at you smiling in your sleep

You were so lovely my heart nearly broke and I thought how very much like Sleeping Beauty a little girl is

When I tuck you in at night, I never know how old you're gonna be when you awake.

One evening you'll run in and jump up in your Dad's lap and throw your arms around his neck

The next morning you might be too grown up for that sort of thing.

You're so quickly approaching the awkward age . . . too young to drive the car, and yet too old to be carried into the house half-asleep on Daddy's shoulder

I have a secret that I've never told you, Sleeping Beauty . . . you are going on a very exciting trip . . .

You're going to travel from yesterday all the way to tomorrow.

It'll be a rapid journey . . . you'll travel light, leaving behind you measles, mumps, freckles, bumps, bubble gum and me.

I promise not to feel too hurt when you discover the world is a great deal more exciting than your ol' Dad's lap.

Yesterday you were blue-jeaned and pigtailed, the neighborhood's best tree climber

Tomorrow you'll be blue-organdied and ponytailed.

You'll view the world from a loftier perch—a pair of high-heeled shoes.

Yesterday you could mend a doll's broken leg with a hug,

Tomorrow you'll be able to break a young man's heart with a kiss.

Yesterday you could get lost one aisle away from me in a supermarket,

Now I have to worry about losing you down another aisle to some
   strange young man.
You see, Hon, just at the point your growing pains stop, that's
   where mine begin.
Tomorrow you'll lay aside your jump rope, tie up lines for hours,
And that little boy that used to push you in the mud,
He'll fight to sit out a dance with you.
I can't expect you to live in a dollhouse forever
Sooner or later a butterfly sheds its cocoon and the smallest bird
   must try its wings.
But when you grow up, out of my arms, and finally get too big for
   your Daddy's shirts,
I'll still recall how you scattered dust and dolls through every room
   of the house, but you shed sunshine too.
The dust is settled, your Mom has picked up all the dolls, but the
   sunshine will always remain in the corners of our hearts.
So, here I am talking to you in your sleep, because if you saw this
   look on my face you'd laugh,
And if I tried to speak with this lump in my throat I'd cry.
Yes, I looked at you tonight and you were a Sleeping Beauty, so I
   tiptoed over and kissed you.
You didn't wake up, I knew you wouldn't.
According to the legend only the handsome prince can open your
   eyes, and me, I'm just the father of the future bride.
So you sleep on, pretty thing . . . tomorrow when you awake, you'll
   be a young lady
And you won't even realize if you've changed courses in the middle
   of a dream.
You might notice a little difference in me though, I'll look a little
   different somehow—a little older, a little sadder, but a whole lot
   richer.
Tonight I kissed a princess, and I felt like a king.

Goodnight, Connie.

My recording of "To a Sleeping Beauty" enjoyed considerable success, and through the years many a father and daughter have told me how it touched them. It always used to upset Connie when she was little, though, and she would come to me saying, "I'm never gonna leave you, Daddy, I'm never gonna leave you!" She would cry, and being the coldhearted, unemotional cad that I am, so would I.

———•———

When Connie was small, we moved into our first home in Arlington, Virginia, which we purchased for a little less than twenty thousand dollars. I remember feeling rather smug going to buy it with our thirty-five-hundred-dollar down payment in my pocket. I thought it was all the money in the world.

And then, in the fall of 1958, my family and I made the move north from Arlington, Virginia, to a big rented house on a two-acre estate near Greenwich, Connecticut. There was still some country up there; the kids needed country, and so did Sue and I. Even though at the time I thought the monthly rent of three hundred plus dollars was outrageous, the four of us stayed there for a year while looking for a house to buy.

The house we finally bought in suburban New Jersey was closer to New York City, in a town called Tenafly, just across the George Washington Bridge. It was a great place, with a really nice neighborhood. Our ranch-style home had five bedrooms and three baths, with a decor I can only describe as early mishmash, with some antiques and a touch of Williamsburg.

Just before we moved to Tenafly, much to our surprise Sue found herself pregnant again. On April 22, 1960, at Columbia Presbyterian Hospital in New York City, she gave birth to our second son, Robert Ray Dean. Not being familiar with the city, I found driving Sue to the hospital a nerve-racking experience. I remember getting lost and turning up one-way streets the wrong way trying to get her there, but we made it.

Robert was a really sweet and affectionate child and an all-around great kid. He would hug and kiss you even when he was just waking up—unlike his sister, who was fussy first thing in the morning. Along with having a good disposition, Robert had an extra sharp mind and a marvelously outgoing personality. He was a real people person, and they loved him to death.

Sometimes you see children who are just too smart for their years, and Robert was one of them. It's scary when you realize that your kid is able to outsmart you, and I knew I was in trouble one day when Robert was about eleven years old. During a meal, when he'd piled his plate up with food for a second time, I told him, "Now, you've got to eat every bite on your plate, because there are children starving in India." He just looked at me and said, "Name one!" And you know, it's hard to punish a kid when you're laughing.

Yachting became one of my family's favorite pastimes since all of my kids were real boat nuts and loved everything to do around the water. We had many great times on our boat, spending about five weeks on it for our vacation every summer, and then whatever time we could in between—about three months a year altogether.

I've run into a few celebrities in boating over the years, and at the risk of sounding like a name dropper, I thought you might find some of their stories interesting. Like the time we were cruising along off the coast of Martha's Vineyard, when we got a distress call from a boat that had run up on a sandbar. When they signaled us for help, we naturally answered the call, and as we got to them we discovered that the famous actor James Cagney had run his sailboat aground. I don't know if he knew me, but I certainly knew who he was. We pulled him off of the sandbar and got him on his way, and I was more than glad to be of assistance to such a show biz legend.

I've also run into people like Geraldo Rivera, Walter Cronkite and Barbara Mandrell on their boats, and there was one encounter with a particular celebrity I'll never forget. Ocean Reef is a beautiful and exclusive private resort on Key Largo in Florida that I belonged to for many years, and every winter my family and I would spend at least a week there on our boat. One year when we were there, it was all the "buzz" that Jackie Onassis was on the island, and my wife Sue—along with every other woman there—was absolutely gaga and dying to meet her.

Sometimes when you're not even trying, opportunities present themselves to you in the most unexpected ways. Since I cook fish better than anybody, my kids had asked me to cook fish for them that weekend, so I told them, "Okay, but I'm not gonna cook fish from the grocery store; we'll cook some that we catch." The next

With Connie, Robert, Garry and friend at the circus in Madison Square Garden

morning, my son Robert and I prepared to go out on a boat we'd chartered for the fishing trip, and as we got there I realized we'd left our cooler of drinks back on our boat, so I told Robert to take the golf cart and go back and get it.

As I stood there waiting for Robert, I happened to notice a woman pulling a lawn chair out of the trunk of an old Plymouth, and then I realized it was *her*. Jackie Onassis was obviously getting ready for a sail. I knew how she felt about her privacy, so I walked over to her and said, "I certainly don't want to intrude on your privacy, but I knew your late husband and had never met you. I wanted to introduce myself, I'm Jimmy Dean." She looked at me rather intently for a moment and said, "Are you the singer Jimmy Dean?" Well, I was flattered to beat all and replied, "Yes, I am." " 'P.T. 109' Jimmy Dean?" she asked, referring to the song I'd recorded about JFK. When I said yes, she yelled to her daughter, Caroline, who was about fourteen at the time, and said, "Caroline, come here. Do you know who this is?" We were introduced, and then Jackie told her, "Go to the boat and get John, and bring him here so he can meet Mr. Dean." After John came over, I stood there chewing the fat with them for quite a while, and had a real nice conversation. They took off before Robert got back, and he sure was disappointed about missing the opportunity to meet them. But no one was more disappointed than Sue. She peppered me with a hundred questions: "What did she look like?" "What was she wearing?" I didn't know anything about that, but I was delighted by how polite and friendly Jackie O. really was.

Discipline wasn't necessarily my long suit as a parent, and I usually left that up to Sue. We tried to teach the kids about earning money through household chores at home and on our boat, but it wasn't easy trying to teach them the value of a dollar. I can remember how I wanted things as a kid when there wasn't money for me to have them, and when you've got a buck or two, you want your kids to have things you didn't have. One of the hardest things I had to do was say no, and though it didn't hurt me to want for things when I was a kid, and probably did me some good, it was still hard for me to refuse my children.

Another problem I had, which I'm sure other entertainers have, was trying to convince my kids that they were no different from others. People have a tendency to treat entertainers' children differently, giving them preferential treatment and making them feel more special than others. I would try to explain to them that my celebrity status made me no better than the next guy, that one man may be a businessman, a plumber, a taxi driver or a doctor, but he's doing that job because it's what he does better than anything. I tried to make them understand that I was an entertainer because it was what I did best, and the way I supported my family didn't make my children any better or worse than other folks.

As a matter of fact, most of our neighbors and closest friends were ordinary people; they were schoolteachers, doctors, lawyers and not other entertainers as a rule. Living in suburbia wasn't a bad environment for my children, although I would have preferred a slower way of life for them in the country somewhere. As they got older, life got more complicated, as it does for most kids. Garry was into everything. He partied a lot as a teenager, and for a while I thought he wasn't going to settle down or amount to anything. But I look at him now and marvel at what a fine man he is.

As he matured, Garry had no ambitions for show business—in fact, none of my kids did. He played the drums well and has always had a good singing voice, but you can't get him to sing—too bashful, I guess. And though Garry didn't take after me professionally, people say he's my spittin' image. They say that about both of my sons; complete strangers have approached them all their lives and asked if they were related to me.

I look at Garry now with great pride, realizing how extremely successful he's become with his La Salsa Restaurant franchise in Fairfield, Connecticut. We call each other regularly, always ending our conversations with "I love you," and he'll occasionally come to visit me in Virginia. I'm grateful that Garry and I are closer now than we've ever been.

As she's gotten older, Connie has also grown to be one of my best friends, although we've always been close. I remember making such wonderful memories with her when she was a kid. She was about twelve or thirteen when we'd sit on the dock at Captain's Marina in

Montauk, New York, eating clams we'd dug—she with a Coke and me with a beer, just the two of us. It was a very special time for me, and one of the sweetest times I can ever remember with her.

Then there was the time I taught her how to water-ski. The first time she was only about eleven and I was pretty hard on her. She couldn't get the hang of it and she cried, so we quit. Then a couple of years later she bugged me to teach her again. So when we went out on the boat that morning, I told her we weren't going in until she learned. Determination took over as she buckled down and soon got up on the skis, and when she did, I'd never seen a wider grin. She was elated and really proud of herself, and to this day I don't know anyone who enjoyed water-skiing more than Connie.

Connie was a typical teenager. She used to love it when I'd pick her up from school on my motorcycle or in my '65 Corvette, and I guess she must have thought I was a pretty cool dad. She also liked for me to braid her hair, or even cut it when she wore it long and straight during those "flower child" days. She had her share of boyfriends and more than a few marriage proposals, and I remember having to console her after one particularly nasty breakup in the tenth grade.

When Connie was eighteen, she decided she wanted to leave home and get her own apartment. She said she wanted a change of scenery, so she and a roommate moved all the way to Florida. Naturally I was a little upset and was inspired to write another poem about her, though it was never recorded.

Connie Left Home Today

Connie left home last Friday, no she wasn't mad
As a matter of fact her last words to me were "I'm really gonna miss you, Dad."
Oh, I thought I handled it pretty well, we kissed and said good-bye
But as I stared at the gloom of her empty room I suddenly started to cry.
Well, that danged fish tank was finally gone and that chirping, squawking bird
And that loud and lousy stereo, the worst I ever heard

But through all this it occurred to me very little did I complain
So I wondered how she could leave me now, the girl had to be
   insane.
Good God knows she had it made, no phone no electric bill
Someone right there to love and care if she ever got ill.
So, Saturday night I sat down to analyze my plight
And I must admit my quandary took me late into the night
Then I recalled many years ago when a young man sat alone
And said, "One way or another, fellow, you're gonna make it on
   your own."
So at three A.M. *I sat back no longer hurt or sad*
I thought, what I saw in my leaving lady was a touch of her dear
   old Dad.
So Connie, your room's all redone now, the furniture's all shiny and
   new
But wherever you go I just want you to know that that room still
   belongs to you.

Thank goodness Florida only lasted about six months, and then Connie got homesick and came back home to live with her mother and me. She went to school and trained to be a medical assistant, before working in several prominent doctors' offices in New York City, and then worked as a secretary where she met her future husband. After a courtship of about a year and a half Connie married Walter Taylor in a huge church wedding in New York City, and had their daughter Caroline three years later, in 1990.

Though she never had any show biz aspirations, Connie's always had a little of her father's "ham" in her. She's ended up on television on more than one occasion: once with the family on my ABC television show, and then in 1990 she and Robert were on the *Regis and Kathie Lee* show, displaying some Elvis memorabilia I had given them.

One afternoon Connie called me and told me to be sure and watch the *Geraldo* show later that day. It seemed that when Jackie Onassis's children decided to auction off some of her possessions at Sotheby's auction house in New York following her death, Connie somehow ended up with tickets to the auction. One of the items on the auction list just happened to be a lot of six 45RPM records called

My daughter Connie
and me, 2001

With my two sons,
Garry (left) and Robert

"P.T. 109" by Jimmy Dean. Connie bid on them and won, and when the producers of *Geraldo* found out she had bought her own father's records at auction for thirty-four hundred dollars, they thought it was a good story. When I tuned in, there she was sitting on a set being interviewed by Geraldo, and doing a darn good job too, really cool and calm.

As Connie gets older, I think she remembers more fondly the things she used to do with her dad. She'll call me sometimes and say, "Dad, something just reminded me of the time we did [whatever], and I just wanted to tell you how much that means to me and how grateful I am that you're my dad." She's one of the very brightest spots in my world, and I wish every father a daughter like Connie.

Since he's grown up, my son Robert has also done quite well for himself, with his own video production company, which actually came about by accident. I had given him the money to start a cellular phone business back in the early nineties, but as a hobby he enjoyed videotaping and production. One day he got a phone call from someone asking him to videotape a wedding, and though Robert had never done it before, he told them he thought he could. It turned out he did such a good job taping the wedding, adding music and editing the tape, that he began to get more and more calls. Robert eventually gave up the cellular phone business, and now his video company with three camera crews is in constant demand in the Dumont, New Jersey, area, where he lives with his wife, Jenn, and daughter, Brianna.

I would be remiss if I didn't mention another "adopted" member of our family. It was about 1965 that we hired a beautiful black lady named Catherine Smith as our housekeeper. Catherine was in her mid-thirties when she came to work for us five days a week, though we really didn't consider her to be an employee, but rather one of the family. I always thought the world of her, and her husband, Frank, too, a wonderful guy and another good soul.

One thing I remember about Catherine was that she made the best peach cobbler in the world—hot and bubblin', with butter floatin' on top, and served with a scoop of vanilla ice cream. It was so good it would make your tongue knock your eyetooth out. I'll also never forget the time I wanted to help Catherine buy a house and Sue hit the roof. All I wanted to do was cosign a loan for her, but Sue said, "What if she walks out and doesn't make her payments? Then we'll be stuck!" Well, I went ahead and did it anyhow, and now Catherine owns her own home. She never missed one payment and has been one of the most trustworthy and loyal people I've ever known. Catherine and I still keep in touch, and I was delighted when she came to visit me a few years ago at my home in Virginia.

Sue and I not only disagreed on helping Catherine, but we didn't see eye to eye on a lot of other things as well. When we were first married I thought our relationship was good, but in retrospect it really wasn't. After almost forty years of marriage Sue and I divorced in 1990. I think the only reason we lasted so long was that it's my nature to not let anything fail, and I was afraid of looking like a failure to other people. It took me a long time to learn that no matter how hard you try, some things just aren't *supposed* to work.

Actually, I think the main problem with Sue and me was that we were really nothing alike to begin with. We're two very different people, with completely different tastes. She loved living in the suburbs, and I always wanted to live on a farm out in the country somewhere. I was a country boy and she was more of a city girl, and as they say, oil and water just don't mix.

Family means a lot to me, though, and I wouldn't take anything for the experiences I've had. I'm sure there's a reason for everything in this life. A reason why I had to grow up without a father—to make me a stronger person perhaps. Or why Sue and I were together all those years without very much in common, though being blessed with three great kids makes me a richer and happier person, and that's certainly reason enough.

~ 21 ~

MY LADY
AND THE BLUFF

WELL, I FINALLY get to tell you about the love of my life, my wife and partner, Donna Meade Dean. It was in June of 1989 that I decided to pay my old friend Ralph Emery a visit on his television show in Nashville, Tennessee. *Nashville Now* was a popular variety and talk show—sort of *The Tonight Show* of country music—and Ralph was the host of the Monday-through-Friday show on the now defunct Nashville Network on cable TV. I had appeared there many times while visiting Nashville, but little did I know that this particular show would change my life forever.

The main reason I booked Ralph's show was to visit with him. I'd do my thing on the show, and then while someone else was performing, we'd chew the fat and have a chance to catch up. When Ralph introduced me that night, I think I sang a number and then joined him for the usual interview in the "hot seat" at his desk. After our on air chat, Ralph introduced the next act and the two of us got down to our real visit.

As a rule, I never paid any attention to the other acts performing on the show, but then I heard *that voice,* and when I looked up at the TV monitor in front of us, I saw her. I said to Ralph, "Whoooo the hell is *that*?" He said, "Well, that's a girl who sings here in town. Her name is Donna Meade." When she finished her number, Ralph introduced us as Donna came over to join him and me on the panel for her interview. She and I didn't have much interaction, but when the show was over, I remember hugging her on the set and telling her how much I liked her singing.

It wasn't long afterward that I wrote Donna a fan letter saying how much I enjoyed meeting her, and that if she was ever touring through Dallas to let me know so I could catch her show. Finally, after several months, I received a reply from her. I had mailed my letter to her record company Mercury-Polygram in Nashville, but they had misplaced it and Donna didn't receive the letter until three months after I wrote it. She wrote back to me apologizing for the delay and told me she wasn't touring at all, but performing six nights a week in a nightclub in Nashville called the Bullpen Lounge. She seemed genuinely delighted to hear from me, though, and invited me to come see her perform the next time I was in Nashville.

Before she recorded for Mercury-Polygram, Donna had gotten her start performing in nightclubs and was the headliner in the Bullpen Lounge for almost nine years. The Bullpen was the most popular nightspot in Nashville back then. Celebrities from every facet of show business flocked there. Most any night you could see country music stars or Hollywood actors, as well as people like G. Gordon Liddy, the governor of Tennessee or the pool-playing legend Minnesota Fats. I had been there for dinner and a show before, but I made it my business to go there for a whole 'nuther reason in December of 1989.

When I arrived in the lounge to watch Donna's show that night, I was escorted to the front of the stage and seated in a VIP booth by the assistant manager, Tex Monahan. I guess you could say it was our first "unofficial" date, because in between her sets she sat with me and we talked about anything and everything. It was great! We hugged good-bye at the end of the night and I asked her for her home phone number, and when I left the Bullpen Lounge that evening, I knew it wouldn't be the last time I'd see Donna Meade.

———•———

Donna stayed on my mind a lot, and all I wanted to do was talk to her. I wanted to tell her that I thought I fell in love with her the night

I saw her face on that television monitor six months before. I pictured the entire scenario, with me spilling my guts and her laughing and saying I was crazy. She would probably be right, but I knew there was something going on in my heart and head that had never happened before. I didn't understand it but I wanted to.

My fantasy with Donna was pretty far-fetched, especially since I was a married man and there was an age difference between us of twenty-five years. And even though I was afraid of making an ass of myself and setting myself up for rejection, I *at least* had to talk to her.

In January I retreated to my boat in Florida and decided to invite her there. One Saturday morning around eight o'clock I called her for the first time since my visit to the Bullpen, forgetting she'd be sleeping after working late the night before. I felt like a cad for waking her up, but she was nevertheless cheerful and sounded happy to hear from me.

"I am on my boat in Palm Beach, Florida," I told her. "It's sunny and eighty-two degrees, and I want you to come here so I can talk to you."

She literally gasped and said, "That's crazy . . . I can't do that!"

"Why not?" I asked. "I haven't killed anybody in weeks."

"It just wouldn't be right," she said. "You're a married man."

I assured her there would be no funny business and that she'd have her own private stateroom, and that all I wanted to do was talk to her. Finally she relented and we made plans for her to arrive the very next day.

On the two occasions I had seen Donna, I couldn't tell much about her figure because of the stage outfits she wore. Her clothes were never very revealing; the long, flowing skirts she wore were pretty, but they covered her well. I didn't care if she was fat, though; there was something about her I was drawn to. When I went to pick her up at the airport that Sunday, I was delighted to see that she was showing off a rather slim figure in her jeans and boots.

When we got to the boat, I invited Donna to settle into her stateroom, change from her winter clothes into something more comfortable and join me on the top deck for a drink. It was a beautiful day topside as we chatted and got to know each other. After a few laughs and some light conversation, I finally asked her, "Just *who is* Donna Meade?"

She looked very serious for a moment. "Well," she said, "first and foremost I'm a spiritual person, and God is at the center of my life."

"I like that," I told her. (Which I later found out was the *right answer*. She's said many times that *that* was the moment *she* fell in love with *me*.)

Donna and I spent two very interesting days together getting to know each other, with her telling me about her life as the only daughter in a musical family of seven children. She said she'd been performing since she was a kid, was once married for three years, with no children, and had lived alone after being divorced six years earlier. She was thirty-six years old.

After Donna returned to Nashville, we saw each other as often as possible during the next several months. She would take off from her job and join me for dinner in Nashville, or fly to Dallas or Palm Beach for a day or two. There I did my best to impress her, wining and dining her at the finest restaurants and introducing her to a few close friends.

I wish I could tell you how long I waited for her . . . all my life I think. Before I met Donna, I thought I knew what true love was, but when she came along, there was a feeling I had never known before. I was positive I had found it with Donna and nothing has changed; it was and still is the greatest thing in my life.

It was at Mario's restaurant in Nashville in March of '90 that I asked Donna to marry me. She said an immediate "yes" that night, but it wasn't until a couple of weeks later that we made it official. We'd planned to have a romantic dinner on her night off so I could present her with an engagement ring, but there weren't very many restaurants open on Sunday night in Nashville.

We ended up at the Jack Daniel's Saloon and Restaurant at the Opryland Hotel—not the most romantic setting in the world but a nice enough place to dine. After handing Donna the small box that held the ring, I'll never forget the look on her face when she opened it up. Her eyes bulged out as she gasped, and then she laughed and cried at the same time. All she could say was "Wow!" As she sat there ogling that ring, I'll bet she said "Wow!" a hundred times.

It really was a magnificent ring—a four-carat marquis-cut diamond that I'd handpicked and had mounted in a gold setting. When

I posed the big question, she again answered "yes", and we then proceeded to plan our future. Naturally there was one "small glitch" to contend with—a divorce from my wife, Sue.

I knew it wasn't going to be easy; after all, at the time she and I had been married for thirty-nine years. But the fact is there are some things in this world that aren't supposed to work, and it took me a long time to admit that to myself. All during our marriage, I had put on a good face, never wanting anyone to know that I'd failed at anything. Mom's words "We don't give up, boy" echoed in my mind, so I hung in there no matter how unbearable it got.

The divorce proceedings were mercifully quick but none too painless. I knew it would get nasty, and because of my business holdings it was naturally expensive. I'll spare you the gory details, but I *will* tell you it wasn't pretty.

The worst part about it was having to deal with lawyers, and to give you an idea as to what kind of a guy my attorney was, his license plate spelled out D-I-V-O-R-C-E. This would be a great place to drop in a few lawyer jokes, but then again as far as I'm concerned most lawyers *are* jokes. I will tell you, however, that I won't say my attorney was dumb, but he didn't know the difference between incest and arson and he set fire to his sister.

The news of my divorce and my relationship with Donna would not elude the press. In fact, we were considered scandalous and became the subject of several articles in the *Enquirer* and *Star* tabloids. One night, while at the Bullpen Lounge, I was sitting with Donna in the VIP booth, when one of the tabloid's photographers was spotted in the crowd with a camera that had a lens as long as a whore's dream. It was Donna's friend Tex Monahan, the assistant manager and acting bouncer, who noticed him taking pictures of us from across the room.

Tex was a big, rotund cowboy who loved Donna and protected her like a sister, and when the photographer tried to leave, Tex stopped him and told him to hand over the film. When he refused, Tex wrestled the camera from the guy and the film hit the floor, just as the house security guard came over and told Tex he had to give it back.

Naturally, the pictures wound up in the next week's tabloids with the story of our affair. Nice try, Tex.

I probably don't have to tell you how relentless those tabloid people can be, and that trying to keep our relationship private was impossible. They even called Donna's parents' home in Richmond, Virginia, and asked her father questions about us. Bless his heart, Mr. Meade was unaware of who they were and was so proud of his daughter that he willingly answered all of their questions and told them whatever they wanted to know.

Once, they even came to Donna's apartment in Nashville while I was there. We'd had a date to go out to dinner that night, and while Donna was upstairs getting ready, there was a knock on the door. A reporter from one of the tabloids identified himself, and I firmly but politely asked him to leave, but that next week the tabloid reported we were living together in Donna's apartment.

Then another time one of their reporters got past security at the Grand Ole Opry House where we were both taping a television show, and they managed to corner Donna in her dressing room. She was terrified! The woman reporter grilled her about our relationship and really raked Donna over the coals.

Finally, *People* magazine called and said they wanted to do a legitimate article about us, so they came to our boat where we were docked in Florida. They did an extensive interview and were the fairest of all the media, reporting just the facts. The way I figure it, those people have to write about somebody, and as my mother used to say, "When they're talking about you, they're lettin' somebody else rest."

———•———

My two sons Garry and Robert took the news of the divorce fairly well, but my daughter Connie was another story. At the time Connie was pregnant with her first child, and my first grandchild, and was no doubt more than a little emotional about the whole situation. She was totally devastated by the split of her mom and me. Naturally she wanted us to stay together, because she loved us and wanted nothing to change, but she also wanted her child's grandfather nearby as she grew up, and not living far away with some other woman.

After a while, Connie warmed up to the situation *and* to Donna. I think it had a lot to do with the fact that she saw how happy she made me and how easily we got along. It was really a phenomenal change of attitude on Connie's part. I think she came to trust Donna as she got to know her better. In short, it's hard to dislike Donna.

One thing that may have softened the blow of our relationship to my family and friends was the fact that it was not me, but Donna who asked for a prenuptial agreement. She insisted that in the event something were to happen between us, she would receive no part of my fortune. Her very words were "I won't have anyone believing I married you for your money." She's always been adamant about being self-reliant, but I don't think she's an independent a person as much as she's convinced that through faith she'll always have whatever she needs.

I'll never forget a statement Donna once made early on in our relationship. Considering our age difference, I asked her how she was going to feel when we were both getting on in years and she would be much more active than me. "Will you still want me when I'm old and feeble?" I asked her, and Donna replied, "I'd rather push you around in a wheelchair than be with anyone else." That to me was the most wonderful declaration of her love for me.

I had asked Donna where she wanted to live after we were married, whether she preferred Nashville, Dallas, New York or her hometown of Richmond, and she really couldn't decide. I think she was going to leave it up to me, but I told her as long as I was with her and near the water, I didn't care. My love for water and trees probably stemmed from my days back in Plainview, Texas, where it really was a *plain view*—nothing but miles and miles of nothing but miles and miles. I at least wanted a place with a pond or some property on a lake or river—anyplace where I could see water. Donna suggested that we just start looking and maybe we'd know it if we saw it.

First we looked around in Dallas but didn't have much luck. There just wasn't much available on the nearby lake at the time. Then we began to look at several places in the surrounding counties of Richmond. After looking at a dozen or more homes, Donna and I hadn't seen anything that really grabbed us—that is until we pulled into a place called Chaffin's Bluff.

The real estate agent told us it was seven acres and a small house with a guest house that wasn't on the market, but she felt sure the right offer could buy it. Neither Donna nor I got very excited until we pulled up in the gravel drive and looked around the side of the house, and there was the most beautiful view of the James River! It was just the most breathtaking view you ever saw. That was when Donna and I looked at each other and at the same time said, "This is it!"

The property was actually the site of a Civil War battle, and Donna and I were totally intrigued by its history. There were earthworks, or gun emplacements, on each side of the house, and the owners showed us miniballs and other Civil War memorabilia that had been found there over the years. The small house was old (built in 1902) but in really good shape. It didn't take long for us to make our decision. We were sold.

We bought Chaffin's Bluff in August of 1990 and proceeded with redecorating and adding on another eighteen hundred square feet to the main house. The property was located in Varina (pronounced va-rye-na), a rural area with no convenience stores or fancy gas stations at the time, and only about twelve minutes from downtown Richmond. Local shopping was done at the decades-old mom-and-pop-owned Carlton's Country Store, complete with rocking chairs on the old wooden porch and full-service gas pumps. Definitely my kind of place. I'd found paradise!

Another great thing about the area was that Donna knew it like the back of her hand. After having been raised about fifteen minutes away, in the neighboring little town of Sandston, Donna had lived in the Richmond area most all her life, before moving to Nashville in 1981. Her mother and father still lived nearby, as did several of her six brothers.

In mid-December, Donna and I moved into our new home. During renovations, we also had some extensive landscaping work done, and while they were at it, we had them place a brick circle in the gardens out back where our wedding would be held. My divorce from Sue was to be final in the summer of 1991, so we scheduled our wedding ceremony for the following October 27.

Among our wedding guests were many of our family and friends that had flown in from all over the country, including producer Jim Owens and his wife Lorianne Crook, of the *Crook and Chase* television show, and the legendary country music performer Rose Lee Maphis. My daughter Connie didn't attend, but my sons Robert and Garry were there standing up for me as ushers, along with my ad agency friend Bob Berry.

Ralph Emery, the TV show host who had introduced us, was appropriately my best man. I remember Ralph telling us how upset country star Lorrie Morgan was with him for coming to our wedding. It seemed that she was also getting married that same day and wanted him to give her away, but he had committed to us first.

The wedding itself couldn't have been more beautiful. October in Virginia can be iffy weather-wise, and planning an outdoor ceremony is always a gamble. But that day the autumn leaves were at their peak, the sun shone brightly and the temperature was an unheard of eighty-two degrees. I'm convinced that a Higher Power had brought us together for a good reason and that the perfect setting was symbolic of our union. I also believe the day was as ordained as I felt our marriage was, because the beautiful weather was short-lived; the very next day it was cold and blustery and the wind blew every leaf off the trees.

For the ceremony, Donna and I exchanged our vows on the brick circle overlooking the James, just as we'd planned. The two hundred or so guests we'd invited witnessed from our lawn, along with at least a hundred uninvited boaters on the river. Since the word had gotten out about the wedding, we had asked the Coast Guard to prohibit boat traffic for those few minutes, but they said it couldn't be done legally. The boaters were actually okay, until they all started blowing their congratulatory horns at the end of the ceremony, prohibiting anyone from hearing the song we sang to each other on tape for the recessional. I guess it's kind of like those helicopters that buzz the Hollywood stars' weddings. There isn't a whole lot you can do about it.

I'll never forget how relieved I was when the ceremony was over. We kissed when the minister said, "You may kiss the bride," but all I wanted to do was hug her. After the wedding, we took pictures on the lawn and then everyone boarded the *Annabel Lee,* a paddle-

October 27, 1991.
The happiest day
of my life

Donna and
me on our
honeymoon
in Maui

wheel showboat docked at our house that we used to cruise down the James River for the reception.

For our honeymoon, we did the traditional Hawaiian thing, with a week planned at the fabulous Four Seasons Hotel in Maui. I had been to Hawaii many times, but it was Donna's first trip to the islands. We enjoyed gourmet dining, took a helicopter ride into the volcanoes, and went to an authentic Hawaiian luau—all in the first three days we were there. As we relaxed by the pool on our fourth day, sipping tropical drinks the size of table lamps, a poolside attendant occasionally sauntered by spritzing our faces with Evian water. It was in this luxurious setting that Donna got the most peculiar look on her face. She turned to me and said, "Can I ask you something? Would you like to go home tomorrow?"

Funny thing was I was as homesick as Donna, but since we'd already paid for our trip, we decided to stick it out. Spending our last four days in paradise was like living out a sentence. We had both come to love Chaffin's Bluff so much that nowhere was more beautiful to us, and we just wanted to go home.

———•———

Our home was truly that special to Donna and me from the start, and it still is. It seems like I've never lived anywhere else. And it's true; I've existed many places, but Chaffin's Bluff is the only place I've ever really *lived*.

A place like the Bluff is so difficult to describe. Take the fireplace in our den built out of river rock straight out of the James—and being the premier fire builder at our house, I don't just build a fire, I build a *farrr*. Because I enjoy it so much and always have, Donna calls me her resident pyromaniac. I used to joke and tell people that when my brother Don and I were young, we built a fire in the house and our dad was furious when he came home. I guess he *was* mad— we didn't have a fireplace!

One thing's for sure, we'll never run out of firewood on our property. It's mostly wooded, with plenty of wildlife: bald eagles, foxes, wild turkeys, otter and deer. And because I have such a fondness for

At home on Chaffin's Bluff

them, our place is more or less a refuge, with no hunting or fishing allowed. We feed the ducks, geese and deer every day, and for the bald eagles I even stock our ponds with carp—their favorite food. At one time we had chickens and guineas, until the foxes got them all. Trying to keep the critters out of our flowers and vegetable garden is a full-time job for our caretakers.

When the weather is nice, we enjoy tooling down the river on our pontoon boat. The James is beautiful and great for fishing and skiing, but not all that wide behind our house. It's forty feet deep, though, and oceangoing vessels pass our house regularly. I enjoy talking to the tugboat and cargo ship captains on my two-way radio and waving to the pleasure boaters going by. A lot of times they'll just cut their engines and hang out, and one time we overheard one of the boaters say to another, "You think that's him?" The other guy said, "Nah, I think he hires somebody to wave for him."

Privacy has never been a real problem for us, though, probably because our property is secluded and at the end of a private road. Although there was the time I was out feeding the chickens in my underwear, and you know that feeling when you *know* somebody's looking at you? Well, there I was out in the yard in just my Jockey shorts and slippers on a beautiful summer morning, when sure enough I looked around and saw a Suburban full of people, with a man leaning over the hood taking my picture. After that I knew I had to do something, so I had several privacy signs posted on our private road.

Donna and I love living in the countryside of Varina and do our best to give back to our community in many ways. I've always been big on the promotion of education and feel something must be done about the literacy level in this country, so for a while she and I "adopted" our local Varina High School. There, we instituted an incentive program called the Dean's List for students and teachers, offering money and prizes for academic achievement and excellence. Some called it bribery, but we were just trying to keep kids in school and learning. We pumped a lot of money into the school, buying an activity bus, curtains for the auditorium and anything else needed that the county could not or would not provide.

The most fun we had with our program was at graduation each year when we'd give away a brand-new car. At the end of the commencement exercises, Donna and I would take the stage with a hat filled with the names of the top 10 percent of the graduating class. After we drew and announced a name, that student would come running to the stage to be presented with the keys to a little red Ford automobile.

Our experiences with Varina High School taught us something as well. We learned after several years that we didn't make as big a difference as we'd hoped to, the main reason being that high school was simply too late to start an incentive program. We learned from a reliable source that it has to start at home and in grade school, so at this writing we are considering implementing the same type of program at one of our community's elementary schools.

As I've said before, I believe there's a reason for everything, and our involvement with the high school led to a very special happening for Donna and me. I'd been tinkering around on the piano for a while trying to write an alma mater for Varina High School and had finally come up with a chorus, and when I played it for Donna, she liked it so much she learned to sing it with me.

One day we were at her mom's house with several of her brothers sitting around and Donna sat down at the piano. She said, "Hey . . . y'all listen to this new song that Jimmy has written for Varina High School," and she began to sing:

> *Varina, dear old Varina . . .*
> *How proudly we wear your gold and blue*
> *Varina, dear old Varina . . .*
> *Forever in our hearts we'll cherish you*

Everyone seemed to like it, especially Donna's brother Danny. He said, "That's really good. In fact, it may be *too* good to just be a school song, so why not make it something bigger?" That was when Donna swung back around to the keyboard, smiled real big and said, "Okay!" She then began to sing:

> *Virginia, dear old Virginia*
> *There's no place on earth I'd rather be!*

That evening, when we got home, Donna continued to write more lyrics to "Virginia." Lying in bed, she couldn't sleep for thinking about it, and got up in the middle of the night with a migraine headache. Guess those lyrics were fighting pretty hard to come out, because by the next morning she had all but finished the song.

Using a melody for another song I'd been tinkering with called "Bend of the River," Donna sat down at the piano and sang "Virginia" for me the next day. After she asked me for my opinion and input, we worked on it for a day or two, fine-tuning each other's efforts until we were satisfied. With Donna's lyric and my melody, we had composed our very first song together.

It wasn't long after we had written "Virginia" that we played it

for our good friends Nelson and Carolyn Bennett. The Bennetts said
they loved our song, and when Carolyn wiped away the tears, we
knew we had something good. Being rather active in Richmond politics, Nelson said, "You know, that would make a great state song.
Did y'all know they were looking for a new one?" We told him no,
and he said, "Well, I have a friend in the state legislature that could
possibly help. I'm going to call Delegate Frank Hall tomorrow!"

Delegate Hall did indeed like "Virginia" and has been trying to
help our song become the new state anthem ever since. However, we
subsequently learned that the issue over replacing "Carry Me Back
to Old Virginny" has been ongoing since the early eighties. Seems
things move kind of slowly in Virginia politics. Our song has gar-
nered a lot of support from the state legislature, though, and Donna
and I still have high hopes for it.

Our "Virginia" song also became quite popular with the public,
and when folks started asking for a recording, Donna and I made a
CD of it. Since it was our intention to donate the song to the people
of Virginia, we never felt right about keeping the proceeds from the
sale of the CD, and because they didn't get their alma mater, it
seemed the only thing to do was to donate the proceeds to our program at Varina High School.

———◆———

Together Donna and I not only have a good marriage, but we also
make a great team. Neither of us performs anymore to speak of, but
we do make charitable appearances on occasion for civic and community organizations like Rotary clubs, Lions clubs and women's
clubs. She sings and plays piano, sings harmonies and accompanies
me while I sing and tell a few stories.

Donna was especially an asset when it came to entertaining clients
and selling sausage, and she traveled with me on business most of the
time when I made appearances and grocery store calls. She also
offered helpful suggestions at times, and it was actually her idea that
I use one of my favorite sayings in a sausage commercial: "I'd rather
explain the price than apologize for the quality."

Business associates seemed to like her too, and many of them said
there was a major difference in me after I met Donna, that my entire

demeanor changed and I wasn't nearly as irritable or quick to anger. They even began referring to me as Jimmy Dean, B.D. or A.D., Before Donna or After Donna. Before she came along, I was fighting the world *and* my first wife, Sue, since we didn't agree on much. Business was a struggle and so was my home life, so there's no wonder I was grumpy a lot and people called me cantankerous.

Nowadays I think Donna just takes me with a grain of salt. She accepts me for what I am—rough around the edges, but as sentimental as, or even more so than most. She'll readily admit she's applied for sainthood, and she may deserve it after having put up with an awful lot from me—especially my outspokenness—but she actually sees right through me, and calls me her "lamb in a lion's suit."

In my opinion, the best justification for marriage is for a person to help another become the best that person can possibly be, and in a good marriage it's completely effortless. Donna and I work to help one another in so many ways, and to continually enrich each other with a sharing of knowledge and wisdom. We laugh a lot too, which is an important part of our relationship.

So now I have the farm in Virginia I always wanted and a wife who makes me feel good about myself, one who knows what it's like to be giving. She's the best friend I ever hoped to have and I wish everybody a friend just like her. The things she does and says and wants are important to me—as whatever I do, say or want is important to her— making it the most relaxed, unselfish relationship in the world.

Together we live quietly with our two miniature poodles Tara and Pepper, and nobody really gives a flip anymore—no scandal magazines chasing after us and no dirt for them to dig up. We both feel we're right where we're supposed to be. I know I am. I'm married to my best friend, living in my dream home, doing whatever I want whenever I want to do it, and if I live long enough, I just might stop pinching myself and saying, "Is this really real?"

ꕤ Afterthoughts ꕤ

YOU'VE NO DOUBT noticed that sprinkled throughout these pages are some of my life's philosophies, which I've enjoy expounding upon. In this section I wanted to share with you a few more points of wisdom that have been passed on to me, and some stories that didn't really fit anywhere else in this book. Hence, a few after-thoughts.

Nowhere does this book sum up my philosophy like Mom's old saying, "Can't never did anything," and whenever I speak on the subject of "I can," someone will invariably say, "That's easy for you to say. God gave you talent." Damned right, He did. He gave each and every one of us a talent.

The thing that frightens me, though, is with all the federal and state aids and various kinds of handouts in this country, that there'll be many people who will never be forced to find out what their talent really is. Nowadays ours is a nation of leaners, and to them I say, "The world owes you nothing."

To me, the most important quality a person can have is a belief in him or herself, and I only wish I knew how to instill that quality in others. I believe in my own judgment, and I don't know if I'm bragging or complaining, but I know of no one who has more tenacity than me—except maybe for a man named Fred Smith.

While trying to get my sausage company off the ground, I was still performing and making appearances around the country, and somehow I ended up in Arkansas. I had gotten a call that someone there named Fred Smith wanted to meet with me to discuss a new business venture. During our meeting, he wanted to know what I thought about his idea of spending forty million dollars to buy several Lear jets to deliver packages and mail overnight. I don't think Fred had even done a feasibility study at the time and I told him I thought he was crazy, which shows you how much *I* know . . . Today Fred's baby, Federal Express, is one of the biggest success stories in the courier business. Now, *there's* a guy who believed in himself and his own ideas.

The Fred Smith story is one of my favorites because it exemplifies how someone with enough determination *can* get ahead in this country. Ours is the greatest country in the world, and it will be good to anybody if they are willing to give of themselves. I pride myself in the fact that I came from humble beginnings, and if I can succeed, *anybody can*. It is indeed my fondest hope that this book will inspire people to say "I can."

Life hasn't exactly been fair all of the time. When I was a kid, I used to think, *Man, if I could ever afford all the ice cream I wanted to eat, that's as rich as I ever want to be.* Well, now I can buy the damned ice cream plant and I can't eat the stuff because of the cholesterol.

Another real disappointment in life I recall came during the time I had my ABC television show. Norman Rockwell was and still is my favorite artist, and the network had lined things up with him to do a painting of me. Unfortunately he got sick before he could get to it, and he passed away shortly thereafter.

———————

If I had any advice to offer someone it would probably be my old motto for the sausage company: Do what you say you're going to do, when you say you're going to do it, and try to do it a little better than you said you would. Nothing frosts me more than when people say they're going to do something at a certain time and don't do it— think building contractors—or when I have an appointment or a meeting with someone, and the other person is late. I said before in this book that my pet peeve is punctuality, and my former family doctor in New Jersey, Dr. Bruce Tapper, is probably one person who can attest to that.

It was one morning when I had an appointment for a checkup with Dr. Tapper that he was running late, leaving me waiting in his reception area for forty minutes after my appointed time. Totally irritated, I left before seeing him and then had my attorney send him a bill. I figured my time was as important as his, and at the time I was making a lot of money, so I prorated my hourly pay for the forty minutes and sent him a bill for eighteen thousand dollars. Shortly thereafter I got a call from him. "Jimmy," he asked, "are you serious?" And I said, "Yes, Bruce, I am."

I left him hanging for a few weeks and then I called him back and said, "Bruce, I'm going to drop this, but the next time I have an appointment with you, I want it to be kept." And it was.

If I have any regrets at all it would have to be that I didn't graduate from high school or attend college, but I was surprised and thrilled when my hometown of Plainview presented me with my high school diploma in 2003. It seems they passed some sort of proclamation in Texas in recent years that said my military service counted toward my education back then, so my diploma is authentic and not honorary.

Something else I wouldn't mind having is an acknowledgment from the Nashville community for my contributions to the country music industry. I think it was in 1993 that my wife, Donna, and I took some

At my high school graduation in Plainview, 2003

close friends on a tour of Nashville, and one of our stops was at the Country Music Hall of Fame Museum. We walked around for the longest time as my friends kept looking for an exhibit that mentioned me or my contributions, but there wasn't any. And then I heard Donna across the way sounding excited about discovering a small theater in the museum that was featuring snippets from old television shows. There on the marquee was "Now Showing! *Town and Country Time*," my old TV show in Washington, DC. But instead of the sign saying "Starring Jimmy Dean," underneath the title it said "Featuring Roy Clark." It damned near broke my wife's heart.

Still, I feel I'm the most fortunate man in the world, and if my luck stops tomorrow, I've had a hell of a lot more than my share. I climbed a lot of mountains and did what I set out to do, and that was to show the skeptics from my childhood that I was every bit as good as they were.

I wish I could go back and find every one of those people who scoffed at me. I would thank them from the bottom of my heart, because every finger that was pointed in my face and every derogatory remark that was made about the house I lived in and the clothes I wore built a fire in me. There was only one way to put it out, and that was to pull myself up by my bootstraps and go out and make something of myself.

Nevertheless, the poverty I grew up in is something I can never forget, and I guess old habits really do die hard. Even today I find myself saving slivers of soap and turning off lights when I leave a room. And still, after all these years, I'm amazed that I can go into any store and buy just about anything I want and not have to wonder if I can afford it. I've seen a lot of people take wealth for granted, but I'm quite sure I never will. I'm equally sure that if I did, Ruth Dean would come back from the grave and smack me upside the head.

Speaking of wealth and making money, I've been involved in a lot of businesses—entertaining, banking, restaurants, real estate and the sausage business to name a few—and it's like I've told a lot of people . . . I'm *still* looking for something I can do. But the one business I've often said I'd *like* to be in is that of buying *some* people for what they're worth, and selling them for what they *think* they're worth. If it was possible, it would hands down be the most profitable business of all.

Certainly the one I enjoyed most was the entertainment business, although I don't have a record of me singing that I can listen to. I hate to listen to myself. Even on "Big Bad John" I can show you a place in that record that's just pitiful.

If it's in your blood, entertaining is something you never give up, and though I'm retired, I still enjoy performing on occasion and playing music with old buddies like Herbie Jones, Jimmy Groves, Johnny Foster, Calvin Garrett and Larry Grossman. And I'm *still* trying to write a song as good as, or that would top, "Big Bad John."

———•———

Like a lot of entertainers, I have been urged by many people to go into politics. In fact, it was Bob Dole, the presidential candidate and Republican senator from Kansas who once asked me, "Jimmy, why don't you run for public office?" I told him, "Well, first of all I'd probably never get elected because I'm too damned honest, and in the second place they don't pay enough money."

I've never been what you might call heavily involved in politics. I believe in the democratic process and I do cast my vote, because if I *didn't* vote, I'd sacrifice my right to bitch. But seriously, this country is very important to me, and I feel that getting to know the people who are running for office is my patriotic duty. Ordinarily I'm drawn to Republican values but call myself a "Demopublican." I've actually been known to contribute to the campaigns of both Republicans and Democrats, and if a candidate needs financial help to get elected, I feel it's my civic duty to support him or her and the issues I believe in. As a rule, I vote for the person or the issue and not a particular political party, and support the person who I feel will do the best job for my state or my country.

During my lifetime I've had the privilege of meeting many of our country's presidents and important political figures, even attending and performing at some of their inaugurations. There's been a few politicians I've really liked, but the majority of them I wouldn't trust as far as I could throw them. To quote Will Rogers, "The trouble with a lot of political jokes is they get elected."

One president I enjoyed meeting was John F. Kennedy. After I'd been living in New York and working on CBS for a couple of years, the folks in Washington invited me back to perform for their Fifteenth Annual International Home Show. Drawing thousands of people each year at the National Guard Armory, the Home Show was exactly that: a show that featured everything for the home, from sinks and stoves to furniture and knickknacks.

With the Home Show being such a big event, it was tradition each year for the star of the show to go to the White House and present a special invitation to the president. I remember the day the limo driver took me to the Oval Office to present the special ticket to JFK. I had known the president from years past as a senator from Massachusetts, when he would sometimes frequent the nightclubs where our band would play. It was no secret he liked to chase the girls a lot back then, and when he was elected president, I told people "what President Eisenhower did for golf, Kennedy will do for sex."

So there I was, being ushered into the Oval Office as his staff member introduced me saying, "Mr. President, this is Jimmy Dean." He said, "Yeah, Jimmy, good to see you again." Going right into my spiel, I said, "Mr. President, I'd like to present you a ticket to the Fifteenth Annual Home Show and certainly hope you'll have the opportunity to attend." "Well, me too, Jimmy," he said, "but there's a huge German delegation in town and I doubt mightily if I'll be able to come." Seizing the opportunity to get in a little joke, I said, "Well, I can certainly understand that, Mr. President, but if something happens and you should be able to come and you lose the ticket, don't worry about it . . . Just come to the stage door and ask for me, and I'll see that you get in."

Obviously appreciative of my remark, Kennedy reared back and laughed at the thought of some redneck country singer having to get the President of the United States in the back door. And when JFK laughed, his whole face turned red. The Irish in him would come out and make his ruddy complexion even redder. He was a good laugher too. I didn't appreciate his politics, but he had a helluva sense of humor.

As far as I'm concerned, George Herbert Walker Bush was one of our finest presidents. He was both tough and fair. It takes much discipline and diplomacy to do that job, qualities I don't admit to having.

I remember a conversation we had one time while he was in office, when I was irate about one of our adversaries and wanted to wipe them off the map. "I'll tell you one thing, George," I said, "it's a good thing I'm not in your shoes." He looked at me, and with a wry smile he said, "Don't you think I know that?"

Both George and Barbara Bush have great senses of humor; they're a lot of fun and are great storytellers too. I have had the pleasure of spending time with the Bushes, either at their home at Walker's Point or aboard our yacht. I remember the year when I got a custom-made Denison, George was so anxious to see it that when we pulled into Chick's Marina, our lines weren't even tied when his security man knocked on our door. "President Bush would like to pay you a visit," he said, so I told him, "Fine." Then he said, "Are there any dos and don'ts aboard?" "Well," I told him, "you don't wear your shoes in the main salon." "You mean everyone has to take off their shoes?" he asked, and I said, "Yes." "Does that include the president?" he asked. "Yes," I told him. His eyes got real big, and then he paused and stammered, "Well . . . *you're* gonna tell him!"

About ten minutes after the first Secret Serviceman arrived, two deep-sea divers came and proceeded to dive under our boat to inspect the bottom for anything suspicious. We could tell the president was getting close to the marina when we looked out and saw guards with rifles standing on the rooftops nearby, then not long after that a crowd started to form around the marina. Kennebunkport is a small, touristy town with plenty of "Bush watchers," and when the Bushes are out and about, the word gets around fast.

It's actually a well-known fact among my friends that I always have white carpeting on my boat, and when George and Barbara arrived that day, I didn't have to tell the president to remove his shoes; he already knew. Now, Barbara was a different story . . . She was in one of her mischievous moods that day, and not only did she wear her tennis shoes into the main salon but she wore two different colors—a white one and a hot pink one. Then to make *sure* I'd see them, when she sat down in the stuffed chair and crossed her legs, she started kicking her foot up and down. Her only remark about her shoes was "I've got another pair at home just like them!" She's a pistol, that girl.

Sharing a laugh with President George Herbert Walker Bush on the TV show <u>Nashville Now</u> in 1992

Aboard our yacht, the <u>Big Bad John</u>, with George and Barbara Bush in 1991 (that's Millie on the far left)

Donna and me with President George W. Bush, in 2001

I've often told Donna that I thought Barbara Bush would've made a good president. She's no-nonsense, honest, warm and tough as the back end of a shooting gallery. She tells it like it is, and I think politics could use a lot more of that. Once when she and the president were aboard our boat, we were watching TV, and the name of a prominent actress came up. I said, "Well, she's just a damned pig," and Donna said "Jimmy!" Barbara immediately chimed in and said, "No . . . leave him alone . . . She *is* a pig!" Love that Barbara Bush.

My favorite memory of George Bush was in Washington, DC, while he was vice president. We had played golf, and afterward he said, "Let's go have some Italian food." As we were eating at the restaurant, the word had gotten out that he was there and a crowd had formed around the front door, so after we'd finished our meal, the Secret Service decided to take us out the back door.

As we were on our way out of the restaurant, the blind girl who had been playing the piano was standing by the door. When I saw her, I introduced myself and said, "Hello, I'm Jimmy Dean, and this is Vice President Bush." Well, when I said that, she gasped, and then she said to the vice president, "Could I look at you?" George said, "Certainly," but in order for blind people to look at you, they have to take their fingertips and run them over your face. That's one picture I'll always retain . . . George Bush standing there patiently while that woman gently ran her fingers all over his face. It was one of the sweetest things I've ever seen in my life.

My relationship with George Bush is one I indeed cherish, and when I told him Donna and I were writing this book he sent me the following letter:

GEORGE BUSH

March 16, 2004

Dear Jimmy,

I understand you are going to print with a new book. If you made
it half as interesting as your life has been, it will be a huge best seller.

I have great respect for your many accomplishments in life. I'll bet a
lot of people wouldn't have predicted that you topped your singing
career with a hugely successful business career. This is the American
dream.

I am very proud of what you accomplished, and I am proud to be your
friend.

All the best,

G Bush

Mr. Jimmy Dean
1160 Riverbend Road
Richmond, VA 23231

Thanks, George. I don't know George W. as well as I do his father, but I've known him since he owned the Texas Rangers and have been around him at the Bush home in Kennebunkport a few times. He's a pleasant guy, but more importantly I think he's been a good president under the most difficult of circumstances.

I don't envy anyone who takes that job. It's a spot I wouldn't give to my cleaners. A politician has to be so many things to so many people—a diplomat, a great communicator—and I really believe most importantly a very good actor. Throughout my career I've played a lot of characters on television and in movies, but I don't think I could have ever been *that* good an actor. I'll kindly keep my hat out of the political ring, thank you very much.

———•——

Actually, I'm enjoying my retirement and feel it's something I've earned, because I worked hard for a long, long time. My days are no longer hectic with constant phone calls in an office . . . Most of my time is spent at home handling business over the phone from our kitchen. I guess it would run most wives crazy to have their husbands around the house all day, but Donna seems to handle it okay. She jokingly says the secret is to keep an ample supply of Valium.

To keep my mind active, I follow current events, work two crossword puzzles a day, and I check my luck playing solitaire every morning. I learned a long time ago that you've gotta try your luck at least once a day, because you could be going around lucky all day and not even know it.

There are many other things I learned along the way, lessons like "Never hire kinfolks to work for you"—especially after the fiasco with my brother Don—and "You can strive for perfection, and sometimes that makes you a miserable son of a bitch." Here are some other observations that I thought were worth sharing . . .

Money makes money.
I've been broke a lot of times but I've never been poor.
Formal education is a wonderful thing, but unless it's sprinkled
   liberally with plain old common horse sense it's not worth a
   damn.

You can't take rejection personally . . . You have to say, "Well, that dumbass just didn't know any better."

Nothing in the world can ever give you the feeling you get from a standing ovation.

Them that's got, gets.

The golden rule is "Them that's got the gold makes the rules."

The older I get, the faster I could run when I was a boy.

If you're that fond of yourself, you don't leave me much room to like you.

You can be on the right track, but if you don't keep moving, somebody will still run over your ass.

You can say anything you want about somebody as long as you say "bless their heart." ("She's the homeliest thing I ever saw, bless her heart.")

Don't make things bigger than they are.

You know you're getting old when you go to more funerals than you do weddings.

The majority of wounds are self-inflicted.

Wealth and success are a state of mind.

And most importantly

. . . God is bigger than most people think.

And you know, I've seen a jillion miracles . . . They're all around. Every green leaf is a miracle. Not long ago I was sitting on the porch in my favorite chair and I noticed a leaf falling, and as it floated down and landed on the porch in front of me, I thought, *Boy what a shame*. It was once beautiful and green and now it's all brown and wrinkled. Then I considered how it had beautified the world and how it would go back into the earth to fertilize and grow more green trees, and it occurred to me . . . I hope I can contribute like that.

As I wind up this epic, I would like to thank first and foremost my pretty and hardworking wife Donna, for the time and effort she has put in helping to write this book, for convincing me that it should be written in the first place and for putting up with a rather uncooperative husband at times. I certainly couldn't have done it without her. Nor could I make this a "tell-all" book and share every secret, mainly because I want to remain on speaking terms with my wife . . . but I *do* hope it has given you some insight into "the farmer."

Looking in the mirror these days, I see a wrinkled old head, but I have to say those wrinkles were a result of more smiles than frowns. I thank you for those smiles . . . You have truly given me a wonderful life and I am forever grateful. May God always bless you and everybody at your house. And for goodness' sake, grin once in a while . . . It's good for ya!

✍ Acknowledgments ✍

OUR THANKS GO out to the following people for sharing their mem-
ories and helping with this book: Willie Bruffy, Ruth Prewitt,
Bob Berry, Herb and Carol Jones, Jimmy and Loretta Groves, Larry
Grossman, Mary Moore, Garry Taylor Dean, Connie Dean Taylor,
Fred Foster, Mike Chase, Laurey Peat, and Diana Burkenfield.

Special thanks to Walt Smith of Record Finder in Richmond,
Virginia, for his help with the Jimmy Dean discography.
www.recordfinders.com

❧ Jimmy Dean Discography ❧

78RPM SINGLES

TITLE/B SIDE	LABEL	NO.	YEAR
Pickin' Sweethearts/Bummin' Around	Four Star	1432	1953
I'm Feelin' for You/Queen of Hearts	Four Star	6313/6314	1953
Sweet Darling/Release Me	Four Star	1654	1953
Glad Rags/Freight Train Blues	Mercury	7774/7776	1957

45RPM SINGLES

TITLE/B SIDE	LABEL	NO.	YEAR
Bummin' Around/Picking Sweethearts	Four Star	1613	1953
Find 'em Fool 'em and Leave 'em/My World Is You	Mercury	70745	1956
Big Blue Diamond/False Pride	Mercury	7742	1956
Hello Mr. Blues/I Found Out	Mercury		1956
Losing Game/The Good Lord's Happy Child	Mercury	71120	1956
Look On the Good Side	Mercury	71172	1956
Deep Blue Sea/Love Me So I'll Know	Columbia	40995	1957
Little Sandy Sleighfoot/Golden Bells	Columbia	41025	1957
Makin' My Mind Up/Starlight, Starbright	Columbia	41118	1959
You Should See Tennessee/School of Love	Columbia	41196	1959
Sing Along/Weekend Blue	Columbia	41395	1959
Counting Tears/Stay a Little Longer	Columbia	41453	1959
There's Still Time Brother/Thanks for the Dream	Columbia	41543	1959
Little Boy Lost/There'll Be No Teardrops	Columbia	41710	1960
It's Been a Long Long Time/Give Me Back My Heart	Columbia	41956	1961
Big Bad John/I Won't Go Huntin' with You Jake	Columbia	42175	1961
Oklahoma Bill/To a Sleeping Beauty	Columbia	42248	1961
Dear Ivan/Smoke, Smoke, Smoke That Cigarette	Columbia	42259	1962
To a Sleeping Beauty/Cajun Queen	Columbia	42282	1962
PT 109/Walk On Boy	Columbia	42338	1962
Little Bitty Big John/Steel Men	Columbia	42483	1962
Little Black Book/Please Pass the Biscuits	Columbia	42529	1962
A Day That Changed the World/Gonna Raise a Ruckus	Columbia	42600	1962
Mile Long Train/This Ole House	Columbia	42738	1963
Funniest Thing I Ever . . . /Thumb Pick Pete	Columbia	42861	1963
Mind Your Own Business/I Really Don't Want to Know	Columbia	42934	1963
Sam Hill	Columbia	43159	1963

Shenandoah/Wait for the Wagon	Columbia	43201	1963
Sam Hill/When I Grow Too Old to Dream	Columbia	42861	1963
The First Thing Every Morning	Columbia	43263	1965
Harvest of Sunshine/Under the Sun	Columbia	43382	1965
Blue Christmas	Columbia	111915	1965
Striker Bill/Things Have Gone to Pieces	Columbia	43540	1966
Once a Day/Let's Pretend	Columbia	43754	1966
I've Been Down Some Roads	Columbia	46039	1966
Stand Beside Me/A Tiny Drop of Sadness	RCA Victor	8971	1967
Sweet Misery/When Somebody . . .	RCA Victor	9091	1967
Ninety Days/In the Same Old Way	RCA Victor	9241	1967
Your Country Boy/I'm a Swinger	RCA Victor	9350	1968
A Thing Called Love/One Last Time	RCA Victor	9454	1968
Born to Be by Your Side/Read 'em and Weep	RCA Victor	9567	1968
She's Mine/A Rose Is a Rose	RCA Victor	0122	1968
And I'm Still Missing You/I'd Like to Be the One . . .	RCA Victor	0600	1968
A Hammer and Nails/I Taught Her Everything	RCA Victor	9652	1969
When Judy Smiled/My Hometown Sweetheart	RCA Victor	9800	1970
Us/Down Comes the Rain	RCA Victor	9859	1970
Aunt Maudie's Fun Garden/Weakness In a Man	RCA Victor	9915	1970
Slowly/Sweet Thang (with Dottie West)	RCA Victor	9947	1970
Everybody Knows/Ain't Life Sweet	RCA Victor	9966	1971
These Hands/Who Put the Leaving in Your Eyes	RCA Victor	273	1971
Your Sweet Love	Columbia	45922	1973
Who's Gonna Love Me/Days When Jim Liked Jenny	Columbia	45981	1974
I.O.U./Let's Pick Up the Pieces	Casino	52	1976

CD SINGLES

TITLE	LABEL	NO.	YEAR
Virginia (with Donna Meade Dean)	River Bend	8897	1997

ALBUMS

TITLE	LABEL	NO.	YEAR
Jimmy Dean Sings His Television Favorites	Mercury	20319	1957
Hour of Prayer	Columbia CL	1025	1957
Big Bad John	Columbia CL	1735	1961
Portrait of Jimmy Dean	Columbia CS	8694	1962
Everybody's Favorite	Columbia CL	2027	1963
Songs We All Love Best (with the Chuck Cassey Singers)	Columbia CL	2188	1964
Jimmy Dean Sings the Big Ones	Columbia CS	9338	1966
The First Thing Every Morning	Columbia CL	2401	1965
Jimmy Dean's Christmas Card (with Robert Dean)	Columbia CL	2404	1965
Greatest Hits	Columbia CL	2485	1966
The Dean's List	Columbia CS	9677	1967

Mr. Country Music	Harmony	11208	1967
Jimmy Dean Is Here!	RCA Victor	3727	1967
Most Richly Blessed	RCA Victor	3824	1967
The Jimmy Dean Show	RCA Victor	3890	1968
A Thing Called Love	RCA Victor	3999	1968
Country's Favorite Son	Harmony	11270	1968
Speaker of the House	RCA Victor	4035	1968
Gotta Travel On	Harmony	11356	1969
The Dean of Country Music	RCA Victor	4323	1970
Country Boy & Country Girl (with Dottie West)	RCA Victor	4434	1970
Everybody Knows Jimmy Dean	RCA Victor	4511	1971
These Hands	RCA Victor	4618	1971
Jimmy Dean I.O.U.	Casino	8014	1976
Big Bad John	Bear Family	15723	1993
Greatest Songs	Curb	77764	1995
Inspirational Songs	Curb	77930	1998
20 Great Story Songs	Curb	77941	1999
American Originals	Columbia CK	45077	1999
Greatest Hits	Columbia CK	65256	2004
The Best of Jimmy Dean	Columbia CK	85872	2004

❧ Photo Credits and Permissions ❧

Photo on page 122 (middle) courtesy of Dean Family Collection
Photo on page 123 (bottom) courtesy of Dean Family Collection
Photo on page 128 (top) courtesy of Dean Family Collection
Photo on page 129 (bottom) courtesy of Dean Family Collection
Photo on page 131 (top) courtesy of Dean Family Collection
Photo on page 131 (bottom) courtesy of Dean Family Collection
Photo on page 135 (top) courtesy of Dean Family Collection
Photo on page 135 (bottom) courtesy of Dean Family Collection
Photo on page 138 by Xenophon Beake Photographer
Photo on page 142 (top) courtesy of Fess Parker
Photo on page 142 (bottom) courtesy of Fess Parker
Photo on page 147 (top) courtesy of Dean Family Collection
Photo on page 147 (bottom) by Donna Dean
Photo on page 151 courtesy of Dean Family Collection
Photos on page 155 courtesy of Dean Family Collection
Photo on page 162 (top) copyright Bill Weaks
Photo on page 162 (middle) copyright Bill Weaks
Photo on page 162 (bottom) copyright Bill Weaks
Photo on page 175 courtesy of Dean Family Collection
Photo on page 203 courtesy of Dean Family Collection
Photo on page 209 (top) copyright Bill Weaks
Photo on page 209 (middle) courtesy of Dean Family Collection
Photo on page 209 (bottom) courtesy of Dean Family Collection
Photo on page 212 courtesy of Dean Family Collection
Photo on page 219 (top) by White Studios
Photo on page 219 (bottom) copyright Star Parade Magazine
Photo on page 225 courtesy of Dean Family Collection
Photo on page 230 (top) by Vicky Burr
Photo on page 230 (bottom) by Donna Dean
Photo on page 242 (top) by Caston Studios
Photo on page 242 (bottom) courtesy of Dean Family Collection
Photo on page 244 by Donna Dean
Photo on page 251 by Jan Garrett
Photo on page 256 (top) courtesy Dean Family Collection
Photo on page 256 (middle) courtesy of Dean Family Collection
Photo on page 256 (bottom) courtesy of Dean Family Collection
Photo on page 264 courtesy of Dean Family Collection

☙ Index ❧